Communicating with Children
and Adolescents

of related interest

Dramatherapy with Families, Groups and Individuals
Waiting in the Wings
Sue Jennings
ISBN 1 85302 144 X pb
ISBN 1 85302 014 1 hb

Listening to Young People in School, Youth Work and Counselling
Nick Luxmoore
ISBN 1 85302 909 2

Making a Leap – Theatre of Empowerment
A Practical Handbook for Creative Drama Work with Young People
Sara Clifford and Anna Herrmann
Foreword by Alec Davison
ISBN 1 85302 632 8

The Child's World
Assessing Children in Need
Edited by Jan Horwath
ISBN 1 85302 957 2

Introduction to Dramatherapy
Theatre and Healing – Ariadne's Ball of Thread
Sue Jennings
ISBN 1 85302 115 6

Helping Children to Build Self-Esteem
A Photocopiable Activities Book
Deborah Plummer
ISBN 1 85302 927 0

Active Analytic Group Therapy for Adolescents
John Evans
Foreword by Peter Wilson
ISBN 1 85302 616 6

Creating a Safe Place
Helping Children and Families Recover from Child Sexual Abuse
NCH Children and Families Project
Foreword by Mooli Lahad
ISBN 1 84310 0096

Communicating with Children and Adolescents

Action for Change

Edited by Anne Bannister and Annie Huntington

Jessica Kingsley Publishers
London and Philadelphia

First published in the United Kingdom in 2002
by Jessica Kingsley Publishers Ltd
116 Pentonville Road
London N1 9JB, England
and
325 Chestnut Street
Philadelphia, PA 19106, USA

www.jkp.com

Copyright © Jessica Kingsley Publishers 2002

Library of Congress Cataloging in Publication Data
Communicating with children and adolescents : action for change / edited by Anne Bannister and Annie Huntington
    p. cm.
Includes bibliographical references and index.
ISBN 1-84310-025-8 (pbk. : Alk.paper)
    1. Interpersonal communication in children. 2. Interpersonal communication in adolescence. 3. Children and adults. 4. Parent and teenager. I. Bannister, Anne. II. Huntington, Annie, 1962-

BF723.C57 C64 2002
362.7--dc21

2002016136

British Library Cataloguing in Publication Data
A CIP catalogue record for this book is available from the British Library

ISBN 1 84310 125 8

Printed and Bound in Great Britain by
Athenaeum Press, Gateshead, Tyne and Wear

Contents

Part I – The Curtain Rises

Part II – Action Across Organisational Divides: Health, Education and the Juvenile Justice System

Part III – Action Methods and Child Maltreatment

Part IV – The Curtain falls

Special note: confidentiality statement

In order to protect the identities of children and young people mentioned in this book their real names have not been used, except in the chapter by Nick Luxmoore where the young people wished their own names to appear. In addition the names of professional colleagues have been changed, where necessary, to protect children. Occasionally, also, personal and family details about some children have been altered, where these could lead to identification.

Part I
The Curtain Rises

CHAPTER I

Warming up
Introducing Action Methods and Work with Young People

Anne Bannister and Annie Huntington

Action methods and child-centred practice

Attitudes to children and young people change over space and time. This is unsurprising when we consider the extent to which childhood can be said to be 'socially constructed', culturally defined and re-defined by actors on the stage of life (Aries 1962). Despite criticisms of the characterisation of childhood as a distinct and separate state from adulthood, and questions about the extent to which continuity or change has defined adult/child relationships, there is some consensus as to the importance of exploring the way we think about childhood and children (Cunningham 1995): not least as competing discourses shape the social spaces within which we engage in our everyday interactions as adults and children. For example, is there a disjuncture between the romantic ideal of childhood and the lived reality of childhood for many children? Are childhood and adulthood distinct and separate, or fused, states? (Cunningham 1995). However childhood is defined, and whether we can pinpoint a 'cut off' point that signals the end of childhood, there is a period of life that can seen as 'qualitatively different from adulthood'(Butler and Williamson 1994, p.1). Further, the 'early years' have been cogently demonstrated to be an important period in the development of any nation's citizens (Brandon, Schofield and Trinder 1998), as has the transition period into adulthood (see Cossa, this volume).

Thinking about and taking children and young people into account is important at many levels – for example, the strategic as well as the local. At the political level we could agree that 'child impact assessment is built into the process of government' (Newell 2000, p.47). Those nation states that have created children's rights commissioners, or are considering doing so, understand the importance of independent representation to protect the interests of children in 'all matters of public policy and administration that affect their lives' (Newell 2000, p.7). This might be viewed as an expression of adults 'speaking out for' rather than 'speaking for' children (Reinharz 1992). At the local organisational level staff working within child welfare services, as well as other sectors like health or education, need to ensure they actively engage their young 'consumers' as services are planned, delivered and evaluated if the rhetoric of 'participation' is ever to become a reality for this group (e.g. Cloke and Davies 1995; Freeman *et al.* 1996). Finally, at the interpersonal level we need to consider how we communicate with children and young people, as many of the authors in this volume clearly have. As we do so we need to ensure that we do not ignore the history of prior adult attempts to engage with children and young people in non-hierarchical, child-centred and empowering ways (e.g. Axline 1947; Axline 1964; Crompton 1980; Hostler 1953).

Many committed and courageous people have attempted to work in child-centred ways whilst occupying a range of professional roles. One example may highlight this point. Francoise Dolto,[1] who died in 1988, was a French child psychoanalyst, doctor and paediatrician. Unusually, for a woman of her time, she regarded children as persons to be listened to in their own right. She discussed family situations directly with children instead of talking over them, or about them, to parents. When listening to and observing a child she would say that she used her intuition, picking up on silences and unfinished sentences, noting gestures and body language. She insisted on the importance of speaking frankly, as one child speaks to another, or as to an adult (i.e. to a subject with needs and desires rather than to an object). This is what Francoise Dolto described as 'talking true' and with which she achieved many successes. Following, rather than always thinking we can or should lead; actively listening rather than always talking; engaging with children on their terms not just ours; being respectful of what they can do rather than largely focusing on what they cannot do (applying the deficit model of child development); or bringing our creativity and knowledge to the interactions we have with them, are all examples of routes to child-centred interactions. Exercising authority and acting responsibly, without abusing the power we have as adults in relationships with children and young people, is crucial if our interactions are to be liberating and appropriate rather than neglectful or oppressive (e.g. Department of Health 2000).

Children, like adults, engage in meaning seeking activities and interactions. As children and young people work to make sense of the world around them adults need to remember to listen to what they have to say about their world, which may mean we need to engage with children and young people using methods that make it more likely that they will be able to communicate what they think and feel to us. Hence the focus of this edited collection, the role of action methods as a route to creative, meaningful and empowering interactions between older and younger citizens.

Action methods – genesis and development

The genesis of 'action methods' in psychotherapy is often credited to J.L. Moreno, the first psychiatrist/psychotherapist to use the concept of 'group psychotherapy'. He was also the inventor of psychodrama, a method of therapy which can be conducted individually or à deux but is usually carried out in groups. Moreno recognised the connections between body and mind which are still not fully acknowledged today. In the early twentieth century, observing children playing in the parks of Vienna, he began to understand that their play was a necessary part of their development and not simply recreation. He realised the importance of spontaneity and how this could be used creatively in action. Many years later, the English psychiatrist D.W. Winnicott recognised that therapy could be described as 'two people playing together'. He also stated that anxiety underlies children's play, and that relieving this through play is essential for their health. He called play 'the gateway to the unconscious' (Winnicott 1964).

Moreno also understood that the interaction between people at play is often on many levels, including mind, body and spirit. He recognised that to communicate fully with others we must make connections on all these levels. He states that the importance of an action method is that 'it is a three-dimensional one and takes place in the present, not removed in point of time' (Fox 1987, p.99). He stresses that it relies on spontaneity, an immediate response by the person which is often felt directly in the body and is likely to be more genuine than a contrived and retrospective narrative. Blatner (1997) points out that many of Moreno's action techniques, which he used in psychodrama, have been incorporated by other therapists, for example the use of 'sculpture' in family therapy and the 'empty chair' in gestalt therapy. These are powerful techniques in which the body plays the major part.

But the discovery of the power of action methods is not confined to psychotherapy. Slade (1995), working in schools before the second world war, used art, drama and dance with children and, in particular, he encouraged them to move around and use their bodies expressively. He noticed that children seemed to need 'personal play' and 'projected play' in order to develop. In personal play he suggests that the child uses the whole body, in running around and so on, and in projected play the child projects feelings onto toys, dolls or other play materials. His ideas were taken up and refined by dramatherapist and anthropologist Jennings (1992) who stressed the power of embodiment. Powerful stories such as myths and legends can only be fully experienced and appreciated as we incorporate them into action and embodiment. Their messages, and the experience which they contain, may need more than words to be fully appreciated.

To return to the theme of play, it is important to note the contribution made by Axline (1947) and her discovery of play therapy. She also used the term 'non-directive therapy' which she states is based on the 'assumption that the individual has within himself (*sic*), not only the ability to solve his own problems satisfactorily, but also this growth impulse that makes mature behaviour more satisfying than immature behaviour' (p.15). It is this belief, in children's own ability for growth and healing, through play, that lies at the heart of our use of action methods.

Why action methods for contemporary work with children and young people?

We believe that action methods, used in an informed and non-directive way, can help children and young people to develop to maturity. The authors, established and new, who have contributed to this book illustrate many different ways of using action methods with children of all ages and abilities in a range of settings. The key components of any action method may be defined as follows:

1. Stating the obvious, 'the essence of action methods is *action*' (Williams 1989, p.16).

2. The method offers a vehicle for creative, spontaneous and life affirming *encounters*.

3. The method is primarily *experiential* and *social* as it enables people to 'create a community to share in the performance of their lives' (Williams 1991, p.1).

4. Use of action methods offers a route to reveal often hidden or unacknowledged aspects of experience in an immediate, fresh and dynamic way as they 'send a verbal narrative into *space and time*'

(Williams 1989, p.16). Personal memories, or collective memories, such as myths and legends are easily communicated in action pictures.

5. Active exploration, experimentation and rehearsal for change is made possible as the method creates opportunities for people to act, reflect and integrate new insights in a reflexive, cyclical and holistic manner that engages *mind, body and spirit.*

6. People are offered opportunities to re-script individual and collective experience *through the articulation of new narratives or the revising of old ones.*

7. Feelings and emotions are expressed through *embodiment.* Body language and facial expression are deemed as important as words. The method offers opportunities to explore emotion, sensation, imagination, beliefs and behaviour.

It will be realised that action methods can, and are, used with adults as well as children and young people. Not just in therapy, but in education, problem solving, people management and artistic projects, action methods are becoming more common. The authors in this volume, however, collectively throw some light on the reasons why action methods are so effective as well as explaining how to use the methods with different kinds of young people in various settings. Finally, they remind us that action methods encompass a spectrum of experiential approaches to exploring and understanding the world around us.

Overview of chapters

Anne Bannister writes about various theories of child development and, in particular, about the effects of trauma upon development. She describes how action methods can replace early attachment processes which may have been damaged or inadequate. She uses new research from neurobiology to illustrate this theme and uses examples from her own ongoing research to show how action methods can also provide the necessary safety and containment.

Mother and son, Sue Jennings and Andy Hickson use their own histories as a background to their philosophies regarding work with children and adolescents. Together with practical explanations of drama games and descriptions of their work, they discuss such essential topics as assessment, engagement and attachment, boundaries and, most importantly, how workers with young people must take care of themselves.

Gail Smith focuses on communicating with young people who stammer using action methods. She describes the application of psychodramatic methods with two young people and draws out theoretical points linked to their experiences. More specifically, she illustrates how psychodrama has been used to help young people disclose their stammering, share their feelings and attitudes about it, work through and resolve some of the difficulties they are experiencing in life.

Kate Kirk describes and discusses the application of action methods as creative therapeutic media, which can be adopted when working with young people who are living with a life-threatening or life-limiting illness. She provides fresh, rich textured descriptions of her work with young people in order to demonstrate that amid the drama of illness art, creativity and spontaneity can exist. Finally, she offers a brief review of the emotional costs, and need for support, for staff working in this area.

Nick Luxmoore offers a clear account of a peer education project that trains, supports, supervises and evaluates the work of school counsellors (aged 17–18 years). The counsellors use active methods to facilitate their, and others', learning. Drawing extensively on young people's own written reports of their experience as facilitators he enables us to 'hear' the voices of young people involved in the project.

Ioanna Gagani and Sandra Grieve explore the application of action methods with young autistic children. Focusing on what children can do, finding ways to follow their lead, working creatively with parents and considering the needs of the 'whole' child form the bedrock of their approach to building bridges with children. Helping autistic children find their way in the world is key to their interventions and the application of action methods the cornerstone of their practice.

Sue Curtis liaises closely with teachers, in the classroom, to help children who are having difficulties at school. Using the medium of dance movement therapy she works with groups of 'junior school' children and her chapter gives clear explanations of the method. She describes how several children learned how to use their whole bodies to help themselves to enter more fully into school life and activities.

Erica Hollander describes how psychodramatic techniques can be used with youthful offenders, and their families, to bring clarity to family difficulties. The action work helps families to understand how the young people have become involved in criminal activity and how the families can help and support them towards change. The violence of some of these adolescents is defused within the enactment and they are able to empathise with their victims.

Mario Cossa uses both psychodrama and sociodrama and incorporates Jungian archetypes into his work with troubled adolescents. Using the creativity of the young people, and keeping within the safety of the metaphor, he introduces challenges, and quests, which the adolescents can tackle together, as a group. His work is reminiscent of shamanic ritual and has powerful resonance with which the young people obviously can identify.

Paul Holmes and his colleagues work with children who have attachment difficulties and who are now in long-term foster placements or adopted. This innovative use of three-dimensional methods combined with family therapy is illustrated in action, with practical examples. This is an area of child protection work which has been somewhat ignored previously. The project that Dr Holmes describes represents a co-operation between departments of Health, Social Services and Education. Its benefits for children and their 'new' parents cannot be overstressed.

Chip Chimera discusses the nature of 'facilitated contact' between parents and children and demonstrates how action methods can be used when working with difficult and painful material in a safe and structured way. She offers a clear practice example to ground her discussion of theoretical issues that need to be taken into account when engaging in this work.

Christina Citron gives powerful illustrations of how action methods, especially psychodrama, can be used with children as young as three years. Using dolls and puppets, she engages the traumatised children with whom she works, in her clinic, and enables them to express feelings about their abuse. They can illustrate their stories in action, even when they do not have the vocabulary for description, and so their experiences can be witnessed and validated.

Annie Huntington undertakes a systemic analysis of issues that may impede adults as they attempt to use action methods in their work with children and young people. She discusses a range of issues as she explores: the impact of wider structuring systems that fundamentally shape the terrain for practice; local social, community and organisational issues that frame adult:child interactions; intra-psychic issues and inter-personal concerns that impact on adult attempts at (re)configuring their relationships with, and ways of relating to, young people.

References

Aries, P. (1962) *Centuries of Childhood.* London: Jonathan Cape.

Axline, V.M. (1947) *Play Therapy.* New York: Ballantine Books.

Axline, V. (1964) *Dibs In Search of Self.* London: Penguin.

Blatner, A. (1997) *Acting-In: Practical Applications of Psychodramatic Methods,* 3rd edn. London: Free Association Books.

Brandon, M., Schofield, G. and Trinder, L. (1998) *Social Work With Children.* London: MacMillan.

Butler, I. and Williamson, H. (1994) *Children Speak. Children, Trauma and Social Work.* London: Longman/NSPCC.

Cloke, C. and Davies, M. (1995) 'Introduction.' In C. Cloke and M. Davies (eds) *Participation and Empowerment in Child Protection.* London: Pitman Publishing.

Crompton, M. (1980) *Respecting Children: Social Work with Young People.* London: Edward Arnold.

Cunningham, H. (1995) *Children and Childhood in Western Society since 1500.* London: Longman.

Department of Health (2000) *Consultation Document. Promoting Health for Looked After Children. A Guide to Healthcare Planning, Assessment and Monitoring.* HMSO: London.

Fox, J. (1987) *The Essential Moreno.* New York: Springer.

Freeman, I., Morrison, A., Lockhart, F. and Swanson, M. (1996) 'Consulting Services Users: The Views of Young People.' In M. Hill and J. Aldgate (eds) *Child Welfare Services. Developments in Law, Policy, Practice and Research.* London: Jessica Kingsley Publishers.

Hostler, P. (1953) *The Child's World.* London: Penguin Books.

Jennings, S. (1992) *Dramatherapy: Theory and Practice 2.* London and New York: Routledge.

Newell, P. (2000) *Taking Children Seriously. A Proposal for a Children's Rights Commissioner.* London: Calouste Gulbenkian Foundation.

Reinharz, S. (1992) *Feminist Methods in Social Research.* Oxford: Oxford University Press.

Slade, P. (1995) *Child Play: Its Importance for Human Development.* London and Bristol, Penn: Jessica Kingsley Publishers.

Williams, A. (1989) *The Passionate Technique. Strategic Psychodrama with Individuals, Families and Groups.* London: Tavistock/Routledge.

Williams, A. (1991) *Forbidden Agendas. Strategic Action in Groups.* London: Routledge.

Winnicott, D.W. (1964) *The Child, the Family, and the Outside World.* Harmondsworth, England: Penguin Books.

CHAPTER 2

Setting the Scene
Child Development
and the Use of Action Methods

Anne Bannister

Introduction: theories of child development

The mysteries of how we develop, from infants to adults, have long intrigued all those who are concerned with the study of human nature, from psychologists to creative therapists and psychoanalysts. Over a century ago Pierre Janet, and later, Sigmund Freud, were developing a psychoanalytic theory of development which stressed sexual drives and 'stages' such as oral, anal and genital. These theories were extended by many others, for example, Erik Erikson (1977), who also recognised that play was 'the royal road to the understanding of the infantile ego's efforts at synthesis' (p.188). In Erikson's awareness of the importance of the somatic process and the societal process of child development, as well as the ego process, he recognised that development was much more than an intra-psychic experience. Melanie Klein (1975) enlarged this awareness by introducing the theory of object relations to child development. She suggested that the baby protects 'good' feelings from 'bad' feelings, by 'splitting' these, both in itself and in the significant other, since it is unable to conceptualise the fact that such feelings may emanate from the same source. Thus she also extended developmental theories to include inter-personal relationships.

Donald Winnicott (1971) also made an important addition to psychoanalytic theories of development. He realised that play and the 'playing space' was vital to the complete development of children. He also understood and recognised the importance of the unique non-verbal communication between parent and child and with his concept of the 'transitional object' enlarged Klein's theories about projection. John Bowlby (1973) and others such as Ainsworth (1969) did much to explain the nature of 'attachments' between a child and

parental figures or other adults. It was realised that these attachments were the
basis for the further development of relationships in the child's life.

J.L. Moreno, who invented psychodrama, was clear that it was the
interaction between parents or adult carers and the child which helped to form
personality. He believed that the child's innate spontaneity, together with this
interaction, aided the formation of the infant's identity. Understanding of
emotions (one's own and those of others) and the ability to make relationships,
are the key to development. Around this time (mid-twentieth century), others
such as Vygotsky and Bronfenbrenner were working to understand the
influence of the whole environment, including wider family and community,
upon the developing child.

Howe (1993) brings together the theories of genetic inheritance (nature)
and the environment (nurture). He states that the brain is programmed with
certain capacities for development but that its potential cannot be achieved
until the environment provides examples and experiences for the potential
state. Moreover, he states, the quality of the examples and the experiences will
uniquely shape the child's eventual realisation of the potential. Thus whatever
the genetic inheritance of a particular child the environmental experiences may
determine the shape of that child in the future. However it is also clear that for
some children the way in which the brain is genetically 'programmed' can be so
deficient in certain areas that 'ordinary' interactions between the mother figure
and the child are not sufficient for the child to understand the nature of
emotions and relationships. Such children are described as autistic, or 'on the
autistic spectrum', with conditions such as Asperger's Syndrome. We now
know that it may be possible to help the development of such children by using
therapy which concentrates upon sensory and somatic experiences (see Chapter
7 in this volume).

Trauma and child development

Many children encounter problems in their development because of the
influence of trauma upon their lives. All trauma, from bereavement to serious
illness, has an influence upon development, but often this is mediated by good
support from parents, siblings and the wider family. In my own work, with
children who have been sexually abused, it is clear that serious damage to a
child's development may be avoided if that child has at least one person who
will give unconditional love and support. It is obvious that if the child is abused
by a family member then it may be more difficult for another family member to

give unconditional support. Typical examples in my own practice are children who have close bonds with a maternal grandmother who may have been their principal carer in their formative years. If such a child is sexually abused by an uncle, often grandmother's youngest son who is still at home, then the grand-mother's loyalty is divided and the abused child feels abandoned and disbe-lieved. A similar situation occurs when an older brother sexually abuses his young sister. In one such case the girl I was working with drew pictures of 'half a house', the other half being absent from her drawing. She expressed her fears that her home had been split and that loyalties had been divided.

A child who is healthily attached to a non-abusing parent, or other caring figures, will have some protection from the damage caused by abuse, even if the adults are unable to prevent the abuse itself. However abusers will often seek to destroy healthy attachment relationships by undermining them. An example from my own practice is of a 'friend of the family' who took a child out regularly for 'treats' at weekends and, at the same time, subtly disparaged the parents who could not afford such 'treats'. This man was typical of many sexual abusers in that he also spent time building his own attachment to the child through play and support. This process is known as 'grooming' the child to be abused (Bagley and Thurston 1996; Colton and Vanstone 1996).

The sexual abuser thus forms an unhealthy attachment with the child. It is unhealthy because a bond of trust is formed and then the trust is betrayed. Trust is basic to the attachment process and when that trust is broken the foundations of the child's world are damaged. Herman (1998, pp.51–52) quotes Janoff-Bulman (1985): 'Traumatic events destroy the victims' fundamental assumptions about the safety of the world, the positive value of the self, and the meaningful order of creation.' A betrayed child may remain more vulnerable to further unhealthy attachments, and to further abuse.

Problems with attachments may also lead to difficulties with identity. These difficulties are also true for those who have been physically and emo-tionally abused, or neglected. Children form their identity in relation to that of their parents or carers. If such carers are abusive or neglectful the child will form a scenario in which he or she is necessarily 'bad' because the carers cannot be other than 'good', since they also provide whatever nurture or shelter is given. This self view is frequently reinforced by abusive parents. In my own practice a six-year-old girl drew herself as a 'wicked witch' since this was how her sexually abusive father frequently described her. This concept of being 'evil' is impossible for the child to contain all the time and so she dissociates frequently. Dissociation, especially during abuse, is a protective mechanism in which children become fragmented and aloof from their bodies. The fragmentation of the child's inner self prevents the integration of identity (Herman 1998). This early separation from the body also causes many of the somatic symptoms which are common in victims of abuse.

It is not surprising, therefore, that a sense of isolation is often reported by adults who have suffered an abusive childhood. Making relationships may be problematic and communication with others may be impaired. In extreme cases this may lead to a diagnosis of 'learning difficulties' in a child. Keeping the child separate from others is often a deliberate tactic in adult abusers and encouraging reliance on the abusive person merely isolates the child further. One ten-year-old girl was isolated at school because she appeared to be unable to communicate. She spoke little and her reading and writing were very poor. In therapy with me she became very controlling and watchful. I waited through long periods of silence, allowing her to explore material in the playroom. Eventually, she took charge of the situation, picking up a marker and writing on a white board. Her spelling was 'imaginative' and difficult to understand until I realised it was phonetic, and expressed her very strong local accent. She wrote a 'story' about an evil king who hurt all the children. Later she acted this out and was able to talk more freely about the father who had abused herself and her siblings.

Action methods and child development

Moreno's theory of child development (Moreno and Moreno 1944; Fox 1987) suggested that personality develops in three stages: the first stage of finding identity, the second stage of recognising the self and the third stage of recognising the other. However, Moreno made it clear that these stages are not inevitable and that they develop only with interaction from parents or carers of the child. Importantly, he suggested that these stages are reflected in the actions of the primary carer for the infant. For instance a mother may talk to her baby, trying to interpret her cry. She may suggest that the child is cold, or hungry and will try to pacify her. Thus the mother 'doubles' the child's expression of feeling in an effort to interpret it, both for herself, and for the baby. This technique of 'doubling' is used extensively in psychodrama. Usually a member of the therapeutic group comes alongside the protagonist (or key player in the drama) and copies her movements or bodily position and also endeavours to vocalise the feelings. The protagonist may accept or reject the words of the 'double' but it is important that the position of the body, or expression of the face, expresses the true feeling more accurately than the spoken word.

This is one of the key components in 'action methods', which are all based on an understanding of the close connections between body and mind. Moreno had a saying – 'the body remembers what the mind forgets' – and this frequently becomes apparent in psychodrama, dramatherapy, play therapy, dance/movement therapy, and many other therapies in which 'talk' is not the only, or even the main medium of expression. These therapies seek to utilise all the means of communication at our disposal, from eye contact to touch. There is recognition that these means were used by the pre-verbal child. So early memories are usually iconic, and sensory. Smells and feelings may be paramount. When another trusted person is able to express those feelings the child feels validated and understood.

Another psychodramatic technique which is often used naturally by a primary carer for a child, is that of 'mirroring'. The adult repeats the words and actions of the child so they can see how they are perceived by others. Of course, this must be done in a supportive and helpful way. In psychodrama the protagonist's behaviour may be mirrored by a group member, if the protagonist is willing. Sometimes several group members may do this (in their own individual ways) so that the protagonist develops a broader view. This 'mirroring' is also a key component in many 'action methods' and it mimics the natural mirroring which an infant receives from parents, siblings and other family members and friends. Both mirroring and doubling help the child with the formation of identity and the expression of feelings.

The third stage of child development, according to Moreno, is role reversal, when the child begins to understand that others have feelings and needs which may be different from the self. From the age of two or three most children act out different roles in their play, by themselves or with siblings. They 'rehearse' potential roles which may become part of their role repertoire. They begin to understand fantasy roles such as cult figures from TV and reality based roles such as 'mum' or 'dad' or 'teacher'. The concept of sharing is learned through the ability to role reverse with the other. This is why most two-year-olds still find sharing difficult.

I suggest therefore, that during the first stage of development, the formation of identity, the child is asking 'What do I feel?' and the doubling reactions of those around her help the infant to understand what those feelings are, and to express them. In the second stage the infant is asking 'Who am I?' and seeing herself reflected through the mirror of those around will help the infant to determine her identity. Finally, and inevitably, the child asks 'Who are you?' as she not only understands that she is a separate person, but that she is uniquely different from others. Through reversing roles she begins to understand the complexity of herself, and others.

Evidence from research

Research is still taking place on understanding how the effects of abuse in infancy and childhood affect the developmental processes mentioned above. Pynoos, Steinberg and Goenjian (in van der Kolk *et al.* 1996) have listed physical symptoms, such as sleep disturbances, which in turn can lead to irritability and difficulties in concentration and attention. In itself this can cause serious learning problems and also relationship difficulties. Pynoos also quotes changes in brain activity which have been noted in various studies (Kagan 1991; Krystal *et al.* 1989). The work of neurobiologist Allan Schore (1994) also throws some light on this. In his detailed and extensive descriptions of the attachment process between the primary carer and the child he states that 'opiates play a unique role in socioemotional, imprinting, and attachment developmental processes' (p.145). He describes the mechanism whereby the emotionally expressive face of the primary carer induces alterations in opioid peptides in the child's developing brain. He states that these changes (usually induced towards the end of the child's first year) make permanent morphological changes in the brain. I suggest that it may be possible that disturbance of the attachment process, which frequently occurs when children are abused in their early years by a person who has some responsibility for their wellbeing, leads to a distortion of parts of the learning process.

This suggestion may also go some way towards explaining why creative therapies that use action techniques which echo developmental processes (for instance 'doubling', 'mirroring' and 'role reversal') are particularly effective with those whose developmental attachment processes have been disturbed. Children who have suffered trauma, of whatever nature, or who have been neglected, negated, or disparaged, may suffer from blocks in expressiveness and creativity. Others, who have also suffered trauma, may have also been encouraged in their creative play. Such children do develop creative ways of expressing their feelings. It seems to be important that such creativity is encouraged in all children to enable them to overcome any earlier 'blockages' and to reach their full potential.

Linked to the neurobiological aspects of child development, and childhood trauma, is the realisation that severe abuse is nearly always accompanied by embodiment, or somatic symptoms of trauma. Young (1992) points to the fact that many of the effects of child sexual abuse concern the body: dissociation, multiple personality disorder (now known as dissociated identity disorder: DID), the eating disorders, somatic disturbances, self-harm and suicide. Dissociation is often described as 'leaving the body' and most victims of severe sexual abuse will experience this repeatedly for many years after the abuse. Although a child or adult may dissociate as a healthy, protective mechanism during periods of extreme trauma, this mechanism can eventually become involuntary and occur with the slightest of triggers at inopportune moments in later life.

Anorexia and bulimia are common symptoms in abuse survivors as are the problems of obesity. Young quotes Briere (1984) who has shown that many young people who have been abused have also self-harmed or made suicide attempts. Young, therefore, recommends that dramatherapy and dance/movement therapy, both of which use embodiment, should be used in reparative treatment. He also mentions other creative therapies such as poetry and art therapy which include aspects of embodiment which may be particularly relevant for abuse survivors.

In fact the ability to be flexible within creative therapies is an important therapeutic aspect. Each child will prefer to express him/herself in a unique way. There are a multitude of creative ways, within play and the arts, and young people can be encouraged to choose the way that they find most comfortable. This choice may depend on the child having been enabled to play and having been given suggestions about artistic expression. Of course the opportunity to play and be creative is essential for all children, not only those who may have been abused. Few children will survive childhood without some traumatic experiences and the naturally healing benefits of play, movement and creativity, must be encouraged.

Play, creativity and spontaneity are closely connected and Kellermann (2000) considers that 'spontaneity...is responsible for the equilibrium of the person' (p.26). Kellermann trained with Moreno who believed that spontaneity was demonstrated by every child during the birth process and that it was essential for development. Trauma can inhibit spontaneity but Kellermann reminds us that psychodrama can 'enable the growth of spontaneity that may alleviate the psychological impact of trauma' (p.26). It is this capability of the creative therapies to trigger the body's own natural healing mechanisms which may be the key to their success.

Returning to neurobiological explanations of emotional development, Schore (1994) states that 'events that occur during infancy, especially transactions with the social environment, are indelibly imprinted into the structures that are maturing the first years of life' (p.3). In particular he stresses the 'interactive' nature of early experiences and how these are not passively received by the infant. They are essential transactions which affect the development of the maturing child. Schore brings together evidence from developmental neuro-chemistry, neurobiology, developmental psychology, psychoanalysis and infant psychiatry to show that 'affect' is transacted within the mother/child dyad and that this is primarily non-verbal. He is concerned not simply with the changing phases and functions of child development but with the structure of relationships which affect the child's behaviour.

He states that face-to-face reciprocal gaze transactions between mother and child induce particular neuroendocrine changes which 'imprint' on the child's brain and cause 'high levels of positive affect and play behaviour, and subsequently the establishment of the capacity to form an interactive representational model that underlies an early functional system of affect regulation' (p.65). It is clear that in his opinion it is the interaction in the mother/child dyad which is the key to healthy development. If we use this research information, together with the research done by Young on embodiment, it seems that an interactive therapy which uses the body may duplicate some of the developmental processes which occur during infancy and childhood.

Herman (1998) presents much evidence to show how traumatic events become frozen memories (pp.33–50). She gives many examples which show that 'traumatic memories lack verbal narrative and context, and they are encoded in the form of vivid sensations and images'. A particularly strong piece of evidence which she quotes is from Lenore Terr (1988) who had documented the histories of 20 children who had experienced severe trauma in their first two and a half years of life (a vital developmental time). None could give any verbal description of the documented trauma. However at around the age of five, 18 out of the 20 were able to re-enact these events in their play with uncanny accuracy. One child, for instance, denied any knowledge or memory of his sexual abuse by a babysitter during his first two and a half years. In his play, however, he re-enacted scenes which showed a pornographic movie made by the babysitter.

I suggest that since these sensory and iconic memories can apparently only be accessed in a sensory and iconic way, such as that provided in play, or creative therapies which use play, then these methods should be utilised to help children who have been abused during their developmental years.

Safety and containment

Any method of therapy or education of children must ensure their safety. The extensive use of metaphor and symbolism within the arts enables distressing or difficult experiences and emotions to be shown or enacted in safe ways. Re-enactment of traumatic events can lead to retraumatisation of vulnerable young people. It is important, therefore, that action methods which portray scenes and emotions should be safely contained. Adolescents in groups often prefer to act out symbolic representations of their difficulties (see Chapter 10 this volume). When they feel safe, they may become able to act out, or talk about, these difficulties. Safe containment of strong emotions, within the metaphor of a story, enables them to be in touch with these emotions without loss of face. Younger children naturally use metaphor within their play and so the continuation of this, stylised into a more adult form of child play, can be acceptable to teenagers who would reject anything which seemed 'childish'.

Therapeutic research groups

This book gives many examples of the use of action methods with children, both as therapy and as communication. The following examples are taken from research undertaken by myself on the effects of creative therapies with children who have been sexually abused, and in them I seek to demonstrate how these methods were safely used to stimulate the children's own capacities for healing. For the purposes of the research two therapeutic groups were set up for boys and girls, aged from 7 to 9 and from 9 to 11 respectively. Each group contained both boys and girls and was run by a therapeutic team of men and women who were psychotherapists, social workers or psychologists. All had several years experience in working with abused children. All the children had been abused by men, the majority, but not all, by someone within the extended family network. Several of the children had suffered other traumatic events such as parental divorce or separation or witnessing domestic violence. The first group was run for 20 weeks but this seemed to be about four weeks too long for the younger children to sustain commitment. The second group was therefore run for 16 weeks.

The aim of both groups was to try to recreate some of the children's developmental stages by using psychodramatic action techniques. Dramatherapy and playtherapy were used to contain these actions in a safe way. Strong feelings were released in the group, and often projected on to the staff, several of whom reacted by somatising these feelings in various ailments and complaints. An interactive, creative approach was used by the therapeutic team. However, an overall structure for the sessions was followed, each week, in the interests of safety and containment. Group sessions started with very active games devised by the children themselves. Forms of 'tag' were popular, together with other well-known playground games. As the groups progressed, the children soon adapted these. For instance a simple game of 'tag', using a wolf puppet as the 'catcher', had rules about 'safe places' (on cushions) where one could not be caught. Eventually the children realised that they could carry the cushions around and so 'take their safety with them'. We believed that innovations such as these were developed by the children as they worked through their experiences.

Expressing feelings and emotions effectively was almost impossible for some of the children, but they were often able to do this through the medium of puppets (Carlson-Sabelli 1998). The puppets were allowed to show their feelings and tell the group why they felt as they did. Thus the children were able to project their own feelings onto the puppets and, through interaction and play, to understand a little about the feelings of others. Later in the group one child felt she should make it absolutely clear what was happening: 'Squirrel is feeling really, really mad today,' she said. Her own face expressed clearly her angry feelings. She began to relate the events which had angered her. 'It's really me that's mad today,' she then explained, 'but Squirrel is keeping me company.'

The main activity during each group session was always artistic and creative. Sometimes it involved the use of clay or paints and often it involved dressing-up and role play. Children worked separately at first with art materials but soon began to share their feelings as they worked. Eventually they were able to co-operate in making a collage. Role play began by individual children, or pairs, dressing up and taking fairy story roles. Later, collaboration with the whole group enabled the children to act out complete scenes, which they devised themselves. In the younger group the children played out mythical scenes which had significance for them. For instance 'mothers' were lost and found and had to make difficult decisions. These scenes echoed real events for the children. Often it was the reactions of their non-abusive parents, after the disclosures of abuse, which reverberated strongly for the young people.

In the older group, eventually, each of the children was able to enact small dream sequences from their own experience, within the group, and other group members were able to play roles. Thus real events were echoed in 'dreams' and contained within metaphors. During the group one child was the subject of renewed investigation by police (of past events) and consequent media attention. This caused additional problems for her and so she continued her therapy on an individual basis after the group had finished. She used the act-ing-out of dreams/nightmares in one-to-one sessions with myself and eventu-ally declared that most of the nightmares had disappeared and she had learned how to cope, herself, with the dreams.

All the children improved on measures of self-esteem and locus of control.[2] Many severely sexually abused children either become over controlling (fearing that a loss of control will lead to further abuse), or they become resigned 'victims' who feel that they have no control whatsoever over their lives. The children in the groups, when assessed at the start, were either over-controlling or too passive, but after the groups their locus of control was more normal. In addition changes to the children's behaviour were monitored by means of 'Strengths and Difficulties questionnaires' (Goodman 1997) given to teachers and parents before and after the group. Overall there was much improvement in behaviours although more assertive behaviour in the children was not necessarily welcomed by parents.

When assessing children for these groups the staff team decided that it would not be appropriate to take children who had been completely unable to make any attachments, or relationships. Such a child could be helped in indi-vidual therapy but would find group work difficult. Some of the children who were assessed were, therefore, referred for individual therapy. However, diffi-culties with identity, emotions, and relationships were common in all group members. For example one boy hit out at a staff member whilst declaring that he was 'very happy'. Although one of the girls could express some feelings through the puppets she frequently said 'I don't know what I feel'.

Another girl constantly expressed difficulties regarding gender. She always wanted to name the genders of the puppets but became distressed when she was not always able to do so. She also became angry at one of the male workers and said he was 'a girl' because he had long hair. She often copied a picture of a graceful Indian woman on the wall of the group room. She asked questions about how the woman in the picture was able to walk so gracefully, carrying a water pitcher on her head. Gender identity seemed to be compromised and this is common with some types of abuse.

Relationships within both groups were often chaotic as children moved between being over-controlling or passive. This led to a great deal of anger. The staff were sometimes the objects of projections of strong feelings from the children. The anger in one of the groups was carried, at first, by one boy, who was aggressive to the other children, and sometimes to staff. Eventually, half way through the group, he decided to leave. Although the children had complained frequently about his aggressive behaviour, they expressed sorrow when he left and made a special card to send to him.[3] The collective group anger was then taken up by a girl who frequently polarised her feelings. Her anger was expressed in biting comments, usually about the boys in the group, but at other times she acted as a peacemaker. Later still, in the same group, another girl sought to control everyone, including staff. It often seemed as if she was afraid of her own anger and that of others.

During both groups the staff made frequent use of the techniques of doubling, mirroring and role-reversal. Staff members would 'double' a child who was having difficulty in expressing feelings. This was often very facilitative and helped to build harmony within the group. For instance one boy was having a minor tantrum about the possession of a certain colour of paint for his art work. The therapist moved alongside him, doubling his body position. 'Shall I be you for a minute?' she asked. No reply. She continued, 'I really need that colour and feel as if I can't wait until Jenny has used it.' The boy nodded, silently, apparently surprised that he had been heard. 'Jenny' looked surprised too but held on to the paint, looking at the boy expectantly. 'Yeah,' he said, 'Okay then. I'll have it next.'

The 'mirror' technique was practised as puppets were used to reflect feelings of the self as well as others. Also, in the use of clay and paints, emotions were expressed through the mirror of art and staff were sometimes amazed at the accuracy with which other children commented on the artwork. For instance one girl painted a fishlike creature. A staff member asked if it was a 'whale'. She made no comment. A younger boy said, 'I think it's an angry shark,' and the girl nodded vigorously. One of the boys made a face from clay which clearly expressed all his anger. An older girl made a clay face, carefully made up with red lips, blue eye shadow and mascara. After admiring it she painted over the mouth with a black moustache and beard and put dark sunglasses over the eyes. 'This is a cool dude in his shades,' she said, apparently satisfied with the change of gender.

Role play and role reversal was practised by all the children who spontaneously created roles for themselves and others. Staff were designated roles by the children. Often these were subservient to the queens and kings or witches and fairies whom they chose to play themselves. They endowed themselves with mythical powers and became confident in expressing this. Like most children of this age they were concerned with 'fairness' and rough, but fair, justice was the rule of the game. After one session all the children attacked a stuffed gorilla who had been designated as 'an abuser'. Together, they threw him out of the room.

One girl acted out a dream where her family were all on holiday where they experienced a volcano erupting. Only a few members of the family survived. This seemed to be an appropriate metaphor for the family disruption which occurs after sexual abuse. Another young person seemed to feel that her voice had never been properly heard, that the fact of her abuse had not been witnessed. Her scene concerned an attack on a girl by someone disguised as a clown. Also in this scene was a witness who was 'deaf' and therefore could not hear the victim's cries for help. Neither could the witness see the attack because he was behind a door. To have one's abuse 'witnessed' by a therapist, or by others in a therapeutic group, is often a healing experience.

Conclusions

Evidence that creative action methods have positive effects on children and adolescents is amply provided in the existing literature and in the chapters of this volume. The amount of positive evidence from psychotherapy research, and neurobiological research, is now increasing rapidly. Children probably now have less natural opportunities to play creatively, and thus to practise self-healing. The introduction of creative action methods in schools and clubs as well as in specifically therapeutic situations must be of benefit to all young people.

For adults who work with children creatively there is a need for support, and adequate supervision, as well as sufficient training. In group work the children's own potential to help each other is increased but, as some of the above examples show, the negative projections of feeling, from traumatised children, can be a heavy burden for staff. It is seldom appropriate for staff to run action groups alone, and it is important to allow time for planning and for adequate staff debriefing. This can be done very quickly, soon after each session, with a colleague, but regular supervision sessions with an experienced child care worker are also very valuable. Nurturing one's own spontaneity and creativity is also essential in ensuring that the self-healing process is a mutual one.

References

Ainsworth, M.D.S. (1969) 'Object relations, dependency and attachment: a theoretical review of the infant-mother relationship.' *Child Development 40*, 969–1025.

Bagley, C. and Thurston, W.E. (1996) *Understanding and Preventing Child Sexual Abuse, Vol.2.* Aldershot: Arena.

Bowlby, J. (1973) *Attachment and Loss. Volume 2. Separation: Anxiety and Anger.* New York: Basic Books.

Briere, J. (1984) 'The effects of childhood sexual abuse on later psychological functioning: defining a post-sexual abuse syndrome.' Paper presented at the Third National Conference on Sexual Victimization of Children, Washington, DC.

Carlson-Sabelli, L. (1998) 'Children's therapeutic puppet theatre: action, interaction and co-creation.' *The International Journal of Action Methods 51*, 3, 99–112.

Colton, M. and Vanstone, M. (1996) *Betrayal of Trust.* London: Free Association Books.

Erikson, E. (1977 reprint) *Childhood and Society.* London: Paladin.

Fox, J. (1987) *The Essential Moreno.* New York: Springer Publishing.

Goodman, R. (1997) 'The Strengths and Difficulties questionnaire: a research note.' *Journal of Child Psychology and Psychiatry 38*, 5, 581–586.

Herman, J.L. (1998) *Trauma and Recovery: From Domestic Abuse to Political Terror.* London: Pandora. (Original work published 1992.)

Howe, D. (1993) *On Being a Client.* London: Sage.

Janoff-Bulman, R.(1985) 'The Aftermath of Victimization: Rebuilding Shattered Assumptions'. In C. Figley (ed) *Trauma and its Wake.* New York: Brunner/Mazel.

Kagan, J. (1991) 'A conceptual analysis of the affects.' *Journal of the American Psychoanalytic Association 39*, 109–130.

Kellermann, P.F.(2000) 'The Therapeutic Aspects of Psychodrama with Traumatized People.' In P.F. Kellermann and M.K. Hudgins (eds) *Psychodrama with Trauma Survivors: Acting Out your Pain.* London and Philadelphia, PA: Jessica Kingsley Publishers.

Klein, M.(1975) *Collected Works, Volume 1: Love, Guilt and Reparation.* London: Hogarth Press.

Krystal, J.J., Kosten, T.R., Perry, B.D., Southwick, S., Mason, J.W. and Giller, E.L. (1989) 'Neurobiological aspects of PTSD: review of clinical and pre-clinical studies.' *Behaviour Therapy 20*, 177–198.

Maines, B. and Robinson, G. (1988) *B/G-Steem: A Self-esteem Scale with Locus of Control Items.* Bristol: Lucky Duck.

Moreno, J.L. and Moreno, F.B.(1944) 'Spontaneity theory of child development.' *Psychodrama Monographs No.8.* New York: Beacon House.

Pynoos, R.S., Steinberg, A.M. and Goenjian, A. (1996) 'Traumatic Stress in Childhood and Adolescence: Recent Developments and Current Controversies.' In B.A. van der Kolk, A.C. Mcfarlane and L. Weisaeth (eds) *Traumatic Stress: The Effects of Overwhelming Experience on Mind, Body and Society.* New York: The Guilford Press.

Schore, A.N. (1994) *Affect Regulation and the Origin of the Self.* Hillsdale, NJ and Hove: Lawrence Erlbaum.

Terr, L. (1988) 'What happens to early memories of trauma? A study of twenty children under age five at the time of documented traumatic events.' *Journal of the American Academy of Child and Adolescent Psychiatry 27*, 96–104.

Winnicott, D. (1971) *Playing and Reality.* London: Routledge.

Young, L. (1992) 'Sexual abuse and the problem of embodiment.' *Child Abuse and Neglect 16*, 89–100.

CHAPTER 3

Pause for Thought
Action or Stillness with Young People

Sue Jennings and Andy Hickson

There are few studies more fascinating, and at the same time more neglected, than those of the teeming populations that exist in the dark realms of the soil. We know too little of the threads that bind the soil organisms to each other and to their world, and to the world above. (Carson p. 62)

Section one

Introduction

Working with children and young people is one of the most challenging areas for people in educational and therapeutic fields. Childhood and adolescence are times of transition and vulnerability, which are manifested in different ways. However it is also a time when we, as practitioners, are stretched to our limits at all levels.

As parents, who have been adolescents, we could both say 'Well, we have been there!' We have been through these stages and struggled with young people's issues over several decades. The fact that each and every one of us has been both child and adolescent must be an underlying theme for this book. Since we choose to write, research and work with young people, this must also have some connections with our own life experience. We have both had our own conflicts and wounds as teenagers, as we do as adults, and have found our own ways to resolve or deal with them. It is perhaps this recognition and continuous re-evaluation of changes that have occurred in us that has helped us to achieve consonance with groups who are struggling with their own expression and communication. When we stop learning we stop living, but what is the point in learning? Will it help me get a job? Will it prevent me from suffering violence?

Sue's journey

I would say that my teenage years included 'silent suffering'; as a war child I had to adjust to the family constantly moving around as my father looked after the practices for doctors who were away at the battle front. This I found a great adventure and have enjoyed travelling and moving ever since. However I was also one of the second half of the family – born when my parents were already middle-aged and seeing that life was not going to be the rosy spectre of child-centred education and a Steiner approach to life. My father challenged all bureaucracy, including compulsory school reports for his children, but he and my mother became very depressed.

Silent suffering means that you keep quiet and don't ask for extra classes because of financial shortage, that you do not query endless discussions about emigrating to a better life. A lot of things are unclear and it is better to keep quiet. Yet what better cushion for this than living in the heart of the country with endless walks and an awakening interest in nature, together with every encouragement to participate in the arts? It is a mixed legacy but one in which I can see the influence throughout my adult and parenting years. I always have attempted to include my children in decision making and planning, and to avoid secrecy, unlike my own experience. However from an even earlier age I tried to provide them with a creative and cultural environment and encouraged their own artistic work.

My journey into the theatre at a very early age had all the support from my parents, but my ideas to apply theatre with people with special needs grew out of a particular need of mine. I was constantly seeing young people needing to make sense of their worlds. I was observing children and adolescents who were not told things or who did not have things explained to them, or about whom there were gross generalisations being made of who they were and what they believed in. I can support teachers and community workers who have reached burn-out as well as empathise with young people who feel at the bottom of the pile and totally hopeless.

I can see that I have always needed to try and build bridges. I seem to work from the idea of 'chaos to clarity'. What do we actually mean through our com-munications as adults to young people? Does it actually have a 'meaning' as such? Or is it a defence, a taking of a stance, or our moralistic viewpoint?

Andy's journey

I spent two years at secondary school in London. At the age of 13, I then spent two years living with my family in the Malaysian rainforest, where I received no formal western education. Then at 15 I returned to England to complete my final year of secondary school. That final year at secondary school has perhaps been the worst year of my life. Surprisingly enough I passed one O level and about five CSEs at age 16, before going on to college to take some more O levels. As well as being painful, school was boring. I wasn't bullied in a physical way but I did find myself to be slightly isolated as I appeared different from the other boys. I was actually embarrassed to be a schoolboy. I thought I was a man.

In Malaysia I was treated as an adult, not a child. I was respected for my beliefs, my ideas were listened to, and I felt a useful member of the society in which I was living. I learned how to speak another language, and to grapple with concepts alien to those I had been taught in England. I learned how to hunt and forage in the jungle, how to fish and set traps in the river, how to build a four bedroom bamboo and wood house with no nails, how to carve wood, build boats, sing, dance and play musical instruments. I learned how to clear a piece of jungle to plant crops, and how to cook, eat and enjoy the fruits of my labour. I learned how to sew, how to punt a boat for miles up a river, I also learned how to make friends. I was never forced to learn anything in Malaysia, but I probably learned more in those two years than I ever have at school or later at university.

My learning experiences in Malaysia took place 'in-action', in other words I was involved in activity which resulted in learning, which is just another way of saying that we learn from our everyday experiences. Our everyday experience is more or less of our own free will, and we are able to make choices. We have a legal obligation to go to school. When we are at school we are often made to learn things that are boring and appear useless or irrelevant to our lives. School is not the only place that we learn things. Learning is one of the things that makes us human, that gives us life. Our experiences, or our learning make us much of what we are. Not all our learning is active though; much comes passively from media such as television. As I learnt in Malaysia without knowing I was learning, I gained a kind of unconscious knowledge. It was not until I looked back at my time there and thought about it, that I realised many of the different things I had learned. This includes ways of thinking too.

Much of the work I am involved in surrounds difficult issues such as racism and bullying, each of which are often intertwined. As a young man I believed that in no way did I or had I ever held any racist views or beliefs. I had grown up interacting with people in a positive way from many different cultures and backgrounds. I remember as a boy discussing girls with one of my black friends, and we both agreed that white girls looked prettier than black girls. How did that thought get into my head and where did it come from? Certainly not from anyone I knew, but it was inside me none the less. It wasn't until this thought came to me that I realised the importance of challenging what we think we already know. In order to learn more about racism, I had to look at my own. I could not deny my own racism even though I found it distasteful. I was lucky that I found a process through theatre and action for this cathartic process to take place. It is a continual process and we never stop learning. In my work I try to role model that there is nothing wrong with making mistakes – the true test is whether we learn from them.

Our working models

SCENARIO 1:

A theatre-in-education play about bullying in schools: the audience is a group of disaffected youth in an inner city, multicultural school; a group of teachers stand at the back, disinterested and disengaged; the young people sit on the window-sill, chat, move around, ignore the play; the head teacher comes in, stops the play, and makes a speech: 'I have never been so ashamed of a class in this school, where are your manners when we have visitors…'. Young people continue to talk through his speech and the play continues. At the end of the day one pupil is excluded.

SCENARIO 2:

The same theatre-in-education play is being presented for a group of multi-cultural backers: bankers, financiers and their guests; they chat amongst themselves throughout the play and call out 'bring on the dancing girls', and laugh at their own cleverness. Despite the fact that they have helped to fund the project, they have no interest in the play whatsoever. They have no curiosity.

The behaviour in the first scene is not shocking; the class are disaffected youth who have become the focus for all the antagonism of the school hierarchy. They are an example of the target group that the programme is trying to address, but with no support from the staff. The staff sent the class along as just something for them to do. The head teacher's interruption made no difference to the situation, there were no bridges. However the second scene gives us some clues about the first. If 'mature' adults cannot show respect or at least basic good manners towards a play about young people and their difficulties, is it at all surprising that young people themselves do not show respect towards other people? Indeed the very disinterest shown by the backers, illustrates this 'cheque book' attitude towards social problems. If we throw money at it then we can salve our consciences, but we are not prepared actually to try and understand the issues. Maybe if we understand the issues, or are even a little bit curious, we may have to change in a more radical way or perhaps we shall get in touch with feelings that we do not want to know about. 'Bring on the dancing girls' is a very sexist and demeaning way of responding to an unfamiliar situation. It is reminiscent of one employer who always referred to the dramatherapist as 'the tambourine lady'.

The above scenes provide the basis for the philosophy of this chapter, together with a belief in the primacy of artistic experience in people's lives. We are not saying that we always achieve these ideals, but they act as a blueprint for our thinking about what we do: whether it is issue based theatre-in-education, community projects with people with special needs, or small group and individual therapeutic intervention with children and young people. We are not being partisan in this, even though many of these views have been adopted by various political parties. We call it an 'ecological model' because it takes into account the context of the individual and their culture, their culture in relation to the reality of global issues, and the human rights that underpin these global issues.

For example: can we possibly get any understanding of issues about bullying when adults who are financing an initiative behave with bullying tactics of ridicule themselves? If these people who are in positions of power cannot grasp the basic human right of respect, can we expect anything to change at either the macro or the micro level?

Our ten tenets

We believe that all our work with children and young people needs the following philosophical basis which is strategically researched, planned and then put into practice:

- work with young people should be based on respect
- work with young people should be contextualised within their values
- work with young people should be part of a wider eco-system

- work with young people should have a core structure of human rights

- work with young people should have a philosophy of creativity and action.

Furthermore, all our work with children and young people is based on some or all of the following methods, structures and theory, which includes both assessment as well as educational and therapeutic activities:

- action methods allow dramatic distance and, paradoxically, deeper understanding

- developmental structures mean age appropriate material, and build-on skills

- performative and playback approaches create a mirror of human experiences

- re-staging our lives ensures the opportunity for second chances and new pathways

- great stories and great plays lead to new understanding.

The philosophical base

Respect: meaning 'to treat with consideration, to avoid interfering with, harming, degrading, insulting, injuring or interrupting' (Concise Oxford Dictionary 1990). It is only through role modelling respect, and other desirable qualities, that we enable young people to acquire them. The example of the head teacher in the introduction shows the futility of haranguing young people to change their behaviour. Once young people have gone down the route of disaffection, it is extremely difficult to reclaim the ground, certainly in terms of mutuality.

One might ask, how can we treat with respect someone who spits and swears at us, who brings in a parent to beat us up, who makes false allegations about us? None of these actions have meaning in themselves, they are all ways of trying to be heard and trying to be seen. In observations of young people, these actions will get progressively more extreme if they are ignored. The task often seems insurmountable once people are in their teens. However a workshop which explores the theme of respect often produces surprising results.

Contextualised values: everybody has a value system and a belief system, and the principles may be very precise or slightly vague and rarely articulated. Nevertheless, the system is there, in the context of each individual. It may be based on a religious system which emanates from the family or from a 'conversion' away from the family. It may be a series of beliefs about the person, the family and the world. It often involves attitudes towards others that have de-valued the person: 'all teachers are dicks', 'all industry exploits people'. Many statements of values may say, for example, 'I believe in the family', yet the rate of family break-up has never been greater. People become disenchanted when they hear pupils express extremist values. However if the values are explored in conjunction with respect, some modification has to take place. We always need to remember that people's value systems will be conditioned through their own deprivation; and teenagers may feel that they 'have nothing left to lose'.

Eco-systems: the eco-system of the individual includes all the ways in which we interact with others and the environment. It goes beyond the 'context' of the previous tenet, and takes in a much wider landscape or map. The individual lives within several spheres of reference including the immediate environment, the society, the region, the country and the globe. All of these impact on each other. Many approaches to therapy emphasise *my* life and *my* needs. Our eco-approach also includes the needs of others, the environment and the global context.

Usually most of our attention is focused on our immediate environment. The wider implications of both our responsibilities, and others' responsibilities towards ourselves, has only recently come into consciousness. If we practise an ecological model of work, it can include issues beyond the individual and the family, and can expand human awareness of the global implications of what we do.

Rights based approach: we accept that everyone has the right to food and shelter and safety – then it starts to get a little blurred. How do we balance the rights of the individual and the rights of the group? A young person says that he has the right to play his stereo as loud as he wants. How does that balance with the rights of neighbours to a reasonably quiet life after 11 o'clock at night? In an attempt to deal with this, new laws have been passed within environmental health. A young woman gets attacked at 11 o'clock at night as she is walking home; a judge tells her that women should not go out after 9 o'clock at night.

Some of the most basic rights that form the basis of this work are: the right to be heard i.e. to have a voice and to be heard without fear of ridicule; the right of personal choice regarding how I live my life, providing it is within the law; the right to carry out my daily life without living in fear: the fear maybe of bullying, domestic violence, abuse, natural disaster, war, poverty and starvation; the right as far as possible to work for my living in an occupation that gives me some degree of satisfaction and to be adequately rewarded for that work; the right to live in an environment that does not damage my health and that allows me to enjoy my surroundings. And we could go on regarding our rights to health, childbirth resources, educational provision, freedom of speech and so on.

Readers will see why 'respect' is put at the beginning of these tenets: because respect acts as a modifier for all the rest. Respect means that there is balance between my rights and yours, between my values and society's values. Respect means that our eco-system has to have consonance and compromise with a world-view. For example: my personal eco-system may believe in loud music while I am writing, so I may have to compromise with the loud music haters of the world. I may have to wear headphones occasionally, or make sure my neighbours are out when listening to loud music - or not subject them to loud music too often!

Creativity and action: Fundamental to our philosophy of work is that dramatic action is not only a means of exploring something, it also has value in its own right. Being active, and therefore using up the energy, is sometimes seen as a way of 'tiring out' adolescents; somehow it will make them more amenable to learning if they burn off surplus energy. This is actually a distortion of another truth. If we 'warm up' physically and mentally, we shall be better prepared and focused to undertake the job in hand. The action needs to relate to the task of exploration. Therefore a very energetic warm-up will make for difficulties for a quiet reflective task. We learn more effectively through drama and action. Active learning is a very efficient way of learning. However, it is not only the action that concerns us, it is also the artistry that is involved in dramatic action. Creative action that stimulates the right hemisphere of our brains, and enhances the release of endorphins (Jennings 2001), and enables us to work with symbol and metaphor, is a health promoting activity. This is why we emphasise that it is not just the dramatic action as a means of doing something, but also the dramatic action in its own right that is crucial to our presentation.

These five philosophical tenets form the basis for what we believe about the work we do with children and young people. They also form the basis for our approaches to training volunteers and professional staff. Whether we are working with groups or individuals, or on theme based theatre projects or therapeutic sessions, they form the basis for our thinking and practice.

In writing this first section we have found it helpful to spend a lot of time trying to articulate a philosophy of work, as contrasted with theory and practice. We found it too easy to say 'Well, of course we believe in respect' or 'Yes, it is a rights based way of working', without actually addressing what it means for us both at a personal level as well as in our professional practice. It is still work in progress and will probably form the basis of more extensive research and writing.

Section two
The five practical tenets
DRAMATIC ACTION FOR UNDERSTANDING:

The game of power

The game of power can be played with large or small groups. The group leader encourages everyone to sit in a circle. Haphazardly within the circle are placed six chairs and one table.

Part One: one at a time, participants are invited up into the space and are asked to create an image with the seven objects. The image does not have to mean anything in particular, and there is nothing to get right or wrong. The only thing that must happen is that the volunteer should make one of the chairs, in any way they want, look more powerful than the other five. Once this has happened he or she sits back down without comment. The group leader asks some of the other participants to say which chair they think looks the most powerful and why. Everything people say is accepted, and this goes on for as long as the group leader feels that it is useful. This process is then repeated with other volunteers, as many as the group leader sees fit.

Part Two: one of the images from part one is chosen, an image where the majority of people have agreed on one chair being the most powerful. Volunteers are now invited, one at a time, to put themselves into the image, trying to make themselves the most powerful person in the image. They freeze in an image within the image without comment. The group leader asks other participants if they are the most powerful person in the image and why. This person stays frozen in the image while others enter the image, one at a time, to try and make themselves look the most powerful. They may not move any of the seven objects or other people in the image, they may only place themselves. People in the image are never asked to comment, only those sitting in the circle. Everyone coming into the image is trying to make themselves look the most powerful – in any way they want. Once the group leader feels enough people are in the image, everyone is thanked and people sit back down in the circle. The group will now see that what is powerful to one is not necessarily powerful to another. Part two is repeated as many times as is appropriate.

Racist cricket

Racist cricket is played in a circle, with everyone standing up. One person is in the centre; this is the batter, the others are the bowlers and fielders. In turn around the circle people bowl a racist statement to the batter. The batter should bat this statement away with another statement that counteracts it. The fielders are there to catch any of the batter's statements and to make holes in it with counter statements of their own. The batter gets two runs for each of the statements successfully batted away without being fielded. The batter is out if they cannot bat the statement away or if one of their statements is successfully fielded.

Unfair Simon Says

The group leader asks the group if they know the game 'Simon Says', usually the group responds with 'yes'; if this is the case then the group leader goes straight into the game. The game starts as normal but then the group leader starts getting people out for undisclosed reasons such as that they have blond hair, or that they are wearing trainers, or that the group leader just felt like picking on them etc. The game is played like this until there is one winner. There will be much hostility and confusion from participants during and after this game. When the winner has been announced the group leader gathers everyone into a circle and talks about what they have just played, what they think the rules of 'Simon Says' are, and what the group leader's rules were. How did people feel when they were out for getting it right? The group leader now talks with the group about people who experience this kind of prejudice every day of their lives.

Blind confusion

In this game, the group is not given any explanation of tasks to be carried out, or of ways to communicate. The group is divided into pairs, each person is either A or B in each pair. All the As put on a blindfold. B now has to get A to do a task that B does not know about. No words may be used, only sounds. B will find that one of the first things to do is get some kind of an understanding in communicating basic things like 'yes' and 'no'. Keep tasks simple at first such as: moving forward in a straight line, finding a chair and sitting on it. After the first attempts, get people to change partners and start more complicated tasks. The group leader should also get the As and Bs to swap over so everyone has a chance at trying to explain a task and trying to complete a task.

DEVELOPMENTAL STRUCTURES

The developmental paradigm of embodiment-projection-role (Jennings 1990, 1998, 1999), which underpins a child's dramatic development from birth to seven years, repeats itself with variations during teenage years. With the onset of adolescence there are not only physical changes in the body but a preoccupation with physical activities which may include sport, dance, and body grooming including hair, clothes, make-up and so on. The preoccupations may be destructive with eating disorders, self-harm, drug abuse. Many young people become absorbed by projective activities such as computer programmes, film and video, as well as artistic activity. Attention is paid to identity and role: role models are important, and roles are tried out and tested. A developmental approach allows these stages to be explored before major life decisions are made, and destructive stages may be changed before they become life threatening to the self or others (Jennings 1995).

PERFORMANCE AND PLAYBACK

Angel High was a show concerning issues around the use of drugs that toured to secondary schools in north London. The play was full of music and concerned the life of a teenager at school who was pushed into dealing cannabis. The play itself did not preach or condescend to young people, it also did not brush the real issues under the carpet. It was hard-hitting and true to life and was followed up with a short workshop that explored the themes brought up in the play.

Extract from the play *Angel High* produced by Tie Tours

Everton:	Look at the state of you.
Tom:	You doing a session now? 'Cause I'm ready.
Everton:	Seems to me that you've already had a session. Too many sessions makes Tom a dull boy.

Tom:	Cut the waffle old man. Race you up the stairs. (He runs up the stairs as Everton enters the lift. He arrives back into the main space out of breath and coughing.) Cheat. It ain't fair.
Everton:	Look at the state of you! What you been doing to yourself? Are you alright?
Tom:	I'm OK, just stop fussing – you're cramping my style. Come on bro let's hit the decks, spin the disc, get some bodies jumping and grooving to the hip hop, non-stop, green cropped sound of 'Nutty T' and brother Everton.
Everton:	Green cropped sound?
Tom:	Do you like my handle Ev? Nutty T!
Everton:	Green cropped sound, Tom – what does that mean?
Tom:	What you chatting about?
Everton:	I told you already Tom, I want this thing to work for me. I'm good at this radio presenting and I can't afford anyone mashing this up for me.
Tom:	And?
Everton:	And that includes you. You can't go on in that state. You're causing danger man. I mean what you talking about a crop of weed for? We'll have the police down here in seconds.

Most of the students who watched the play said 'yes, it was true to life' and provided the following opinions. It was realistic, real, this happens every day, it would be a 'normal' life situation, this has happened to people I know, and because that is what people do.

Many of the students referred to the realistic and everyday language used in the play. The teenage attitude/mindset portrayed by the actors was accepted; some said that the characters looked real and that the play itself didn't leave out anything and showed how people use people. Some stated that this would be the 'thing' people would go through when getting involved in drug abuse or drug dealing.

The majority of students on the evaluation sheets stated that they learned about the danger of alcohol or the danger of leaving a drunken friend alone. They also learned various aspects about the dangers of taking drugs such as: how drugs can affect the psyche as well as the body, how easy it is to get addicted, how drugs can ruin lives, how drugs can damage your reputation and how drugs can change your personality. Some simply stated not to try drugs because they can kill or that they are bad and can lead into big trouble and ruin lives. One person stated, 'Even women can be dealers, dealers can beat you up and in some cases kill you, not only by selling you just the drug either.'

2bl was a play that tackled the issue of bullying, racism and cross-cultural understanding. It is a play that is written in both Japanese and English, about 50 per cent of each language in the show. The play includes song, dance, story-telling and ritual. *2bl* toured to secondary schools, colleges, youth centres and theatres across England and Japan, and was followed up with workshops to explore the themes involved. This piece was very challenging, particularly the use of two languages which served many purposes. Not only was the play accessible to both Japanese and English speaking audiences, it also challenged audiences to find ways of understanding other than through language. One interesting and subtle difference between some English speaking audiences and those whose first language was not English, was the seeming lack of respect shown towards something that they could not immediately understand. This is seen through the examples at the beginning, when contrasting them with another secondary school in north London where the audience was predominantly Muslim and whose first language was Hindi. The Hindi audience liked the play immensely, but they also gave it respect, and in doing so were able to enjoy it through their own interpretation.

The English translation of the Japanese text is in brackets and italics and is not spoken by the actors.

Extract from the play *2bl* produced by Tie Tours

Tomoko enters at a distance.

Tomoko:	Yoshiko. (*Hey Yoshiko.*)
Yoshiko:	A… (*Oh no.*)
Tomoko:	Kocchi oideyo, isshoni ikayo. (*Over here, come over here.*)
Yoshiko:	Un chottomatte… (*Hello. Yeah, just coming.*)
Tomoko:	Hayakukinatteba! (*Hurry up!*)
Mario:	Where are you going?
Yoshiko:	(She points at Tomoko.) They just turned up, sorry Mario.
Mario:	Don't do this Yoshiko.
Tomoko:	No, asobini ikayo. (*Come and join in our picnic.*)
Mario:	Iccha dameda Yoshi. Aitsura nanka mushi surebaiinda. (*Just ignore them.*)
Yoshi:	Come back.
Yoshiko:	I can't ignore them Mario, they are my friends.

Tomoko: Naniyatten-no? Daijobu? Aitsugananika ittekuruno? (*Is that boy harrassing you?*)

Yoshiko: Chigau, chigau, imaikukara mattete. (*No no, it's okay I'm coming.*)

Mario: You're making a mistake Yoshi.

Tomoko: Ja hayaku shinatteba! Watashira datte isshowa matteran-naiyo. (*Hurry up. Get a move on. We won't wait for you forever, you know.*)

Mario: Yoshiko, party desuru? (*What about my sister's party?*)

Yoshiko: Let's talk later. Gomen. Sonokotowa mataatodehanasa…watashi min-nawo mataseterukara ikune? (*Mario, I can't deal with this, can we talk later? I need to go over to see them.*)

Mario: Doshita Yoshiko. Dokonimo tomodachiga inakunattemo oreha itsumo

Yoshiko: No Tomodachi dazo. (*What's happening, am I only good enough when there is no one else to be friends with?*)

Yoshiko: Onegai Mario. (*Please Mario.*)

Tomoko: Nanka Yoshikono atarashii kareshi wa Philipinejin mitaiyo. Che saiaku. Yoshikomo kitanaijinshuno nakamani nacchattanda! (*It looks like Yoshiko has found herself a new lover. A Filipino lover. She's starting to mix with the dirty people!*)

Yoshiko: Watashi ikuyo. (*I've got to go home.*) I'm going home.

RE-STAGING

Through action we are able to re-stage our lives and make choices about the way forward. Especially if we are working in a developmental model as described above, we can create a series of stages that are age appropriate through which individuals and groups can create their own journeys. There may be periods from the past that need to be re-visited in order to address unresolved issues, there may be current stages or future ones that can be placed within a theatre structure – the stage. On this stage we can create narratives of past, present and future, from the imagination and from reality, within the metaphor of a play. Dramatic distance is created in order, paradoxically, to come closer to our lived lives, both as individuals and groups.

GREAT STORIES AND GREAT PLAYS

With virtual reality, instant living, life itself turned into entertainment, and non-actors groomed for soap stardom, we are in danger of blurring the borders between everyday reality and dramatic reality (Jennings 1998). People shy away from myths and Shakespeare and say 'People won't understand', 'People

don't talk like that anymore' (of course they never did!). I have created *Hamlet*
with five-year-olds, Noah's Ark for an entire school where communication had
broken down, and produced *Romeo and Juliet* with people with learning disabilities. The great stories not only assist us with language and expression of all
kinds, they address the issues of our own lives in unique ways. They indeed
help us to be great! The following example is an ancient myth from the Temiar
people of Malaysia which was adapted within a Tie Tours play, *Silent Scream*.

Extract from the play *Silent Scream* Produced by Tie Tours

Once upon a time there lived this huge snake, her name was Tagou Relai. She
lived high up on a mountain within one of the lush forests of Malaysia. Tagou
Relai lived many many years ago. There were very few people in Malaysia then,
just beautiful, lively forests, crystal clear waters and fine days. There were so
many species of animal that you'd spend the rest of your life naming them. It
was a fantastic place and Tagou Relai lived in harmony with it all. One day as
Tagou Relai lay stretched out in the topmost branches of a tree, soaking up the
sun, a strange man came up to her and said 'I want that tree'. So she moved to
the adjacent tree. 'I want that one too,' he said. So she moved to the next one
along. 'Look, just clear off, snake,' he said. 'I'm having all these trees round
here, ha ha ha.' Tagou Relai was quite upset, this was no way to behave. Why
did this strange ghost-like man have to be so greedy? Couldn't he use a tree that
was unoccupied? There were lots of trees, more than enough for everybody,
so...

Tagou Relai went off in search of a tree; on the way she met Arek, Abillum
and Tengah. They were members of the Golden People who lived in the forest
and who shared all the joy that was around them with anyone who crossed their
path. The Golden People were more black than gold and when the sun clipped
any part of their skin it would send off shimmering golden particles, a gold so
deep that it held within it all the colours of the rainbow. 'Where are you going?'
asked Tengah. 'I'm trying to find a tree,' Tagou Relai replied. 'One that's far
away from the ghost-man.' Tengah then whispered the following riddle into
Tagou Relai's ear: 'To domineer, to slaughter or to fear, whichever way you go is
forwards and all holes will be filled, Tagou Relai, my friend.' Tagou Relai
thought for a minute since she always took what Tengah said very seriously.
Amongst other things Tengah was a great healer. A seer, he could see things
that others could only look at. 'Thank you, my friends,' Tagou Relai finally said.
'If you are looking for food, I saw some lovely fruit on the large gabag tree.'
With that she slipped further off into the forest, to look for that one special tree,

away from the ghost-man. She combed the forest for five hours and eventually came to a little brook. Next to the brook was a flowering cheb cheeb tree. It had space all around it and stretched high above the canopy. Tagou Relai slipped up the trunk, right up to the top she went, taking in the scent of the beautiful lilac flowers. The sun shone wonderfully on her back as she slept. Tagou Relai slept for twenty five thousand years, give or take a day. How could she sleep for that long? It was the path she chose to take.

The shock of hitting the ground is what woke her. She opened her eyes, next to her lay the tree, chopped down. There was no brook, there was no gold, just a dull greyness…and the ghost-man. That was the last thing she ever saw, the hole she was now lying in was steadily filling up with concrete. No one ever heard her last words. There is a legend that Tengah is still alive; yes, to this day. Many people seek him but that's another story.

What do we sense?

We may observe that a person is physically malnourished or that their eyes are glazed; he or she may be fidgeting, pacing, restless, rocking; they may be absolutely still and seeming to be 'cut off', or they may be flooding with tears, self-harming, muttering threats or hearing voices that we are unable to hear. Or they may be lashing out, fighting others (see ground rules), or trying to drown us out with noise. If we are assessing an individual for creative or therapeutic work we have to make choices regarding the appropriateness of what we have to offer. As we stay with someone 'in the moment', we are observing and noting with all our senses; we are aware of what we feel we can assist with, within our own frame of expertise, and what needs further specialist help. We may be pondering the involvement of the person's GP, family, community psychiatric nurse, church or self-help groups. We are assessing the situation, and making use of any networks that we know the person may already have, or that could be helpful to them.

We ourselves may feel we need some advice, time for reflection, supervision or colleague collaboration. We have to be aware of the eco-system both of ourselves as well as the young person, which includes a whole range of professional people and family members who may assist in drawing a basic 'map' of where the person is at right now and what we might have to offer. Already we are assessing the person, the situation and our own skills: indeed, a lot of assessment happens in situ and we are not aware of it as a formal process.

However, little assessment can take place unless we can meet the person 'in the moment'. R.D. Laing was asked while visiting Chicago to examine a girl who was diagnosed as schizophrenic: she was in a locked, padded room and sat naked, rocking herself. Laing, to the surprise of the staff, removed his clothes, and sat with her in the cell, rocking in the same rhythm as the girl. A little while later she began to speak for the first time in many months.

If we are planning a group then we may assess all the individuals before the group begins, and even then use the first two or three sessions for observation. In schools it is often a very different matter: we are handed a class, often because they are 'difficult' or 'impossible' as described below. We are then assessing in the moment what might be remotely possible with such a group. It is a useful guideline to always ask the individual and the group where they think they are at – what they would find useful and enjoyable – and find ways to take their ideas into account. A jointly planned session will stand a great chance of engagement and attention.

Our work in assessment is in a variety of settings with children and young people. Obviously the approaches used in day-to-day therapeutic work contrast with the more formal requirements of, for example, court assessment. Nevertheless, we always involve creative methods which may include: sculpting with stones, shells, small toys (spectograms); representations of the person's family tree, eco-system or world view, through drawing, painting, sandplay or mandalas; explorations of selfhood, feelings, relationships, or the crisis itself, through masks, puppets, landscapes, pictures of clay (Jennings 1999). Assessment is about trying to understand where the person is at, within the creative and therapeutic space. This space may be symbolic or actual. We may have to create it in the moment, or it may be contained in our workroom or studio, wherever that may be.

Our philosophy of assessment is to try and discover the strengths of the person in order to try and build greater health, rather than exclusively focus on the difficulties and perceived 'weaknesses'. We do not judge what is right or wrong, only saying that what is right for one person is not necessarily right for another. Likewise we try not to use the word 'problem'! Therefore, when people are feeling very vulnerable or angry, it is not denied or dismissed, but they are usually able to also recall a time when they felt less vulnerable or full of rage. They can often get in touch with some strength and recall their own resilience that they were able to use to help them deal with a difficult situation. If it is an extreme way of 'coping', such as beating the person up or bullying because they themselves have been bullied, new strategies can be explored through action. By looking back to a different time in life, young people can sometimes see that their life is not 'inevitable'.

There are various assessment tools which use creative approaches. Lahad's *Six Part Story Making* (6PSM) analysed by BASICPh (Lahad 1992, 2000), Gersie's *Ninepart Story* (personal communication), and Jennings EPR (1998, 1999) each open up new ways of working.

What do we try to develop in our work?

HEALTHIER ATTACHMENTS

In a 'health' rather than a 'problem' approach, we can explore relationships within the dramatic action. We aim for trust to be developed as an ethos within the group as well as appropriate balance between dependence and independence. Through the role young people can see the effect of their behaviour on others (how it may be inhibiting their relationships) as well as other effects on themselves. The power struggles in *Coriolanus* or *A Midsummer Night's Dream* are examples of great plays with major attachment themes.

RESILIENCE IN DEALING WITH THE WORLD OR 'SURVIVAL TACTICS'

Resilience is our self-stabilising means of dealing with trauma and crisis, of meeting the world in ways that reasonably cope with adversity. Recent studies of resilience have been based on health or adaptive development in the face of stressful situations, rather than using 'disturbance' models (for a brief history of stress and coping, see Lahad 1992). People have different ways of 'meeting the world', and a method that can assess our coping skills will enable intervention that builds on our strengths and things that are familiar to us, rather than having a system imposed on us. Young people often show extraordinary levels of resilience which can be interpreted in negative ways – they are being stubborn or difficult – rather than being seen as their ways of 'meeting the world'. Creative drama work can help adapt more extreme forms of 'coping' without being destructive.

ENGAGEMENT

When working with young people we need to engage them in ways that they can relate to rather than imposing what we think they should be doing. There are many ways to do this – a bit of research talking to young people about what they want is one way to start. One project that Andy is currently involved with is geared towards secondary school students creating workshops for primary school pupils to help with the transition from primary to secondary school. The students create and run the workshops – staff are there to give ideas and direction when needed or requested.

CHOICES

Young people need to feel that they have a choice; positive learning will not take place when they feel they are being forced to do something. Sometimes young people may not be able to see what choices are available to them, and sometimes their choices have been deliberately hidden because it is thought that this will make life easier for the teacher.

MOTIVATION

Motivating seemingly bored and disinterested young people can seem like a difficult and thankless task. One group Andy worked with a few years ago refused to participate in any activity that was presented to them. So Andy and his co-worker worked on their own for 30 minutes, then one by one four of the group of seven young people came over to see what was happening. They then joined in for the remaining 30 minutes of the workshop.

NEGOTIATION OF BOUNDARIES AND GROUND RULES

Some rules are important and must be discussed and understood by the group; a verbal or written contract may be negotiated and agreed. The group leader should be aware of what these roles are and what limitations they will put on behaviour. There are also rules that one might want to negotiate with the group. For example, one non-negotiable rule is safety for ourselves and others within the group. Other rules might be: no physical contact between people (when dealing with violence), no out of context racist language to be used, and so on.

What about the workers?

Some cannot handle working with disaffected young people. We are often given the classes that are labelled as the most difficult in the school, containing students that noone else can work with. 'You won't get much out of them', is often the comment teachers might make in passing. Some of the actors that we train to work with these same young people, often don't seem to handle it well either. Their work is excellent, but they often still take personally what some young people may say to them. This can affect their work, especially on a gruelling tour of two shows and two workshops, five days a week plus travelling.

It is essential for there to be a balance in our work. Workers need both supervision and support and a realistic programme. We need to be careful not to get into a 'saviour role' (Lahad 1999) and to realise that there are some things that we cannot change – at least on this occasion!

Closing thoughts

The re-awakening of creativity for everyone can be the most healing of all processes: creativity is essential for survival.

References

Carson, R. (1965) *Silent Spring*. Harmondsworth: Penguin Books.

Dallas, G. (2000) *Angel High*. London: Tie Tours.

Hickson, A. (1998) *Silent Scream*. London: Tie Tours.

Jennings, S. (1990) *Dramatherapy with Families, Groups and Individuals*. London: Jessica Kingsley Publishers.

Jennings, S. (1995) *Dramatherapy with Children and Adolescents*. London: Routledge.

Jennings, S. (1997) *Dramatherapy Theory and Practice 3*. London: Routledge.

Jennings, S. (1998) *Introduction to Dramatherapy: Ariadne's Ball of Thread*. London: Jessica Kingsley Publishers.

Jennings, S. (2001) 'Re-stage your life.' *Avalon Autumn 2001*. IOA Foundation.

Lahad, M. (1992) 'Story-making in Assessment Method.' In S. Jennings (ed) *Dramatherapy Theory and Practice 2*. London: Routledge.

Lahad, M. (1999) 'Supervision of Crisis Intervention Teams.' In E. Tselikas-Portmann (ed) *The Myth of the Saviour in Supervision and Dramatherapy*. London: Jessica Kingsley Publishers.

Lahad, M. (2000) *Creative Supervision*. London: Jessica Kingsley Publishers.

Laing, R.D. *Website 2001* (unofficial).

Tajim, S.S. (2001) *2bl*. London: Tie Tours.

Part II
Action Across Organisational Divides: Health, Education and the Juvenile Justice System

CHAPTER 4

Freeing the Self

Using Psychodrama Techniques with Children and Adolescents who Stammer

Gail Smith

Introduction

Talitha[4] began to stammer[5] at the age of four. In her early childhood it took the form of multiple repetitions of sounds, words and phrases at the start of sentences. These dysfluencies[6] were free from muscular tension and she showed little awareness or concern about the interruptions in her speech. Talitha's parents were not particularly concerned about it since she was a talkative and confident little girl.

As Talitha got older, the nature and severity of her stammer changed. Although her repetitions were less, they were accompanied by tension in the muscles of the face and lips as she struggled to push sounds out of her mouth. Talitha became increasingly aware that her speech was different from other people around her. In school, children started to laugh and tease her about it. She began to feel self-conscious and embarrassed, particularly when she was asked to talk and read out loud in front of her peers. These were times when she stammered the most. To avoid stammering and the ridicule that often accompanied it, Talitha began to substitute words before speaking. She would swap what she considered to be difficult words around in her head for ones that were easier to say. The classroom quickly became a place to be feared. Talitha was so ashamed of her stammer that she felt unable to talk about it with her parents or her teachers.

By the time she had turned 13 years old Talitha had changed from being a confident and chatty young girl into a withdrawn and depressed one. She no longer chose to answer questions in class, and had formed a habit of making regular trips to the toilet to avoid situations in which she might be asked to speak out loud. Her experiences with stammering had become so bad that she had found approaching others and talking with her friends extremely difficult. Eventually, she asked her parents for help after many months of suffering verbal teasing from other pupils. They contacted their doctor and a referral was made to the speech and language service.[7] Talitha came to see me at her local health centre. She complained of feeling misunderstood by her teachers and generally isolated from her peers.

Fifteen-year-old Connor had been known to the speech and language service since the onset of his stammering at age three. It began soon after he started to attend at the local nursery. His mother had picked him up at the end of the day and noticed he was stretching out some of his sounds at the start of words (sound prolongation) and repeating several others. These dysfluencies continued to appear in his speech on a daily basis. Connor was aware of his difficulties and showed this by stopping to re-start the sounds he had stammered on again. The more he struggled, the more sounds became stuck in his mouth behind tightly closed lips (blocking). Connor would try to push them out by stamping his foot and screwing up his face. At times he would become so frustrated that he would give up on his speaking attempts altogether. His mother shared her concerns about his speech with the nursery teacher and a referral was made to the speech and language service. Connor received individual therapy[8] at his local health centre to help him speak with less effort and tension. On-going parental advice and support sessions were also commenced.

As Connor grew older his stammering occurred more frequently. Like Talitha's, the severity of it increased and he developed greater muscular tension in his face, lips and tongue causing the sounds to become even more blocked in his speech. Although he no longer stamped his foot, he replaced this with rapid eye blinking and other behaviours such as fist clenching and slight head nodding in order to push through his speech blocks. Since Connor had received on-going support for his speech difficulties from both his speech and language therapist and his teachers, he had developed confidence to say exactly what he wanted in class. Connor was generally a happy boy, popular with both his peers and his teachers. However, he found his stammer to be embarrassing as he felt it made him look stupid. He developed several 'escape behaviours'[9] in response to his stammer, to avoid getting stuck and to prevent people finding out about it. For example, like Talitha, he substituted words he found difficult to say for easier ones. Connor would also get his friends to buy things for him in shops and to purchase bus tickets on his behalf, to avoid speaking. This meant that at times he had walked home instead of catching the bus, thus avoiding his fears about his stammering.

Connor had not been seen for the past four years as there had been no reported concerns from his parents, school or by Connor himself. A referral was made by school, asking for him to be seen as a result of difficulties he had experienced during his work placement. He had chosen to go to a local travel agency as leisure and tourism was of particular interest to him. He attended for only three days before walking out and deciding not to go back. His teachers discovered that he had been asked to make a couple of phone calls to customers. Like many other people who stammer, Connor was terrified of using the telephone. He rarely answered the phone at home and only occasionally made calls to his friends. Since Connor held a lot of negative feelings towards himself in relation to his stammer, he had felt unable to discuss it with the manager at the travel agents. Therefore, he had been unable to get the help and support he needed to complete his placement. His fear of stammering on the phone with strangers had become so great that the risk of using it was far greater than failing the placement. Connor did not return to the travel agency.

Introducing these young people here gives you (the reader) some insight into the experience children and adolescents who stammer may have. Their experiences can be very painful and isolating, impacting on important areas of their life. This chapter is about communicating with young people who stammer. Talitha and Connor will be discussed in more detail later to illustrate how psychodrama has been used to help them to disclose their stammering, share their feelings and attitudes about it, as well as to begin to work through and resolve some of the difficulties they are experiencing in life. First, some general information about the condition of stammering is given in order to show where psychodrama can be of benefit in working with young people.

What is stammering?

Many definitions of stammering can be found within the literature (e.g. Shapiro 1999; Van Riper 1982). Peters and Guitar (1991) define it in the following way:

> Stuttering is characterized by an abnormally high frequency and/or duration of stoppages in the forward flow of speech. These stoppages usually take the form of (a) repetitions of sound, syllables, or one-syllable words, (b) prolongations of sounds, or (c) 'blocks' of airflow and/or voicing in speech. Individuals who stutter are usually aware of their stut-

tering and are often embarrassed by it. Moreover, they often use abnormal physical and mental effort to speak. (Shapiro 1999, p.9)

This definition gives some description of the overt physical and audible manifestations of stammering. However, it does not cover other features of the condition such as the psychological aspects or the additional (secondary) speech behaviours and body movements that can also be present. Shapiro (1999) views stuttering as, 'a diagnostic label referring to a complex, multidimensional composite of behaviours, thoughts, and feelings of people who stutter' (p.14). Currently, there is no single definition that is all-inclusive.

Aetiology

'Etiology, yet unknown, is conceptualized to relate to the interaction of physiological, psychological/psychosocial, psycholinguistic, and environmental factors' (Shapiro 1999, p.14).

The symptoms and underlying causes of the stammer appear in different combinations for each individual (Guitar 1998; Rustin, Botterril and Kelman 1996).

Presentation of stammering

Stammering has been likened to the image of an iceberg by Joseph Sheehan (1958), an American speech and language pathologist. Like an iceberg, it consists of a part above and a part below the surface of the water.

Above the water level

Features that lie above the water level are referred to as 'overt' aspects and are visible and audible. These can include behaviours such as repetitions of phrase units ('I like – I like – I like meat'), words ('What – what what's that?'), parts of words ('Mummy can I have a bi-bi-bi-biscuit?') and sounds ('Are we g-g-g-going to see grandma today?'). Prolongation, which involves lengthening a sound such as ('I Sssssssssssssssaw you at the doctors earlier'), and blocking behaviours (involuntary withholding of the sound within the mouth or larynx) can also occur. There may also be a disruption in the pattern of breathing, for instance, running out of breath before finishing a sentence or rapid intakes of breath before speaking. Complete cessation of airflow is typical during episodes of blocking and the person generally experiences tightening in the muscles of the diaphragm, chest, neck, mouth, jaw and face.

SECONDARY BEHAVIOURS

Other behaviours may occur such as reduced eye contact, facial tics and grimacing, or extra body movements such as fist clenching and foot or hand tapping. Typically secondary behaviours are adopted in response to the stammering as strategies for controlling, concealing, or coping with it. Over time they become integrated into the stammer itself.

In young children, speech dysfluencies can usually be seen and heard by others (features above the surface of the water). Awareness of their difficulties and general level of concern is momentary, it exists only at the time the dysfluency occurs.[10]

Below the water

The part below the surface of the water is known as 'covert' and consists of feelings, thoughts and behaviours that are less likely to be seen or heard by others. This part is concerned with the psychological and social impact of stammering upon the individual. Its development starts as the child becomes increasingly aware and anxious about his/her speech. Children begin to pick up on verbal and non-verbal responses made by others and perceive these as negative in relation to their speech difficulties. This growing awareness can lead to feelings of anxiety, fear and self-consciousness around speaking. A child may start to anticipate difficulties with certain sounds, words, people or specific speaking situations.

AVOIDANCE BEHAVIOURS

This growing realisation that their talking sounds different to that of other people often produces attempts by the child to stop or conceal his/her stammering (Turnbull and Stewart 1996). Children quickly become skilled at developing strategies of avoidance and concealment that can be quite effective on a short-term basis. For instance, avoidance of answering questions in class or pretending not to know the answer. Some children will respond to questions with initial enthusiasm, but then quickly feign forgetfulness if they anticipate or start to stammer. Forgetting one's homework may mean that the child can escape from having to read his/her work out in class. Others may begin to show a disinterest in out of school activities. They may become less chatty and start to withdraw from social interaction with others, thus reducing their social contacts and support networks. When these strategies are relied on, they can have a negative impact upon how children learn to manage their stammer on a daily basis in a variety of speaking and social situations. Thus, spontaneity of response gives way to rigidity.

There are other strategies of avoidance that are directly related to the act of speaking, for example, changing difficult words, phrases or sentences for easier ones. This was mentioned earlier in relation to Talitha and Connor. Also, adding words such as 'well', or 'well, erm' to the start of a sentence in order to prevent getting stuck on the first sound of a word. This is quite a common strategy adopted by children who stammer and its use can quickly become excessive.

Some children become so adept at techniques of avoidance and disguise that even professional speech and language therapists can struggle to detect any signs of stammering. The covert part of the icebergs of such children can be massive. Since many children suffer experiences of teasing and bullying (Guitar 1998; Shapiro 1999), they will do anything to conceal the problem. This is particularly difficult as Turnbull and Stewart (1999) point out:

> as with an iceberg, the most dangerous part of stammering is not what can be seen but the unseen, hidden part... It is this part which acts as a foundation stone for the maintenance of stammering as a disabling disorder. (p.53)

However, like other types of coping strategies, techniques of avoidance and disguise have a protective function. Finding ways of reaching children without pulling down or disregarding their defences is an essential task for any therapist who works therapeutically with children (Hoey 1997), including speech and language therapists.

EMOTIONS

Children who stammer may begin to feel a whole range of negative emotions in relation to their stammering such as fear, embarrassment, anger, shame, annoyance and frustration. Connor and Talitha both felt embarrassed by their stammer. Many children report feeling guilty, since they believe that if they tried hard enough they could stop the stammer from happening. When their efforts fail them they begin to feel helpless. Fear is a powerful and common emotion felt by children who stammer. It can keep them trapped behind walls of defence and can maintain their strategies for self-protection, making them unable to do or say exactly what they want. For the reasons stated, it is crucial for therapists to acknowledge the inner emotional world of children in therapy and to support them to work through some of the difficulties they experience.

A more serious and entrenched problem that also lies beneath the water level is the child's construing of him/herself, especially with regards to his/her self-concept and self-image. For children who continue to stammer a process of integration of the stammer into their sense of self gradually takes place. The child stops thinking about the stammer as something that he/she does and starts to think, feel and believe that he/she is a 'stammerer' (Hayhow and Levy 1989; Turnbull and Stewart 1996). Negative thought patterns and firm beliefs about the 'self' quickly become established. For example, 'I am stupid and other people think I am stupid because I stammer', 'I will never be normal', 'I will not be successful in finding a job', 'I can never be a good communicator.' Once this happens, it can often be difficult for the child to believe that change is possible. The child starts to evaluate him/herself and his/her life events in relation to the stammer. When things go wrong, the stammer becomes the sole focus for blame and the child believes that life would be 'fine' if only the stammer would disappear.

Psychodramatic applications within stammering therapy

In therapy children require a holistic and eclectic approach to intervention (Guitar 1997; Rustin, Botterril and Kelman 1996; Shapiro 1999). Each child who stammers presents with his/her own unique representation of the iceberg. Whilst some children will display more overt features (behaviours above the water level) and require a focus which aims to reduce the frequency and severity of the behaviours, others may show very little overt stammering. However, the nature, severity and frequency of a child's overt features should not be used for judging whether or not the stammer is a problem for any given child. It does not offer a full insight into how the stammer is impacting on the child's psychological state or to what degree it affects his/her life. Van Riper (1982) points out:

> It is difficult for those who have not possessed or been possessed by the disorder to appreciate its impact on the stutterer's self concept, his roles, his way of living. Once it has taken hold, after a period of insidious growth, almost every aspect of the person's existence is coloured by his communicative disability. (p.1)

Therefore, it is important to attend to both the overt and covert aspects of the stammer. It is specifically in relation to the features below the surface of the water that I believe psychodrama to be of most benefit. The method can be applied for the purpose of exploration, reparation and prevention. In working with children there are two particular aims that need to be part of any intervention. First, to reduce overall sensitivity towards the stammer in order to speak openly about one's feelings and attitudes towards it. Second, to prevent the child from developing covert features in order to reduce the possibility of the stammer becoming a disability in life.

In the examples below, the use of psychodrama with Talitha and Connor is discussed to demonstrate how it enabled them to share their inner world of thoughts and feelings. Descriptions are given of how specific techniques were applied in order for them to re-experience issues from the past or present, with the aim of understanding, clarifying and changing these. The techniques of re-enactment, future projection and role training in the 'here and now' have offered these children ways of practising new behaviours in relation to old situations. They have also offered opportunities for exploring ways of handling possible future events.

Talitha's story

Remember Talitha, at the start of this chapter; when she first came to me for therapy she was withdrawn and depressed. Her overall confidence and self-esteem were low, she tried hard to keep herself from stammering in front of me. She had learnt that speaking was risky, especially at school and in front of strangers, which included me. For the first few therapy sessions, Talitha arrived to find me sitting at my computer huffing and puffing out of exasperation. I was terrible at resolving any problem I had with it. Information technology and word processing were subjects she knew well. They were used in school and she had been given a computer of her own a few years back. I was genuinely in need of her help and pleased to accept it. Since she willingly accepted the role of 'problem solver' this allowed her to engage with me on a more 'person-to-person' level. She was able to witness my struggles with the computer and to hear my experiences of frustration, anger and helplessness. Furthermore, Talitha was empowered in her role as problem solver offering me, the adult professional, real assistance.

The quality of the therapeutic relationship between the therapist and the child is paramount. Developing a warm and equal relationship within an environment that fosters safety, trust and mutual respect is crucial before any therapeutic work can begin (Bannister 1991; Bannister 1997; Hoey 1997; Yalom 1995). When children come for therapy, they are at different starting points in terms of their readiness for dealing with their problems. Therefore, it is vital that we (as therapists) are sensitive to their individual needs and ready to adjust our behaviour accordingly. Both the child and therapist need time and space to feel comfortable with each other, in order for their experiences and feelings to be communicated with ease and openness. Karp (1998) states, 'When the room has its arms around you it is possible to be that which you thought you could not be, and to express that which seemed impossible to express' (p.3). The process of establishing the kind of therapeutic relationship described above corresponds to the stage of 'warm-up' within the psychodramatic process. Its importance should not be underestimated. It assists both parties in reaching a state of readiness for exploration of real life issues in action and facilitating the process of change (Karp 1994, 1998).

In later therapeutic sessions, the psychodramatic techniques of future projection, role reversal and role training were used to help Talitha confront and own her feelings about her stammering. For example, in one session she used empty chairs and various objects around the room to create an audience of teachers and peers to whom she could speak openly for the first time, about her experiences with stammering. Talitha spoke about her helplessness and despair each time she was bullied or teased by other pupils. She expressed her anger at her teachers for displaying what she perceived as a lack of understanding and intolerance of her stammering in class. As she spoke, Talitha clenched her hands into a fist behind her back. Standing up to double her, I asked, 'Can I be you for a moment?' Talitha nodded. I stood next to her, assuming her body position with my hands also clasped behind my back. Gritting my teeth I let out an almighty growl of anger. 'How dare you treat me like this! You ask me endless questions and then when I can't say the answer you tell me off for not knowing it.' As I let my anger come forth, Talitha began to join in, expressing her feelings to those who mattered. She had never done this before. 'You should try having a stammer then you'd know what it feels like. I can't stand it when you finish my sentences off for me. I can speak for myself if you give me a chance. I can't stand coming here anymore, I hate it!' Talitha burst into tears, covered her face with her hands and turned her back on her audience. I stood beside her and placed my hand on her upper back to comfort her. For the first time in her life, she allowed her tears of pain and sadness to be expressed.

The psychodramatic technique of doubling performs two essential functions, emotional holding and stretching of the protagonist's internal world (Lousada 1998). Physical and emotional holding occurs as the double accurately copies and tracks the protagonist's[11] (in this case Talitha's) body posture, and assumed internal emotional state and thought processes (Smith 1999b, p.8). This requires a great deal of sensitivity and empathy for the protagonist's position. Doubling was useful for Talitha. Initially it gave her the opportunity of feeling heard and understood. Having a witness to 'hear' and 'fully comprehend' our personal story is a valuable and essential part of the therapeutic experience (Bannister 1997). It also provided her with the experience of being emotionally held whilst she voiced and acknowledged some painful feelings that had never been disclosed before. Doubles strive to express thoughts, feelings and non-verbal communications that the protagonist is holding back (Blatner 1988; Holmes 1991; Lousada 1998). As Talitha's double, I picked up on the contained anger in her fist. I was able to verbalise this and by doing so, enabled Talitha to release these emotions for herself.

During this same piece of work, Talitha learned through the process of role reversal, that her teachers interpreted her quietness as a lack of interest in particular subjects. 'Role reversal is a powerful and central technique of psychodrama. It requires the protagonist to step into another person's shoes, to experience him/herself and the situation from this other's perspective' (Smith 1999b, p.9). Significant shifts in understanding and changes in one's behaviour can occur as a result of this process.

Talitha was asked to assume the role of her English teacher. In role, she explained that she had never seen Talitha stammer in class and had not picked up that she had any difficulties with her speech. She had simply assumed that she was not interested in the topics being taught. 'I'm sorry you didn't come to talk to me about it. But now I know I'm happy to help you in any way I can', remarked her teacher. Having heard from the teacher, it was important for Talitha to hear these messages directly. She was reversed back into her own role whilst I took the role of her teacher. She was able to hear her teacher's point of view. From this position, Talitha was able to acknowledge to herself the responsibility she had for informing others about any problems she was experiencing. Her initial thought about her lack of support from teachers was challenged. 'Role reversal is an essential part of learning about relationships' (Lousada 1998, p.214). Talitha went on to create future scene enactments. She rehearsed approaching various teachers, about her problems with speech, in several different ways. Bannister (1991) suggests that 'through re-enactment the process of desensitization can occur' (p.87). Gradually Talitha became more open to discussing her stammer.

Connor's story

Connor was also introduced earlier. When he walked out of his work placement, his teachers became very concerned. Although they had been aware of his stammer, they had not understood how, or to what extent, it affected him in situations outside of school. Since Connor performed well academically, answered questions in class and was a popular lad with peers, they had not thought that he would have any difficulties during his placement.

Connor had agreed to see me. When he came for therapy he was initially angry. Not only had he construed the work placement in a negative light, but the way he construed himself in relation to his stammer was also negative and entrenched. He felt he was a failure for having to repeat his work placement and considered himself to be stupid and abnormal. 'Nothing good can happen,' he had told himself, 'until I get rid of this stammer!'

Since the placement incident had been a harrowing experience and something that Connor had been asked to repeat, he had been keen to look at this first. He used chairs, tables and objects available to reconstruct the office at the travel agency as accurately as possible. 'I was doing really well until he asked me to use the phone,' Connor explained through a deep sigh. 'Can you show me what happened when your manager came into the office?' I asked. Connor agreed and took on the role of manager willingly and I took on Connor's role. As the manager, he explained he had been in the job for eight years and had seen many students come and go. He had warmed to Connor from the beginning since his enthusiasm and interest in the job had been evident through their discussions together. He reported Connor to be a confident young man who picked up new information quickly.

Initial scene setting and interviewing of a protagonist in a role, in this case Connor, are common procedures in the psychodramatic process. They serve the purpose of deepening the warm-up for the protagonist to the presenting issue, thereby generating a more authentic emotional response during situation re-enactments. Additionally, it enables the 'problem', to be enacted as closely and realistically to the protagonist's perspective as possible.

In role as the manager, Connor re-enacted the scene in the office that had taken place in real life. The manager walked into the room, briefly asked how Connor was getting along, then proceeded to tell him about several phone calls that needed to be made to customers. Having seen the situation from the manager's role, it was now important for Connor to show how he had responded. He was reversed back into his own role and I took the role of his

manager to re-play the scene exactly how Connor had shown. Upon receiving
the task from his manager, Connor's face drained of colour. Once the manager
had left the office Connor jumped to his feet and began pacing up and down
the room. Stepping out of the manager role and back into therapist role, I asked
what he was thinking and feeling. Connor shook his head and repeated over
and over, 'I can't do it, I can't use the telephone, I can't do it!' Connor had
waited until his lunch break before escaping.

What became evident in therapy was that Connor only had one response
for dealing with threatening situations: he fled from them. As people in school
and at home were familiar with his stammering, Connor was rarely placed in
difficult speaking situations. He never stepped out of his comfort zone and had
not had many opportunities for practising new ways of coping. Bannister
(1991) states, 'The opportunity to practise future roles and not to be punished
for making mistakes is an important part of psychodrama. Young people, in
particular, need practice at assuming roles they have never experienced' (p.87).

Psychodrama was used with Connor over subsequent therapy sessions for
many purposes. First, it provided a way for Connor to externalize and then
explore the different aspects of himself. He was able to look at his system of
internal roles and consider how well these functioned in everyday life. These
intrapsychic explorations allowed dialogues to occur between roles. By
assuming some of these, I was able to challenge several of Connor's negative
attitudes, feelings and beliefs held about himself and his stammer. Hoey (1997)
reports, 'The whole psychodrama technique depends, for its healing power, on
the director's ability to honour the protagonist's inner world and, from within
it, to make challenging and extending interventions in a non-manipulative
way' (p.5).

Second, through the technique of future projection, we were able to create
a scene in which Connor explored the manager's response to his disappearance
from the office. Consequently, an appreciation of the manager's feelings and
perspective was obtained. Through role reversal, Connor was able to experience the confusion and disappointment felt by the manager. A future scene in
which Connor returned to speak with the manager to discuss his difficulties
with stammering was created, and he was able to experience the consequences
of his actions. His initial beliefs about how the manager would have responded
to his stammer were put to the test.

Finally, Connor's difficulty disclosing the stammer to others was worked
through in action over several sessions. A variety of work placements were
psychodramatically created and Connor was given the chance to rehearse how,

when and where to make his disclosures and to begin to ask for help when he needed it. 'This kind of repair work enables old scripts, messages and behaviours to be changed' (Smith 1999a, p.8).

Follow-up

Talitha and Connor were both followed up six months post therapy. Although both teenagers still stammered, several important changes had taken place. Both had taken on some responsibility for acknowledging difficulties with their speech to their teachers, rather than continuing to hide them. Thus, teachers were more willing to inquire about how things were going, thereby detecting problems and working in partnership to resolve them. Additionally, Talitha reported that her teachers now consulted her first if they felt certain tasks in class were likely to cause her any problems.

Both Connor and Talitha were taking more risks in difficult speaking situations and their teachers felt that their overall confidence levels had improved. Connor's attitudes and feelings towards his stammer remained negative. He still construed himself as a 'stammerer.' He had further work to do at a later date. However, he did go on to repeat his work placement. Prior to its commencement, both Connor and his teacher had a meeting to discuss the problems he had previously experienced and 'safety nets' were put in place. I later received a card from him to say he had completed his placement successfully.

Summary

Helping young people to address the covert aspects of their stammering can be a difficult challenge. Turnbull and Stewart (1999) see this as no easy task and advise therapists to proceed with caution. Whilst some children are able to share their feelings openly and are willing to look at the ways in which they avoid or try to keep their stammering hidden, others deny that these aspects exist. They may find it extremely difficult to admit that they have a stammer, even to themselves, and they may report that 'everything is fine'. Therapists are wise to respect the child's readiness for such explorations and to follow the pace he/she sets. Hoey (1997) warns us about pushing past a child's self-protective barriers, since this usually leads to resistance and can be very damaging to the therapeutic relationship.

The three phases of psychodrama, warm-up, action (enactment) and sharing can offer a structure that enables young people to explore some of their feelings, thoughts and behaviours in a gradual and non-threatening way. The therapeutic process, inherent within this structure, has allowed me to move alongside a child, to experience and to participate in his/her individual journey at a very real level. Talitha's encounter with me at the start of her therapy (as presented earlier) required time and space for an equal partnership to be formed before any exploration around her problems could begin. This was part of her initial warm-up phase with me (her therapist), moving slowly towards action. The warm-up helps the child to reach a state of readiness for disclosing and then exploring difficult and painful issues. Hoey (1997) writes in detail about the therapeutic relationship between the child and the therapist. She spells out the implications if not enough attention is paid to this phase of the psychodramatic process.

The action phase offers opportunities to explore any aspect of a person's life, past, present and imagined future, within the 'here and now'. We are able to go back in time and look at 'what could have been'. We can also consider 'what can be' through the use of future projection. Exploration and repair work is possible on these many different levels. You will remember Connor's story. He used the technique of future projection to look at what might happen during further work placements. In action he was able to explore difficulties that might arise and to rehearse ways of dealing with them, developing spontaneity of response rather than using previous rigid behavioural responses (please refer to earlier description). Bannister (1991) has used future projection and rehearsal techniques widely with young people who have been abused. These children required time and space to practise new roles of relating to adults, for developing trust, self-confidence and assertiveness.

Intra-psychic and inter-personal relationships can also be explored in action. These are important since children who stammer have usually developed many negative thoughts and feelings in relation to their stammering. To externalise and confront the part of oneself that stammers and one's belief system can be a turning point in therapy. Additionally the child who stammers is part of a number of social networks and therefore, the stammer has usually had some effect on relationships within many different contexts. These may need to be explored and worked through. Talitha experienced difficulties in her relationships with her teachers. The technique of role reversal was used to explore these and to consider possible resolutions. This particular technique enables a child to experience and to re-evaluate his/her situation from another's perspective. This is exactly what Talitha did. Also, through doubling, I have been able to join the child in their inner emotional world by assuming an aspect of their internal self. This has allowed me to support and challenge their thoughts and feelings from within in a sensitive and respectful way. I see this process as being unique to the method of psychodrama and it can give a child the feeling of being really heard and understood (Bannister 1997).

Sharing is the final part of the session. In a group, it offers the opportunity for participants to share aspects of their own life experience in relation to the work they have just witnessed in action (Smith 1999a, p.9). By doing this, group members can gain insight into their own life difficulties and the protagonist often feels understood and not alone with his/her issues. Therapists can choose to join in with the sharing at their own discretion. In individual work with a child I have at times shared some of my own life experience at the end of the session, thereby deepening my identification with him/her on a more person-to-person level. This has allowed the child to feel that he/she is not alone in his/her struggle. This is important since many young people who stammer often believe that children (people) who do not stammer are good communicators and do not have difficulty with interacting with others around them. My sharing has enabled some children to hear how my life struggles are similar to their own. There are many contradictions within the psychodramatic literature about therapists 'sharing'. Ruscombe-King (1998) writes about the benefits and potential dangers of doing so.

I have described how the method of psychodrama and its specific techniques were of benefit to Talitha and Connor, when applied during their individual therapy sessions. I have only been able to offer a taster of the enormous benefits I believe this approach can offer the field of stammering therapy. Its potential is yet to be unleashed!

Acknowledgements

A special 'thank you' to all the children with whom I have worked. You have taught me about the need for respect, openness and equality in therapy. To all my family, thank you for your love and encouragement. A special thanks to Annie Huntington and Anne Bannister, to the tutors at the Northern School of Psychodrama, and to Dr Trudy Stewart, Jackie Turnbull and Monica Bray, for your belief in me! The on-going support, love and encouragement you give, as I continue to integrate psychodrama into the profession of speech and language therapy is deeply appreciated.

References

Bannister, A. (1997) *The Healing Drama: Psychodrama and Dramatherapy with Abused Children*. London: Free Association Books.

Bannister, A. (1991) 'Learning to Live Again: Psychodramatic Techniques with Sexually Abused Young People.' In P. Holmes and M. Karp (eds) *Psychodrama: Inspiration and Technique*. London: Routledge.

Blatner, A. (1988) *Acting – In: Practical Applications of Psychodramatic Methods*. New York: Springer.

Guitar, B. (1997) 'Therapy for Children's Stuttering and Emotions.' In R.F. Curlee and G.M. Siegel (eds) *Nature and Treatment of Stuttering: New Directions*. Needham Heights: Allyn and Bacon.

Guitar, B. (1998) *Stuttering: An Integrated Approach to its Nature and Treatment*. Baltimore: Lippincott Williams & Wilkins.

Hayhow, R. and Levy, C. (1989) *Working with Stuttering*. Oxon: Winslow Press.

Hoey, B. (1997) *Who Calls the Tune? A Psychodramatic Approach to Child Therapy*. London: Routledge.

Holmes, P. (1991) 'Classical Psychodrama: An Overview.' In P. Holmes and M. Karp (eds) *Psychodrama: Inspiration and Technique*. London: Routledge.

Karp, M. (1994) 'The River of Freedom.' In P. Holmes, M. Karp and M. Watson (eds) *Psychodrama Since Moreno: Innovations in Theory and Practice*. London: Routledge.

Karp, M. (1998) 'An Introduction to Psychodrama.' In M. Karp, P. Holmes and K. Bradshaw Tauvon (eds) *The Handbook of Psychodrama*. London: Routledge.

Lousada, O. (1998) 'The Three-layered Cake, Butter with Everything.' In M. Karp, P. Holmes and K. Bradshaw Tauvon (eds) *The Handbook of Psychodrama*. London: Routledge.

Peters, T.J. and Guitar, B. (1991) 'The Nexus of Stuttering: An Introduction.' In D.G. Shapiro (ed) *Stuttering Intervention: A Collaborative Journey to Fluency Freedom*. Texas: PRO-ED.

Ruscombe-King, G. (1998) 'The Sharing.' In M. Karp, P. Holmes and K. Bradshaw Tauvon (eds) *The Handbook of Psychodrama*. London: Routledge.

Rustin, L. Botterill, W. and Kelman, E. (1996) *Assessment and Therapy for Young Dysfluent Children: Family Interaction*. London: Whurr.

Shapiro, D.G. (1999) *Stuttering Intervention: A Collaborative Journey to Fluency Freedom*. Texas: PRO-ED.

Sheehan, J.G. (1958) 'Conflict Theory of Stuttering.' In J. Eisenson (ed) *Stuttering: A Symposium*. New York: Harper and Row.

Smith, G. (1999a) 'The role of psychodrama.' *Signal: The Newsletter of the Special Interest Group in Disorders of Fluency, 11*.

Smith, G. (1999b) 'Creative possibilities: using psychodrama with children and adolescents who stammer.' *Signal: The Newsletter of the Special Interest Group in Disorders of Fluency, 12*.

Turnbull, J. and Stewart, T. (1996) *Helping Children Cope with Stammering*. London: Sheldon Press.

Turnbull, J. and Stewart, T. (1999) *The Fluency Resource: A Practical Manual*. London: Winslow Press.

Van Riper, C. (1982) *The Nature of Stuttering*. New Jersey: Prentice-Hall.

Yalom, I.D. (1985) *The Theory and Practice of Group Psychotherapy*. New York: Basic Books.

CHAPTER 5

Where there is Drama there can also be Art
Using Creative Media with Children Living with Life-Threatening Illness

Kate Kirk

Introduction

A diagnosis of life-threatening illness in the life of a young person or child can be a dramatic and devastating experience. This chapter will explore the practical applications of action methods as creative therapeutic media with young people who are living with a life-threatening or life-limiting illness, in order to demonstrate that amid the drama of illness art, creativity and spontaneity can exist. The chapter opens with working definitions related to my understanding and use of the terms, life-threatening or life-limiting illness, action methods and creative therapeutic media. Three case studies are used to demonstrate a variety of interventions used with young people who have very different types of illness and prognoses[12] and who are at different stages in their illness. The case studies are drawn from my work as a psychodramatist in a palliative care service and private practice. Each case study is followed by a short commentary relating aspects of the case material to practice and theory. The practicalities of using action methods with this client group will be explored, whilst recognising that sometimes the choice is simply influenced by the vigour or frailty of the child. The chapter ends with a brief review of the emotional cost and support needs for workers who engage in this work and concludes with a discussion of some of the ideas that underpin it.

Working definitions and the background to this work

Over the past thirty years there has been increasing interest in using action methods and creative media for therapeutic purposes (examples from the literature would include: Gersie 1991; Hoey 1997; Kipper 1986; Meekums 2000; Parks 1990). Other literature looks more specifically at using these methods with adults (for example Aldridge 1998; Kirk and Lever 2001) and young people who have life-threatening illness (Councill 1993) or who are dying (Perkins 1976; Tate 1989). Examples of the range of application of creative media with young people who are ill can be found in a recent volume of *The Arts in Psychotherapy*. Among the articles were those which dealt with the use of art therapy with young people who have cystic fibrosis (Fenton 2000), young people undergoing bone marrow transplantation (Günter 2000) and who have diabetes (Raghuraman 2000).

Living with life-threatening or life-limiting illness

Receiving a diagnosis of any illness will have some sort of impact on the person and their life. However, because of reality, myth, stigma and mystery, some illnesses carry a heavier penalty. A diagnosis of any illness, no matter how mild or severe, can feel as though the person's life is threatened. I believe that the differences between life-threatening and life-limiting illness are as follows:

- Life-threatening illnesses are those that actively and continually threaten the person's life; for which there may be considerable and effective treatment, yet cure is either unlikely or not necessarily guaranteed. For example: cancers, diabetes, motor neurone disease and AIDS.

- Life-limiting illness does just as it says. It limits the person's day-to-day life experience and limits them in achieving their potential had they not had the illness, whether this is through the restrictions arising from the impact of the illness on their body or through the constant reminders of medication, diet and use of appliances to aid their continued health and mobility. Life-limiting might also include life-shortening from complications that are secondary to the condition, for example: cystic fibrosis, multiple sclerosis, and rheumatoid arthritis.

This may be fine in theory, but what actually counts is how the person makes sense of the diagnosis and what their illness actually means to them. Exploring the illness stories from the person's life, their family (DeMaria, Weeks and Hof 1999; Schützenberger 1998, 2000) and social context (Radley 1993) can enable the worker to understand why a person is responding as if their life was being threatened though their illness has a seemingly benign influence; or, conversely when the person is responding as though their life is not under threat although the prognosis is poor.

Action methods, creative therapeutic media and life-threatening illness

For the purpose of this chapter, the term 'action methods' is 'used to describe ancillary techniques from psychodrama such as role reversal and doubling – and related methods such as timelines, sculpting, social atoms and spectograms – which are used by people in learning situations...' (Batten and Wiener 2001, p.2). The application of action methods in this case, combined with creative therapeutic media, is for therapeutic effect. Creative therapeutic media include tools, materials, music, drama, and games used to enhance therapeutic work. Blatner (1992) states that 'creative art therapies offer a range of vehicles for promoting healing, and often provide experiences for patients that are not available through the more traditional types of verbal or behavioural therapies' (p.409).

Gersie (1991) suggests, amongst other things, that creative-expressive activities matter because they enable the person's current situation to be looked at indirectly, 'gently easing our attempts to control the healing process' (p.235). She believes that creating something new gives some form of mastery over the person's current difficulties and in symbolising the 'unthinkable' the person's tolerance for the 'actual' is increased (p.235). The structure inherent in the therapeutic process offers the person a degree of control in exploring difficult areas in their life. She specifies two other beneficial reasons for using creative-expressive processes. The first is that, in the process of symbol-making, 'the products which have been made, increase our awareness of ourselves and others. We learn to see and hear differently' (p.235). The second, perhaps most relevant to working with young people, is that:

> When we are engaged in symbolic-expressive activities we do not have to accommodate ourselves to external demands or models; there are neither coercions nor sanctions and this enables the assimilation and therefore the transformation of experienced reality. When this reality is grievous it is even more important that this process occurs. (Gersie 1991, p.236)

The importance of using creative media when working with young people is in its ability to tap into the freedom and spontaneity that are inherent in young people (Segal 1984). Through the expressive nature of art, dance, music, drama etc., young people are free to express verbally and non-verbally their repressed and difficult feelings. The playful nature of these processes enables young people to return to their natural expressive element: games and plays. In adult therapeutic endeavour, talking and articulacy are prerequisites for healing. Young people need media that are both familiar to them and will enable them to express what feels impossible to articulate given their limited vocabulary of words. This next section contributes to our understanding of the application of action methods. It also demonstrates the flexibility and responsiveness of creative media when working with young people who are physically vulnerable.

Case studies: Clare, Jenny and Jack

This section introduces three young people and their experiences of life-limiting or life-threatening illness. They include: Clare who had had the chronic life-limiting condition of ME[13] for several years; Jenny who had recently been diagnosed with systemic lupus erythmatosus (SLE);[14] and Jack who had leukaemia[15] and was undergoing chemotherapy with a view to a possible future bone marrow transplant. They were chosen because each demonstrates the use of creative media in action. I have tried to present the case studies as stories using the young people's words where possible. Inevitably, they are only snapshots of the therapeutic process, which in Clare's case consisted only of one session.

Clare: Big Bird and ME

Her mum, who had heard that I used art and psychodrama to help people who were ill, referred Clare to me. Clare was a painfully thin young girl of 12 years old. It seemed surprising that she was able to find the strength to walk across the room, so slow and weary was her progress. She lowered herself onto the sofa, trying to protect her bony joints with the surrounding cushions. In a monotone voice she told me that she'd 'been like this for the whole of her life, at least three years anyway.' Her parents had taken her to the family doctor who had, in turn, referred her to the local paediatrician, who then referred her to the regional hospital where she'd seen the 'nerve doctor' (neurologist). She had had a battery of intrusive, uncomfortable and pointless tests, pointless because they'd proved nothing, but excluded lots of things.

One day her mum had read an article in a woman's magazine about something called ME. This started a whole new series of tests, not only in hospital but also with some very odd people, 'Weirdoes', who, according to Clare, looked into her eyes, took samples of her hair, pushed on her arms as she tasted different foods, gave her strange diets and 'did something with magnets and electricity.' This she grudgingly admitted seemed to be 'not too bad'; she'd had some more energy afterwards. She felt that she had been 'trawled around like a prize pig', she did little complaining though, because 'what's the point when mum and dad are trying so hard to help me get better?'

So here she was with me, another odd person to see. She didn't 'mind exactly', she was 'just really tired.' I asked her what she had tried to do for herself in all this. She was surprised by the question, as though her illness was none of her responsibility, it belonged to the doctors, therapists and her parents: 'I just suffer from it.' I suggested that we might look at a way of helping herself, so that even when people were doing things to help her, she could do something to help herself. She appeared to cheer up at this idea. I explained that, because of the way I work, I ask some pretty weird questions; if she was doubtful about anything she must just ask me why or what I'm doing. I suggested that this probably put me in her 'weirdo' category. She smiled.

If she could think of a way of explaining what ME looked like in her body, what would it be like? She thought for a few minutes and decided 'it would look like grains of corn scattered throughout my body because it just seems to be everywhere inside me.' So if grains of corn are scattered what would pick them up? 'Hens or some sort of bird.' If she needed something to pick up the grains of ME corn what might that be? 'Big Bird from Sesame Street.' Why Big Bird? Because 'I really like him, he's very sensible and helps the other people and the puppets in the show. He's good with children too.'

Conscious of her physical state, I asked her if she could become Big Bird for a minute. She stood up straight with her neck stretched a little forward. I asked her how, as Big Bird, he could help Clare with all these grains of corn called ME? 'Well, I could peck them up and gobble them away.' I told Big Bird I was worried that, if he gobbled up all the grains, that would mean he'd get ME as well. Big Bird realised that was not a good idea. 'I will peck up the grains and when I have a full beak I will give it to the grumpy character that lives in the dustbin. Nothing ever touches him so it would be safe to put it in the bin.' I asked Clare to return to her place on the sofa, keeping the image and words of

Big Bird in her mind's eye. What did she think about Big Bird's idea? She was really pleased; 'I think it's great.'

I said that we could try and enact Big Bird's suggestion in two ways: physical enactment or visualisation. I wasn't sure which suited her best, only she knew how much energy she'd got to do this. She immediately said, 'I want to do it like a play, then, afterwards, I can save the pictures in my head.' I was surprised at the fervour of her response. We set up the scene; gently shaking her arms and legs to dislodge the ME from her body, she sprinkled imaginary grains of ME corn. We used the wastepaper basket to denote the dustbin. She then role reversed to become Big Bird; slowly and silently she picked up all the grains and deposited them in the bin. In the role of Big Bird she appeared to have lost some of the rigidity and weariness in her movements, which appeared more fluid. As Big Bird she explained, 'I have to be careful and pick up all the scattered grain, I don't want anybody else to become ill.'

After we had established that all the grains of ME corn had been picked up and dumped into the bin, I wondered if Big Bird had any special message for Clare to remind her of what she'd done today and her illness. Big Bird suggested, 'Clare has found that she could do something for herself and she should practise a bit more doing this and other things for herself.' When Clare was sitting back on the sofa I asked her what she'd thought about the message from Big Bird? She replied, 'I will think about him picking up the grains of ME again. I think I have got so used to being ill that I've forgotten some of the things I can do. So, instead of being cross at all the things I can't do I'm going to try and find things I can do.' Post script: sadly, I was only able to work with Clare for this session, she ended up spending time in London having more of the 'magnets and electricity'. This happened some years ago, before ME became well recognised in adults, let alone in young people.

COMMENTARY

Clare illustrates the restricted role repertoire that can develop in chronic illness: the role of 'patient'. In young people this role is compounded by powerlessness, demonstrated in Clare's account of being passed around from expert to expert. Described as the drive towards the fulfilment of desires at the core of the self (Blatner 1997, p.84), her act hunger to be more powerful and mobile can be seen in her energetic role reversal as Big Bird. Not only does she find some of her own power but also she finds herself as her own healer in the role. Clare's action was a monodrama, that is an encounter with different aspects of the protagonist and without auxiliaries (other participants) (Blatner 1997, p.20).

Clare's experience as Big Bird picking up the grain was very different from her passive experiences at the hands of others.

A significant process that informs this work is found in psycho-neuroimmunology (PNI). This is a developing science that seeks to uncover the mechanisms between stress, immunology and disease progression (van den Boom 1996). The relationship between the mind, the body and immunity is highly complex; its forebears are found in ancient beliefs about the mind-body connection and the development of biofeedback studies (Kiecolt-Glaser and Glaser 1989). Beliefs in PNI would suggest that when working with metaphors in illness the body is changed (Gruber *et al.* 1988). Simply, that Clare's enactment and belief that Big Bird can dispose of the grains of ME will effect some sort of change in her body; whether this is at cellular, enzymatic or hormonal level, something will happen. In psychodramatic terms, Clare's role reversal with Big Bird released her from some of the grip of the 'patient' role.

Finally, even when working in metaphor the therapist has to have an eye on reality. Clare as Big Bird ingesting the grains of ME would have been counter-productive; hence the need to dispose of them, keeping them away from Big Bird and out of Clare's system.

Jenny and the Wolf

Jenny was a bubbly young woman of 15 who had been diagnosed with SLE. She was a member of a school drama group who, in exploring other uses of drama, were experiencing a number of psychodrama sessions. Themes that had been previously explored in the group were related to families and relation-ships, loss and issues about growing up. The warm-up phase had been exercises to make physical the stresses and strains of daily living and to represent the times when people feel over-stretched. Jenny emerged as the protagonist. She was tearful as she explained what had acted as a catalyst to her becoming the protagonist. 'Part of the trouble was those exercises; I felt the usual restrictions in my body because of my condition.' Her upset was related to the forthcoming holidays when she and her family were going abroad. 'I just know that this'll mean I'm banished from the sun to the shade and I'll be covered up. Because of SLE and steroids, my skin is really sensitive to the sun. I'm really just very, very, fed up with fighting this all the time.'

Tapping into the war metaphor, I wondered if we could set out her fight. She chose a person to represent each part of her body affected by her SLE, setting them out in a line down one side of the room. As she enrolled the auxil-iaries, she sculpted them into a shape suitable for her needs and gave them a sentence to say. I asked her to set out the opposing side; who was left to stand opposite and fight? She chose other people to represent her thoughts (e.g. 'I hate my body, there's always something wrong', 'I want to be different', 'Why me!') and feelings (e.g. fear, anger, anxiety, stress) about having SLE. Again each auxiliary was assigned a sentence.

We joined the audience to wait for the battle to commence. Each line called, then shouted, the words they'd been assigned. As she watched and heard the battle, Jenny became more tearful; 'This is just like what's inside me.' I wondered if she'd noticed anything about the battle. She asked what I meant; I asked her who the real enemy was? She said, 'It's my illness.' I then wondered where SLE was in the battle? 'Nowhere and everywhere,' she replied. I wondered whether we could find something to represent her illness: the real enemy. 'A wild animal.' I asked whether she knew that 'lupus' meant 'wolf' in Latin. She said 'ideal'. She assigned a role to a large young man with a particularly wild expression that she liked. One by one we approached the auxiliaries, assigning them with new words to shout, not at each other this time but at the wolf: lupus.

We rejoined the audience and watched the redrawn battle lines. This time when action was called Jenny was delighted to watch as the wolf got his comeuppance. The audience were infected by her glee and cheered the champions. I asked her which of the auxiliaries she would like to role reverse with. She chose to be her heart, she fought with her body allies against the wolf. In a second role reverse, this time from the other side of the lines, she chose to be her anger. She fought vigorously with lots of loud angry roars. Her heart and anger auxiliaries had got additional information, so we went back into the audience to watch the renewed battle. She said, 'I feel like a heroine a million miles away from being that miserable victim.' So we gave her a heroine's welcome home from the war.

In the sharing phase four young people revealed their own experiences of acute and chronic illness. They included: Ted, whose brother had Still's disease (juvenile rheumatoid arthritis) and how his illness limited the whole family; Emma, whose father had chronic leukaemia, felt his treatment programme dictated her life; Mike, who had coeliac disease, who was fed up with not being able to eat just whatever he wanted; and Winston, whose family were vulnerable to sickle cell anaemia, and was always waiting for the bad news to hit him.

COMMENTARY

When using action methods the therapist has to be conscious of health and safety, as can be seen in Jenny's story. Physical limitations that may create problems or cause harm to the individual have to be identified early on in the life of the group. In order to protect participants' bodies, part of establishing the safe therapeutic space for action methods includes the permission to modify or to refuse exercises.

There were a number of therapeutic factors that are relevant to Jenny's psychodrama; the first was in externalising her problem. White and Epston (1990) believe that externalising 'encourages the persons to objectify and, at times, to personify the problems that they experience as oppressive. In this process, the problem becomes a separate entity and thus external to the person' whereby the stuck qualities of the problem are 'rendered less fixed and less restricting' (p.38). It was startling to find the war zone metaphor so accurately reflecting the auto-immune condition Jenny's body, which was effectively fighting itself. Sitting in the audience enabled her not only to witness the current state of war in her body but also to create an alternative story in which a unique outcome is plotted (White and Epston 1990, p.16).

Two therapeutic factors described by Yalom (1985) seem particularly relevant. The first, apparent in the sharing phase after the action of psychodrama, was 'universality'. The discovery that you are not unique, because others have similar struggles and feelings, leads to a reduction in isolation (pp.7–9). The second factor, 'altruism', is implicit in the process of the psychodrama. Altruism is the gift of being helpful to others without any motivating gain; in the psychodrama group it is found in 'not only the reciprocal giving-receiving sequence but also from the intrinsic act of giving' (p.14).

Jenny was motivated to look at the issues related to her illness and in doing so opened up others to reveal and vent feelings connected to their own struggles related to illness. None of the young people had expected to unburden themselves at school in this way. Each student who had shared with Jenny thanked her; they were both surprised and pleased, because they had not spoken out before. As a consequence they experienced the concern, care and support of the other group members and Jenny felt less isolated.

The Devil and Jack's Bones

Jack was a boy of ten, referred to a community palliative care service. He had been diagnosed as suffering from leukaemia and was undergoing a chemotherapy programme. By our first session he had had his first three doses and 'wasn't feeling too bad, though dead sicky most of the time and tired' and very angry. He told me the story of his illness, from the gentle insidious signs of it through to the moment he got the surprise of the diagnosis. He impressed me with his use of the medical words, saying 'I want to be a leukaemia expert, so I always ask the doctors to tell me the proper words for treatment.'

However, all this did not really help because lying on the bed while they infused the 'chemo' was 'plain horrible. I know I'm going to get sicker and my hair will drop out, bits have already. I'll end up looking like all those sad kids with baseball caps to cover their bald heads.' The whole thing was 'evil' and he was dreading each session. What did evil mean to him? 'The Devil, that's what "chemo" is. The Devil, I have to fight the effects all the time.' Normally people did have to fight the Devil, but in this case it seemed that he was going to have to do something different because the Devil was on his side in that it was fighting the bad blood cells.

We explored what he could do differently between Jack and the Devil. We came up with the idea that dancing with the Devil might be the best. Dancing with the Devil was inevitably uncomfortable – he was the Devil after all – but at least they were on the same side. We set up a scene for him to dance; he chose some heavy metal music, as being the 'jangly' sort of music the Devil would dance to. He became the 'Devil Chemo' and had a deep voice. Sounding very strong like a tyrant, Jack said, 'I'm going to rule these blood cells and knock them back into remission.' I asked the Devil Chemo what were Jack's orders? 'Jack has to join me and dance to my rhythm. If he does this he will win the fight. Jack is my second-in-command but he had better toe the line. I am the boss, if my wishes aren't obeyed then I will spit hell fire.' They practised the dance ready for the next 'chemo' session.

Back in his own role, Jack was very pleased: 'I like the Devil spitting hell fire, it's really cool.' In his own role he was exhausted but pleased with the music and the dance. 'I'm going to borrow Ed's (brother) heavy metal tape and listen to it on my Walkman when I have chemo next, this'll remind me of my dance with the Devil.'

Towards the end of treatment Jack became very frail, he was placed in an isolation cubicle because of the risk of infection. There was talk of his brother acting as a bone marrow donor. He had games and cards, colouring pens and papers to keep him occupied. Drawing and listening to story tapes were about the only things he could do. Just holding a book to read was hard work for him. In a short session we looked at what his bone marrow might look like at the moment. He drew a cartoon bone, brown, fractured and disgusting with black speckled bits in the grey bone shaft. Then we thought about what his bone marrow would look like with his brother's transplanted in it. He drew a brilliant white bone with sparkling gold bits. 'I think that to get the old bone to become like the new, I have to fill up the old bone, slowly rinsing out all the debris and bad stuff, replacing it with the new sparkling cells. It has got to be slow, so that none of the old cells would be left.' We created a visualisation with these images, the old bone being the starting point. There was a tube filling its centre with a sparkling liquid until it started to overflow. Gradually because of the liquid, the bone became cleaner and purer, and the cracks were repaired. This image was continued until the new bone was completely rebuilt.

Jack was very satisfied with his ideas and leant back on the pillows. 'This is my prescription, I will think of this three times a day.' Jack went on to have his bone marrow transplant, which appears to have been successful.

COMMENTARY

Jack's story illuminates a common experience for people who are suffering from, and treated for, life-threatening illness, that the physical effects of treatment are often worse than the effects of the illness itself. Jack's act hunger (see Clare) was to be the expert, in control and in charge. Playing the Devil amplified this desire to become an ultimate controller. His control of therapy was implicit in the process where I, the therapist, followed him in the dance. In the role of the Devil he was able to express some of his accumulated anger through spitting fire and stamping around as he danced. From his monodrama came a practical plan to deal with his subsequent sessions of chemotherapy. Taking his Walkman and music not only perpetuated his collaboration with Devil in keeping the dance alive but also took his action from the symbolic into the actual, into his attendance at the chemotherapy session.

Chemotherapy regimes are time-consuming for the young person and their parents; they mean frequent and regular hospital attendance. One thing that is not apparent in this case study is the amount of disruption to the therapeutic relationship caused by planned and unplanned hospital admissions, appointments for urgent investigations and the rigidity of treatment regimes. Consequently, the therapist has to be mindful that each session is discrete and self-contained and yet part of the whole process. It is hard to predict when the client will be called away at short notice and for how long.

About the impact of the work

It is fair to say that sometimes the impact of this work on the therapist is shocking. The first and most immediate shock is that certain illnesses and their subsequent treatment can be both brutal and destructive. It is hard enough to view the effects of illness on adult bodies; how much harder it is for the therapist to overcome the feelings of pity and distress when children present their disfigured and scarred bodies. The challenge is how to manage our own emotional responses in ways that are respectful and truthful.

It can be difficult when you follow the child and their family post-diagnosis, with all the hope of a cure, through to the end of their life, offering either continuous or episodic care. When the child has a poor prognosis, or is in the terminal phase of their illness, a significant difficulty for the therapist is being confronted by their own helplessness to rescue and heal.

There are a number of coping strategies that the therapist can use to deal with the impact of this work. The first is to work with different types of clients in their caseload, balancing clients who have a poor prognosis with the newly bereaved carers or those who are post-diagnosis. The second strategy is to have good quality, regular supervision, preferably from a supervisor who understands just what this work entails. Increasing personal therapy or withdrawing temporarily, or ultimately permanently, from the work are ways of dealing with the stress incurred. Time out enables the worker to make sense of it all and replenish their resources.

Having said all this, working with young people who have life-threatening illness illustrates the unpredictable nature of life. One learns not to take life for granted and to realise that all is not certain; also to value relationships, families and friends, especially the young people amongst them.

Conclusions

Many adults who find themselves in the restricted role of 'patient' rail against their loss of power, becoming either angry or compliant to deal with the process. Young people, already disempowered and disenfranchised in the world, become even more so through illness. Adults not only dictate what is happening in young people's lives but, with illness, also what will happen to their bodies, their private selves. The intrusiveness of illness and treatment and, in the case of young people, their powerlessness to have some say in what is happening, cannot be overemphasised.

Young people, with less experience of the world, have to rely on the adults who surround them for interpretation of the facts. All this might be at a time when the significant adults are dealing with their own emotional reactions to having a child with a life-threatening illness. The world as a safe and dependable place has been lost, leaving the child and the family disorientated. Factors that may assist them to find equilibrium will depend on learning gained from recovering previous life experiences and their current resources to ride this storm.

The therapist assigned to working with the child and/or family may arrive at any stage in the illness. Immediately post-diagnosis, the first tasks might be to debrief the delivery of the diagnosis and to inform as to the nature of the illness and treatment. The worker balances information and support, rather than overloading the already stressed family. It is easy to see how the child's needs get lost within the family's turmoil. A problem for the worker is identifying who their client is: family or child? This will, of course, depend on their professional role and contract, but, where possible, the young person's needs should predominate.

One reason for giving the child space on their own arises from the complex family dynamics. Through having this illness, the child may feel responsible for inviting chaos into their family and therefore say little to promote it further. They may feel loyal to their parents and other adults (who must know best) and therefore repress criticism of what parents and doctors are asking, although it feels wrong to them. They may collude with the parents' desire for hope and a cure without having the opportunity to explore the alternative: the hopelessness that they may at times legitimately feel. The young person may feel compelled to take up the infantilised patient role because their parents, wanting to nurse them and wrap them in cotton wool, are unwilling to allow them to be a young person first, an ill person second.

It is here that Gersie's (1991) statement is most meaningful: being engaged in symbolic-expressive activities the child does not have to accommodate 'to external demands or models; there are neither coercions nor sanctions and this enables the assimilation and therefore the transformation of experienced reality' (p.236). In addition to attempting to redress the power imbalance through collaboration, action methods create a vehicle via which complex issues connected to illness are explored, and which may otherwise remain unheard.

References

Aldridge, D. (1998) 'Life as jazz: hope, meaning, and music therapy in the treatment of life-threatening illness.' *Advances in Mind-Body Medicine 14*, 271–282.

Batten, F. and Wiener, R. (2001) 'Editorial.' *The British Journal of Psychodrama and Sociodrama 16*, 1, 1–3.

Blatner, A. (1992) 'Theoretical principles underlying creative arts therapies.' *The Arts in Psychotherapy 18*, 405–409.

Blatner, A. (1997) *Acting–in: Practical Applications of Psychodramatic Methods.* London: Free Association Books.

Councill, T. (1993) 'Art therapy with paediatric cancer patients: helping normal children cope with abnormal circumstances.' *Art Therapy: Journal of the American Art Therapy Association 10*, 2, 78–87.

DeMaria, R., Weeks, G. and Hof, L. (1999) *Focused Genograms: Intergenerational Assessment of Individuals, Couples and Families.* Philadelphia, PA: Brunner/Mazel.

Fenton, J. F. (2000) 'Cystic fibrosis and art therapy.' *The Arts in Psychotherapy 27*, 1, 15–25.

Gersie, E. (1991) *Storymaking in Bereavement.* London: Jessica Kingsley Publishers.

Gruber, B., Hall, N., Hersh, S. and Dubois, P. (1988) 'Immune system and psychological changes in metastatic cancer patients using relaxation and guided imagery: a pilot study.' *Scandinavian Journal of Behaviour Therapy 17*, 25–46.

Günter, M. (2000) 'Art therapy as intervention to stabilize the defences of children undergoing bone marrow transplantation.' *The Arts in Psychotherapy 27*, 1, 3–14.

Hoey, B. (1997) *Who Calls the Tune? A Psychodramatic Approach to Child Therapy.* London: Routledge.

Kiecolt-Glaser, J. and Glaser, R. (1989) 'Psychoneuroimmunology: past, present and future.' *Health Psychology 8*, 6, 677–682.

Kipper, D. (1986) *Psychotherapy through Clinical Role Playing.* New York: Brunner/Mazel.

Kirk, K. and Lever, M. (2001) 'Palliative Care Counselling: From Diagnosis to Death.' In K. Etherington (ed) *Counselling in Medical Settings.* London: Jessica Kingsley Publishers.

Meekums, B. (2000) *Creative Group Therapy for Women Survivors of Child Sexual Abuse: Speaking the Unspeakable.* London: Jessica Kingsley Publishers.

Parks, P. (1990) *Rescuing the 'Inner Child': Therapy for Adults Sexually Abused as Children.* London: Souvenir Press.

Perkins, C. (1976) 'The Art of Life-threatened Children: A Preliminary Study.' In R. Shoemaker (ed) *Creativity and the Therapist's Identity.* Baltimore: American Art Therapy Association.

Radley, A. (ed) (1993) *Worlds of Illness: Biographical and Cultural Perspectives on Health and Disease.* London: Routledge.

Raghuraman, R.S. (2000) 'Dungeons and dragons: dealing with the emotional and behavioural issues of an adolescent with diabetes.' *The Arts in Psychotherapy 27*, 1, 27–29.

Segal, R. (1984) 'Helping children express grief through symbolic communication.' *Social Casework: The Journal of Contemporary Social Work*, 590–599.

Schützenberger, A. A. (1998) *The Ancestor Syndrome: Transgenerational Psychotherapy and Hidden Links in the Family Tree.* London: Routledge.

Schützenberger, A. A. (2000) 'Health and Death: Hidden Links through the Family Tree.' In P.F. Kellerman and M.K. Hudgins (eds) *Psychodrama with Trauma Survivors: Acting Out your Pain.* London: Jessica Kingsley Publishers.

Tate, F. (1989) 'Symbols in the graphic art of the dying.' *The Arts in Psychotherapy 16*, 115–120.

Van den Boom, F. (1996) 'Methodological and theoretical reflections on PNI, HIV and coping.' *Patient Education and Counselling 28*, 85–91.

White, M. and Epston, D. (1990) *Narrative Means to Therapeutic Ends*. New York: W.W. Norton.

Yalom, I. (1985) *The Theory and Practice of Group Psychotherapy*, 3rd edn. New York: Basic Books.

CHAPTER 6

Can We Do Something?
Young People Using Action Methods to Support Each Other in School

Nick Luxmoore

Introduction

So much of school involves listening, watching, reading: simply sitting and listening and watching and reading. Young people get fed up. They fidget. 'Miss, when are we going to do something?' They talk, tip back on their chairs. 'Can we *do* something?' Someone tips too far, falls, there's a crash, laughter and, at long last, action as the teacher moves to confront a spread-eagled, smirking student.

This chapter is not an argument against those vital skills of listening quietly and concentrating hard and, when they can, many teachers do seek out more active methods of enhancing young people's learning. But there is potential for young people themselves, provided they are carefully supervised and supported, to use active methods to facilitate each others' learning. This chapter describes one such programme, drawing extensively on young people's own written reports of their experience as facilitators. Throughout the chapter they tell their stories of nervousness and relief doing the work, of difficulties experienced and overcome, of the delight and responsibility of the work and of the lessons learnt.

In developing citizenship in schools, I believe the emphasis needs to be on giving young people a positive *experience* of citizenship, rather than merely an academic understanding. That means finding all sorts of opportunities in school for students to take responsibility for each other and for the things that matter. There is, after all, much that is mutually therapeutic about older young people supporting and working with their younger peers (Luxmoore 2000). Coren (1997) argues that this learning from peers provides a necessary developmental bridge in young people's separation from parents. For even discounting hours spent in school lessons, young people spend about twice as many waking hours with their peers as with their parents or with other adults (Gordon and Grant 1997) and they learn more readily from each other than they do from anyone else (Cowie and Wallace 2000). They learn by interacting: learning to play, learning to listen, learning to trust.

Peer education has therefore been widely developed in and out of schools as an effective means of addressing important issues such as drugs, sexual health, conflict and self-esteem. Finn (1981), quoted in Cowie and Wallace (2000), defines peer education as 'the sharing of information, attitudes or behaviours by people who are not professionally trained educators but whose goal is to educate' (p.20). The chapter will explain the context in which this particular peer education programme took place before going on to describe the training provided for those young people responsible for its delivery. It will outline a three-part structure used by the young people as the basis for each session, using extracts from their written reports. It will describe the crucial need for supervision to support this work and will, again, use the young people's own reports in evaluating the success of their work. Some concluding thoughts about how this work might be developed will end the chapter.

In developing this work, my own thinking has come from the philosophy and practice of psychodrama (Moreno 1987) with its sense of interactive, *group* experience as vital for a species so reliant on each other, and with its emphasis on *activity* as a sure way of learning. Having been a teacher and a youth worker, I am also well aware of young people's need for structure in order to feel safe enough to learn. There's an old saying which ought to be emblazoned on every classroom wall: 'Tell me and I'll hear, show me and I'll see, involve me…and I'll understand.'

Context

The student counsellors are drawn from Year 13 (17 to 18-year-olds) at Bartholomew School, Eynsham, Oxfordshire. (I am grateful to the Headteacher, Bill Berry, for permission to publicise this work and grateful to the counsellors for permission to quote directly from them throughout this chapter.)

After selection and training, the student counsellors work with younger students in a whole variety of ways, one of which is through running formal, structured groups during those lessons in the week sometimes called 'tutorial', 'guidance' or 'personal, social and health education' lessons. Working in pairs or alone for between four and six consecutive weeks with a single-sex group of between 8 and 16 students from a mixed ability tutor group, the counsellors aim to establish an atmosphere in which younger students can begin to talk about important things such as families, friends, enemies, sexuality and so on. These are things which rarely get talked about in whole-class lessons but which remain important nevertheless, gnawing away, affecting relationships all the time and therefore affecting students' learning.

The way the student counsellors establish that atmosphere is through carefully selected, highly structured, active and involving exercises designed to be fun and to allow younger students to get to know each other differently. The groups are not compulsory but it is rare for younger students to decline the offer or drop out once a group has started.

After each session, the student counsellors meet (individually or collectively) for a further session to debrief with their adult supervisor, a role I've played for many years, as the school counsellor, but which could equally well be played by a committed teacher. These sessions are also a chance to think carefully about the underlying processes and issues emerging in each group and choose appropriate exercises to use the following week. After the final session, the counsellors write a report about their group. With their permission, I have used extracts from these reports to describe exactly what happens in the groups because they were the ones present, and can tell the story the way it happened.

Training

The student counsellors are trained for this work by firstly doing all the exercises that I suggest they use themselves with their groups of younger students. There is not space in this chapter to describe many of these exercises in detail. Most of them are mine, culled from other practitioners, from books, workshops, experiential groups. Sometimes the counsellors contribute their own exercises, remembered from drama lessons, parties, even playgroups. If exercises seem inappropriate at first, our discussion centres on how to adapt them so that they remain fun and keep everyone involved. Whenever possible I ask a counsellor who already knows the exercise to introduce and run it with the rest of us. We then offer feedback as to how clearly the exercise was explained, which bits we did not understand, how confident we felt about doing it and what the counsellor did or said which made us feel more or less confident. In this way the counsellors develop a wide repertoire of exercises to use in the coming weeks and get better at the crucial task of introducing them so that younger students will feel safe and enthused.

In most cases teachers have been happy to allow the student counsellors to run these groups and happy for them to work with whatever concerns emerge from the younger students. Sometimes, where teachers have decided to do a particular module (on sex education, for example), the counsellors have joined in and run their own groups, covering the same subject matter. Teachers and counsellors have then trained together for the task: all joining in the exercises they will subsequently use to explore the topic with younger students.

Basic structure of sessions

Action methods make learning fun and effective but only when young people feel safe enough to join in and contribute. Each session the student counsellors run is therefore carefully structured with a warm-up phase, a main or 'serious' part of the session and a closing exercise. The counsellors learn that, until a group is ready, there is no point in going on to more personally challenging or 'serious' work.

A. Warm-ups

Some groups, anxious and wary of each other, need a lot of warming up, so we think very carefully in supervision before and after each session about what a particular group is ready for, about the level at which we can fairly expect them to contribute. Trying too much too soon scares people and, when that happens, they retreat, naturally enough, into anxious, defensive behaviour. Unless a group is first allowed to establish some degree of trust it is much harder for them to contribute at a level that means something.

> The girls in the group were quite quiet when they first arrived. I had already put eight chairs in a circle and so I asked them to take their coats off and sit down. I decided that as they were quiet we would do a warm-up which involved moving around. This woke them up a bit. After this we did an activity which would get everybody thinking about each others' lives and feelings. (Sam Lees)

Most groups begin with a name-learning and then a chair-swapping exercise which, because it is fun and active, relaxes the group so that they are then ready for something more thoughtful. This works with most groups:

On the whole the group enjoyed the more active exercises, in particular 'Sharks'. This exercise consisted of Hannah playing both a shark and a lifeguard and shouting 'Sharks!' at regular intervals, forcing the other group members to jump onto the nearest chair to avoid being caught. Laughter and shrieks were plentiful during the game and the boys expressed their enjoyment of this exercise. They were then very keen and responsive when asked to volunteer for exercises after that. (Alan Brown)

The group seemed to prefer more active exercises. Quieter exercises made them fidget. This tendency might have been caused by the strict structure of secondary school compared to primary school which gave them more 'playtime'. They seemed to miss primary school and miss having a way of releasing energy in an informal way. This theory was tested in the last session when we did an exercise called 'Caterpillars' where the boys, working in teams, had to roll over each other like caterpillars to reach the finishing line. They really enjoyed this exercise. (Hannah James)

Thinking exercises went down well alongside physical activities. A notably successful activity was 'Snails' where each member has to hold hands and then wrap round each other in basically an organised hug. Such activities are a 'street cred' way of making contact with other members and it also requires teamwork. 'Snails' was very popular. (Paul Richards)

Things are not always straightforward:

We did an activity which involved all holding hands, promoting physical contact. This was really good and the girls wanted to do this a couple more times. However, the second time we did this activity I got accidentally head-butted very hard so I decided we wouldn't do it again. (Sam Lees)

Knowing when to end a warm-up was something Emma learnt:

Our second warm-up was not as successful as the first because it didn't really get rid of a lot of the energy that they came in with and made them restless. The problem with this warm-up was that it was a short one but we definitely ran it for too long. From this we learnt that we had to have a specific time for the exercises so that they would not fizzle out and become boring. (Emma Thompson)

Alison approached her Year 8 group with the same intention of warming them up for more thoughtful work but her life was made difficult by an unwitting teacher:

The first of the five weeks was the worst! Nobody spoke, moved or even breathed throughout the whole 40 minutes. I tried to be really enthusiastic and friendly, only to be stared at blankly – how embarrassing! Worse still was the fact that the previous teacher in the class had scrawled across the blackboard 'SEX EDUCATION' which the girls sat and faced throughout the whole first session. (Alison James)

She persisted:

I tried to be really organised in how I ran the group. I wrote out what I was doing each week on a blank piece of paper, so I could glance at it if I forgot! The girls always got there too early for me to set the chairs out in a circle before them, so we did it together. I found this a good way of starting conversations and getting to know the girls and I think they began to trust me which was a nice feeling... One difficulty we did have that may have added to the group's initial anxiety and questions was that the person I was running the group with was away for three weeks with glandular fever. We felt it was right to tell the group on the third session that she wouldn't be joining us now, even if she did come back to school. This was a good move as they stopped expecting her and may have stopped their feelings about the group not being complete yet.

Although most groups relish the chance to have some fun, not every group is so easy. Ben was working on his own with a particularly suspicious group of Year 10 boys, drawn from different classes:

I had prepared quite well for the session and began with two warm-up exercises. Calling them exercises and not games seemed like quite a good ploy as using the term 'games' seemed to be giving the wrong impression, exciting them too much. We were doing an exercise called 'Heroes'. Whether it was anxiety or cockiness, four of the group claimed to have no hero, which made doing the exercise much more difficult... (Ben Rollinson)

In supervision Ben thought hard about how to begin his next session, now that he had met the boys and got some sense of what they might need:

The next week my preparation was better. Out of experience I made sure I could set up my room in the youth centre earlier so I could be mentally prepared and all mats and the television were removed so the room was pretty much empty and made me feel more secure that they would have less opportunity to mess around. I was also able to be sitting in the room when they entered which I felt gave them an impression that the sessions were structured and more disciplined than they imagined. I remembered their names and was able to greet them individually which I think made them slightly more at ease.

Little by little, Ben's group began to contribute.

Paul and Hannah ran a boys' group together:

> We felt the boys needed to bond together and overcome some of the extreme individualism which had been apparent in our first session, both physically in the boys' appearances and in their opinions on most things (the group often got sidetracked into the football versus rugby versus cars versus don't care debate!) We did a few more activities to do this, such as a game called 'Tangles', and a more demanding challenge on the trust front: building a human coffee table. (Paul Bonham)

Having warmed the group up, the student counsellors in a first session then invite group members to suggest and agree a set of rules they can all abide by. Some groups spend a long time on this, carefully paving the way for work which can go on to become more personal once a sense of safety is established. No name-calling, not laughing at people, trying to be honest and keeping things confidential are often agreed as rules. The counsellors always explain that, under some circumstances, they will not be able to keep everything confidential. Sometimes they get each group member to sign the large sheet of paper on which the group's rules have just been written down.

B. Main exercises

For each session, the student counsellors select from a repertoire of 'main' exercises designed to get an honest discussion started:

> For the main activity in this session we prepared a number of possible situations associated with friend and boyfriend-related issues, for example, 'Your friend asks to copy your homework. What do you do?' or 'Your friend tells you that she tried smoking at the weekend', or 'Your friend says she fancies your boyfriend.' The students then worked in pairs and had to act out to the rest of the group the wrong way to handle their situation and then the right way. The group as a whole then discussed whether they felt the pair had given a 'good' solution or not. This exercise worked well. Giving the wrong solution helped to lighten the atmosphere, which enabled students to focus on what the 'right' solution might be and talking

about other people's situations was easier than talking about their own. (Rebecca Wadcock)

The main bit of our session took the form of an exercise in which we encouraged everyone in the group to think of someone or a group of people who angered them. This met with some very emphatic replies, not least from Amber and myself! We then pulled an extra chair into the circle in which we were sitting and explained that this chair was in fact THAT person or THOSE people who upset them. What we were trying to do was to get everyone to take a turn at addressing the person(s) they felt angry with for whatever reason and therefore let themselves explain their feelings in a way which would not hurt the person involved (often it was people close to them) or further inhibit their relationship. I began this to give an example of what we meant. Amber and I found, however, that although everyone was willing to talk about their feelings, most of them felt slightly put off by the prospect of shouting at a chair and rather self-conscious. We continued discussing the subject but the chair was not used very frequently. It was an interesting exercise, and we did cover a lot, but we felt afterwards that perhaps we had used the wrong format for discussion. (Ruth Everett)

As Ruth suggests, it is important in this work that action does not happen for action's sake. Willis (1991) points out that 'action' in a group does not always have to be physical. Talking matters too:

We were unsure what to do with the varying personalities in the group. So to cater for everyone we did an 'open' exercise. There was a hot seat and the person sitting there had to try and move out of it. To do that they had to say something that they guessed had only happened to them, such as 'I reckon I'm the only one who hates my younger brother.' The object of everyone else was to keep the person in that seat, so to keep them there they had to say whether or not what the person had said applied to them. This worked in that people were made to feel supported and not alone, which obviously was unintentional by the rest of the group. Some things said were only for the sake of it, such as 'I'm the only one who ate pizza and jelly for breakfast', which was fine at the start but got tedious for those who were being more serious. (Naomi Cook)

This week we divided the group into two and got them to draw onto paper the changes that happen to boys and girls during puberty. This was meant to explain to them changes they and their friends would be going through. It was also good fun drawing the pictures. (Jonny Room and Sam Bentley)

The main exercise was chosen because of their inability to conflict with the overall opinion of the group. The exercise was basically set up so that each individual was paired randomly and had to argue either for or against a statement we gave them. We were pleasantly surprised that the group we had now been with for three weeks dramatically changed. Possibly because of the introduction of competitiveness (as each person wanted to win the argument even though it sometimes contrasted with their true feelings) and possibly because of the lack of intimacy in the argumentative situation, all of the individuals were contributing and with some thought. (Andrew Glossop)

Becky was back and I was glad the group was complete on the last week. We did an exercise where we all sat in a circle and there was a spare chair. The person next to the empty chair started off and asked someone else in the group to come and sit next to them for a reason. If the other person didn't think it was a good enough reason they didn't have to move. Most reasons given were things like, 'Come and sit next to me because you're a really nice person.' Whenever someone moved, then there was another empty seat and the exercise went on. I particularly enjoyed this as we could hear what others thought of each other and what they thought of Becky and me. At the end of the session I felt really good as we had had a good time, a good laugh but been serious as well. (Claire Speedie)

The student counsellors learn to be patient:

'We started the 'statements' exercise to try and get some debates going. However, they agreed with each other about every statement and it seemed that nobody dared to be different, even though one of our statements was 'being different is good' which everyone agreed with! (Ed Shrimpton)

One statement we used for a discussion exercise was 'Boys are only after one thing.' We felt afterwards that it was too mature for them as they immediately started talking about how their brothers wanted two things for Christmas so the statement wasn't true! (Beth Roberts)

As they become more confident, the student counsellors are able to adapt exercises to suit the emerging needs of a group. In an early session, Paul and

Neil had used a chair-swapping exercise that involved boys calling out numbers to each other:

> A particular success this week was an adapted numbers game. This time the players had to play using compliments. Each member sat in a seat with a word such as 'nice', 'gorgeous' or 'wonderful'. Many of these words are feminine – unusual to lads – but the boys made the exercise work and, unconsciously or accidentally, offered each other a range of compliments. (Paul Richards)

When their boys' group struggled to discuss a series of controversial but abstract statements prepared for them, Paul and Neil adapted the statements:

> We introduced statements only about football but related them to everyday situations. They all understood and enjoyed this because it was about a subject that most of them were interested in. This exercise took up most of week two. (Neil Evans)

The student counsellors describe adapting to all sorts of situations. Aaron was running his groups in the school library:

> This week we had fun with an exercise where the kids each had to be a different sexual word. After much fun with saying the words a teacher came in, complaining that we were being too noisy, so to quiet them down I decided instead they had to act out the words they were in silence. I won't go into detail as the results were unrepeatable and quite frankly rude, which of course was half the fun. (Aaron Duke)

Alison was using some health education booklets to help her girls' group get information about their bodies:

> I got asked the most embarrassing question: 'What's masturbation?' First I copped out by asking whether anyone in the group knew and could explain, then some horrid person said, 'Why don't you explain?' I gave the booklets out again and got someone to read out the bit about masturbation and tried to explain. (Alison James)

Paul and Jonny had to negotiate a similarly tricky moment during the less formal lunchtime group they were running:

> One boy's entrance ruined the group as he burst in declaring, 'The king has arrived!' tripping over the table, spilling coffee and eventually choking on a Wham bar. (Paul Bonham)

C. Endings

The student counsellors try to end each session in a deliberately structured way, even if that only amounts to going round the group with each person saying one thing they have enjoyed or will remember about the session. Talking at the end can be a way of integrating the active learning which has been taking place. When a group comes to the end of its final session, the atmosphere is often more charged and there is an even greater need for a considered ending (Salzberger-Wittenberg, Henry and Osbourne 1983):

> The last session didn't go as well as the others and the boys arrived with a silly attitude, knowing it was the last and perhaps therefore shouldn't be serious. They did, however, beg for an extension and one lad was worried that they were going to be replaced. It seemed that our group had become a very important part of their week and also a solid commitment as all the sessions were attended by all eight boys. Although at times they treated the sessions as just fun, such as the last session which focused on role-playing scenarios such as asking a girl out, dumping someone, making up with friends and so on, it seemed the group actually was very important. (Paul Bonham)

> At the end of each session we did an activity to end it. In the very last session we all had a piece of paper with our name on it and everyone had to write something on it about that person which they thought was good. I think this was a beneficial activity because they were able to take away something positive from the group. I also felt that I benefited from this activity as I also went away from the group feeling positive and more confident about doing more groups in the future. (Hayley Jones)

> In the last session, I allowed the group to choose their own warm-up exercise. However, along with the fact that people may have had mixed feelings about the fact the group was ending, this meant they seemed slightly more boisterous and less attentive to the rules. The main exercise in this session was a role-play. The group immediately warmed to this and obviously put a lot of effort into their scenes, so I allowed the exercise to overrun at the expense of another. Then I did an exercise which allowed people to express their feelings about themselves and others. This reassurance also provided the group with a sense of closure and resolution. (Phillippa Howarth)

Supervision

The student counsellors have an immense ability to do this kind of work (as their reports demonstrate), but the work is only as effective as it is structured and supervised. My role has been: first, to train the counsellors, making sure they feel confident and clear about a range of exercises and situations; second, to liaise with teachers about prospective groups of younger students, about venues and timings, and third, to supervise the counsellors each week.

For every session the student counsellors run they have a further supervision session with me, debriefing, thinking and planning. It saves time and is a richer experience if I meet with several counsellors at a time so that they can hear how other groups are going and contribute to each other's planning. Typically, we hear what happened in a particular group: which exercises went well and which backfired. We hear what the group members were saying, what they enjoyed and what seemed to make them anxious, what teasing there was, for example, and what words were being used to tease, which may betray the group's underlying anxieties. Sometimes we think hard about a particular student in a group. We invite one of the counsellors to become this student and we ask questions of that counsellor in role, searching for insights into the younger student's behaviour, thinking what might be going on below the surface. From all this we think about what the *underlying* issues might be for each group, what they are struggling to talk about, what seems to get stuck in their relationships with each other and we plan the following week's exercises deliberately but subtly to address these issues.

Sometimes we get stuck in supervision and have to improvise, inventing or remembering new exercises which we quickly practise with each other. Sometimes we end with only a broad outline of a group's next session and the counsellors must go away and plan the details: writing a series of provocative statements for discussion or choosing a particularly physical warm-up from their repertoire.

As the Crick Report (Advisory Group on Citizenship 1998) observes, it is important to give young people meaningful responsibility for others but, in my experience, to do so without adequate support is unfair. Without that support, the danger is that young people have a bad experience and in future shy away from ever taking responsibility again. Without reliable and consistent supervision it is better not to embark upon this kind of work at all.

Evaluation

Although they are often nervous at the prospect, the student counsellors invariably report at the end how much they valued and enjoyed the experience of running a group and seeing it develop over a period of time. A lot of learning takes place for the group members (Yalom 1970) and for the counsellors:

> For our group the main underlying issues were the anxiety of growing up and the feeling that being different means that you will be excluded and not accepted for who you are which we found to be the opposite and there was a lot of acceptance in the group at the end of the four weeks. (Emma Thompson)

The student counsellors evaluate their work constantly through their thinking in supervision sessions. Their reports indicate the depth of that thinking and learning. Kate and Ed had decided to split their girls' group in half for one exercise. Kate writes:

> The group that went with me was the seemingly more mature friendship group who wore make-up and talked about boys a lot. The ones who went with Ed were the more childish members of the group. When they came to sessions some of them had small toys with them and got excited when we used a teddy bear when playing 'Pass-the-object'. They appeared to cling to Ed. This could be because they saw him as a parental figure or that they themselves were playing with the idea of boyfriends. Ed being older and in a position of authority meant that he was safe, so that they could experiment with the idea. (Kate Mansell)

Another Kate and her partner Gillian had a difficult third session with their group:

> The girls left the group with a wealth of information about sexual health but the group process, the life of the group, lay struggling on the ground. The part I played in this was that I tried to fit too much information into four short sessions, not paying enough attention to the group processes which had naturally only just begun to develop at this stage of the group's life. The only choice we had was to review session three and pay close attention to group building and considerably less to content. Fortunately this proved to be successful and we revived the group. (Kate Bruce)

> Even though this group didn't go anything like the last one, I did learn something. We'd been told not to expect our new group to be like the old one and in a way I did and I ended up feeling disappointed. (Hayley Jones)

Younger students usually regret the fact that their group is ending because it has been fun and it has been worthwhile. They have felt valued. It has been possible to have conversations that would not otherwise have happened. They ask for more groups and then, when they are older, many of them volunteer to become student counsellors themselves.

Developing the work

The programme I have described in this chapter happens to use Year 13 students to run the groups but the young people do not have to be old or academically able to be capable of doing this work successfully. Nor do they have to be model students. I have organised exactly the same kind of work for Year 10 (14 or 15-year-old) students to run with Year 8 (12 or 13-year-old) students, for Year 8 students to run with Year 6 (10 or 11-year-old) students and so on. What matters is finding appropriately active but structured exercises which engage young people and providing the degree of training and supervision the young people delivering the work require. Knowing that the work will be so carefully supervised is what often convinces otherwise sceptical teachers to allow it to take place.

Conclusion

When adults behave as if they are the only ones capable of looking after and educating young people, they maintain a dependency which always turns sour as the young people fight – quite rightly – to take back responsibility for their lives. Most young people have massively untapped potential to do the kind of work described in this chapter, provided the task and the support is appropriate. For some, it is the first time they have ever been given worthwhile responsibility and they amaze teachers with their ability to think about and support others.

Afterword

I am grateful to the many student counsellors who, over the years at Bartholomew School, have been committed to supporting younger students and have been prepared to try things out. By no means all of them are quoted in this chapter.

References

Advisory Group on Citizenship (1998) *Education for Citizenship and Teaching of Democracy in Schools (The Crick Report)*. London: QCA.

Coren, A. (1997) *A Psychodynamic Approach to Education*. London: Sheldon Press.

Cowie, H. and Wallace, P. (2000) *Peer Support in Action*. London: Sage.

Finn, P. (1981) 'Institutionalising peer education in the health education classroom.' *The Journal of School Health 51*, 2.

Gordon, J. and Grant, G. (1997) *How We Feel: An Insight into the Emotional World of Teenagers*. London: Jessica Kingsley Publishers.

Luxmoore, N. (2000) *Listening to Young People in School, Youth Work and Counselling*. London: Jessica Kingsley Publishers.

Moreno, J.L. (1987) *The Essential Moreno*. New York: Springer.

Salzberger-Wittenberg, I., Henry, G. and Osborne, E. (1983) *The Emotional Experience of Learning and Teaching*. London: Routledge.

Willis, S.T. (1991) 'Who Goes There? Group-analytic Drama for Disturbed Adolescents.' In P. Holmes and M. Karp (eds) *Psychodrama: Inspiration and Technique*. London: Routledge.

Yalom, I.D. (1970) *The Theory and Practice of Group Psychotherapy*. New York: Basic Books.

CHAPTER 7

Let's Make A Bridge!
Working in Action with Autistic Children

Ioanna Gagani and Sandra Grieve

Introduction

We work with children who have an autistic spectrum disorder using psychodramatic principles and interventions. According to J.L. Moreno, its founder, 'psychodrama can be defined as the science which explores the truth by dramatic methods' (Moreno 1994). The most important thing to be said about what we do, is that we have a deep love for the children we work with that nurtures and affects the way we are with them, which in turn affects the way they are with us.

This chapter begins with a short explanation of autism, followed by a discussion about our views regarding working with children with autism and how psychodrama fits into our work. We then move on to present our ways of being with the children, which is the most significant aspect of the work that we do; everything else stems from that. We share with you psychodramatic interventions that facilitate and strengthen our connection with the children. We also discuss how those interventions facilitate the children's learning and development by showing how a psychodramatic intervention can help children experience a developmental stage that they have not yet reached. Ideas about how to educate and help the rest of the family to be auxiliaries to their relatives with autism are also presented.

What is autism?

According to the American Psychiatric Association (1994) autism is classified as a pervasive developmental disorder. Wing (1996) describes autism as a spectrum, with children manifesting severe impairments accompanied by intellectual disability at the lower end of the spectrum and less severe symptoms and learning difficulties at the higher end. Symptoms usually become apparent during the second or third year of life, when the children begin to clearly show the triad of impairments that characterise autism: qualitative impairments in social interaction, in communication and imagination and a markedly restricted repertoire of interests and activities (Wing 1996; American Psychiatric Association 1994). The way that those symptoms manifest themselves varies greatly from child to child and what strikes people the most is how different children with autism are from each other (Randall and Parker 1999). So children may range from having a total lack of interest in social interaction to a difficulty in understanding the subtle rules and cues that govern social interactions. In the same way, children may have a total lack of desire to communicate through to poor skills in reciprocal conversation. Children might have receptive language (understand what others say) but no expressive language (they themselves do not talk) or they may be echolalic (exact repetition of the words spoken by others). They might range from a total lack of pretend play to repetitive play with no imagination or creativity or to restricted and stereotyped activities. They might show interest in toys but in a non-functional way, for example focusing on the wheels of a toy truck and constantly spinning them. Other stereotyped activities may range from smelling everything and everyone, twisting and turning their hands or objects close to the side of their eye through to head banging and self-biting.

Autism is a developmental disorder, which means that as children get older, some of their behaviours may disappear and other behaviours may develop (Randall and Parker 1999). For example, I, Ioanna, work with a girl who, with the onset of puberty, became very interested in her sister's friends, wanting to play with them and asking for them when they were not around. Her ability to initiate and maintain an interaction with them did not improve but her desire to do so and to be involved in their activities greatly increased with puberty. Thus, knowledge and an understanding of childhood development are necessary in working with children with autism. We have a duty, as workers, not only to be with them in a way that they can enjoy and thus develop their social skills, but also to help them experience to the best of their abilities the important developmental stages that they have not yet reached because of their autism.

How we see a child affects how we relate to a child

In life, people often focus on the negatives, on what is missing in their life rather than what is present. This mistake is often made when thinking about one's child too. When parents or workers are faced with autism, they can easily fall into the trap of only seeing what the child is not doing. When meeting an autistic child, do you see their autism or do you see the whole child? If you see their autism, you would say that little Tom, for example, has no eye contact; he does not recognise his own name; he is obsessed with spinning tops and that is all he does if left alone. If you see the whole child, however, you would see a beautiful five year-old boy who has a captivating smile and really loves spinning tops: let's see, will he turn and look at you if you start spinning around yourself? These are interesting questions.

Having knowledge of autism and normal childhood development, combined with the psychodramatic principle of spontaneity, with its focus on the moment, is extremely valuable to our work. Moreno (1994, p.67) maintained that 'a spontaneity theory of child development evaluates the growth of the infant in positive terms, and in terms of progression, rather than in negative terms and in terms of retardation and regression.' When we work with the children we forget their autism and everything that they are not doing. We focus on what they are doing and on ways that we can assist them to develop in a progressive way. Every step forward, small as it may be, is a bridge between their autistic world and the social world.

Psychodrama and autism: the beauty of action

Psychodrama, being an action method, can be a bridge between the autistic world and the social world because it does not rely on language alone in order to communicate and connect with people. Numerous writers and researchers have emphasised the importance of play in childhood development (Piaget 1962; Vygotsky 1962; Winnicott 1971; Dolto 1994) showing that children learn, interact and deal with the world through play and play can only be done through action. It is crucial to speak the children's language when working with them. Psychodrama involves *therapeutic* action[16] (Moreno 1994), a way of being and acting with the child that will assist him or her to function in more progressive ways. With psychodrama everything is possible. The child can learn at his or her pace, without even realising that he or she is learning and more importantly the whole experience will be enjoyable. As psychodramatists we focus on the present and on any interest the child has at any given moment. We can act from a spontaneous and creative state to find a way to meet the child in his or her world, connect with them and start building a relationship with them. Our connections with the children and the relationships we build with them are the most important stepping stones of their treatment. It is only when there is mutual interest and enjoyment between the worker and the child that the child enjoys and is motivated to learn.

Connections and learning through psychodrama: three case studies

Moreno (1994) said that every human being at any given moment exists in relationship with another person or object. It is through relationships that children learn; relationships with their parents, friends, teachers and many others. A child in isolation can develop their somatic[17] roles, they can learn to be a walker, a breather, an eater. Their genetic make-up will make sure that they blink, swallow or make vocalisations. Here lies the difficulty for children with autism because they exist in isolation even when surrounded by people and they lack the motivation to form relationships. They withdraw from social contact and therefore miss out on everything that is learned through relationships with other human beings.

Case study 1: Alice and the development of play (Ioanna Gagani)

Alice is three and a half years old. Her receptive language is very good but she is still non-verbal. I worked with her for a year and a half for an average of six hours a week. The example I present here occurred within the first months of her therapy. Although we have made a few significant connections through play, they have been short lasting and have not altered her reaction every time she sees me; the moment I walk through the door she starts crying.

In terms of normal play development, Alice is in the stage of pretend or symbolic play. Simply explained, pretend, or otherwise called symbolic play, is a simulative or non-literal behaviour (Fein 1981), acting 'as if' something is the case when it really isn't (Leslie 1987). Her limited interests, however, lie still in manipulation play, a common type of play in autistic children whereby they manipulate objects in a stereotyped way (Tiegerman and Primavera 1981). On rare occasions Alice also engages in functional play, which involves the appropriate use of an object or the conventional association between two or more objects (Ungerer and Sigman 1981). Generally, however, if Alice engages in any kind of play, it is with particular cause and effect toys (for example, a toy where you push buttons and different things pop up) that have captured her interest and with which she follows a repetitive and stereotyped pattern. She also solely engages in solitary play[18] withdrawing from or pushing anyone that attempts to play with her.

I put Alice's favourite video on television, Cinderella, and doubled her as she was watching. Doubling is a psychodramatic technique, which allows the person who is doubling to enter into the inner world of the person being doubled (Sternberg and Garcia 2000). It is a very good technique to use with autistic children because it is not confrontational. The children do not have to do anything; it is the person who is doubling that does all the work. In addition, if one doubles them in the traditional way, taking up their body posture and doing exactly what the child is doing, the children can experience what it is like to have a companion, one that does not ask for anything or push them but stays with them without having any expectations.

As I doubled Alice during the video, I was able to see that she was connecting with the animals on the screen, becoming very excited when they appeared and withdrawing when there were people on the screen. When the video was finished, Alice started looking through her Cinderella book, fully immersed in her own world and ignoring my presence. It was time for some role taking on my part. Since I had just doubled her, I knew what I was going to do. I got on the floor next to her and started taking up the roles of different animals in the book. I became a dog, sniffing, licking and biting her softly, a horse, pushing her around with my head, a mouse, tickling her all over. Alice was having so much fun, that we soon ended up rolling around on the floor with me becoming every animal I could think of. The end of the game found us both lying breathless side by side on the floor with cheeks bright red. It is at that moment that Alice looked at me and for the first time I got the sense that she really saw me.

This was a huge breakthrough for Alice, I had never seen her have so much fun before whilst being so present. The role-play was also very significant for Alice's development. First, the connection that was created between us was so strong that it did not disappear. Alice was always very happy to see me after that; she came to me for comfort and easily let me into her world. Second, in terms of play development, Alice was able to engage in age appropriate pretend play. She might not have taken up a pretend role herself, but she was able to recognise that I was being an animal and relate to me at that level. This of course does not mean that from that day on Alice engaged in pretend play, but she did show the capacity for it and became very willing to play with me after that. That is where the most significant change occurred. Whereas until then Alice was only engaging in solitary play, after my intervention she slowly became more and more willing to participate in associative play, first with me and then with the rest of the family. From this time on, Alice wanted me to be with her and interact with her during activities that in the past she only wanted to do alone. This was a huge progression in her development.

Case study 2: taking turns with Alex (Ioanna Gagani)

Alex is a beautiful seven-year-old boy, who is very interested in little things. He can sit and observe the ants on the ground for a long time, or explore the dirt in the garden. He is otherwise quite withdrawn, spends most of his time in his own world, has limited expressive language and when frustrated makes loud and very metallic vocalisations. I usually meet Alex outside where he is at home playing with dirt and ants.

Our time together usually starts with me doubling him (by being next to him and doing exactly what he is doing). This helps Alex get used to having me there. Alex then starts making his metallic vocalisations. I then adopt another psychodramatic technique, mirroring. Sue Daniel (2001) explains this technique as follows: 'Mirroring is when we present a picture in words or action to a person, which provides a mirror for their verbal and non-verbal communication.' With Alex, mirroring involved us sitting opposite each other with me imitating exactly what he was doing, including his, sometimes loud, metallic vocalisations. This is how our connection began. Alex often came and sat on my lap baby-like making strange sounds, which I mirrored. He found my sounds very interesting and pleasurable and he often showed great affection towards me in those moments. He put his hands on my face bringing it very close to his and looking straight into my eyes or he touched my cheek very gently with his mouth.

Mirroring Alex continued to be effective. One day we moved into taking turns with the sticks we were holding. Alex was sitting on the ground holding a stick that he tapped on the ground at different places. I noticed that the sound the stick made when it tapped the ground differed from place to place and concluded that this was what Alex was interested in. I mirrored him by picking up another stick and tapping it on the ground. After a while I tapped my stick on Alex's stick to show him that this made a different sound and then rested my stick on the ground. Alex wanted more of that sound so he put his stick under mine and lifted my stick up to show me that he wanted more. The first few times I complied and tapped my stick on his. Then I mirrored his action by placing my stick under his and lifting his stick up. Alex was very amused at this, he clearly understood that now I wanted *him* to tap *my* stick, that it was his turn. We took turns for a significant amount of time, tapping each other's stick. Instead of saying 'my turn' and 'your turn', we used Alex's way of communicating.

This is another example of how a psychodramatic technique can help a child experience an important aspect of their development in a fun and non-provocative way. Turn taking is a skill required not only for social play (Wolfberg 1999) but also for conversation (Frith 1989). Turn taking begins in infancy with normally developing children (Wolfberg 1999). Alex might have had a few turn taking experiences as an infant, which, as he got older, would have gradually decreased until they disappeared. He could have learned to take turns under different circumstances too, by doing a puzzle for example. It is very likely, though, that he would not have enjoyed the experience because it would have been artificial. It wouldn't have emerged from something that he was personally involved and interested in. Therefore, it would have been harder for him to initiate it spontaneously. Here lies the beauty of action, as Alex was able to participate and thoroughly enjoy taking turns with me.

In summary, working psychodramatically allows me to work *with* the children rather than against them, following their lead, finding out where their interests lie and making an intervention that will create a connection and a relationship between us whilst facilitating their development. These things are vital for the children's functioning in the social world.

Case study 3: co-operating with Cole (Sandra Grieve)

Cole is lively five-year-old boy who was diagnosed autistic when he was three years eight months. In order to help him make sense of the world, I needed to find a connection into his. Words would not be enough. He had a very limited vocabulary of mostly nouns and, being able to copy words is not talking (Janert 2000).

I still remember that first session vividly. He came happily into the playroom with me. When he ran in circles, I ran in circles. When he lined up his trains, I lined up my trains. When he lay face down on the floor, I lay face down on the floor. He paid me no attention at all. Then, all of a sudden, he started to shout and scream and began throwing his railway track at the wall, so I began throwing bits of track at the wall, while making a lot of noise. He stopped and looked at me. I stopped and looked at him. He smiled. I smiled. He then began making faces, not at me, just because that was what he liked to do. So I started making faces at him. We connected. A brief and fragile connection, but a connection, nonetheless. And so it began, my tentative journey to his world and his first few steps toward the bridge into the world.

It was important to his family that he developed sufficient social and cognitive skills to be able to attend and benefit from a mainstream primary school. One of his biggest challenges and strengths is that he has a lot of determination and tenacity. Co-operating with others is not often tempting for him. He had come a long way in the first year of us working together. His receptive and expressive language had improved and his play was almost age appropriate. However, if he didn't feel like doing something, he just didn't. He avoided, withdrew or tantrummed. He did not co-operate.

In common with other autistic children, Cole found it difficult to 'mind read' (Baron-Cohen 1995). That is he found it hard to imagine what another person might be thinking or feeling. He also found it hard to understand or communicate what he was thinking or feeling. We developed a 'Can I be?' game, using psychodramatic doubling. He loved Thomas the Tank Engine. As he played with Thomas and his friends, I would initially double Cole in order to build on our connection. As our play progressed I would ask, 'Can I be Thomas, for a minute?' I would become a very co-operative Thomas, making train noises and leading the rescue team to avert another disaster, often caused by Gordon (another train). I would then role reverse with Gordon, making their relationship explicit. Cole thought this was hilarious. As we progressed, I would ask him if he could be Thomas for a minute and the co-operation between Thomas and Gordon developed. This became a ritual for us, I would add new dimensions to the relationship, explain how Gordon was feeling and why he needed help from Thomas, and in time so did Cole. In this way he was gaining experience of turn taking and empathy.

Autistic children love rituals. It is their security, their way of making sense of the world or tuning it out or controlling it whenever that seems necessary for them (Tustin 1990). They have that love of rituals in common with all young children. Where they differ from other children is often in the nature of these rituals. They tend to be more rigid and less easily evolved or learned from. Psychodrama also loves rituals and it adds some spontaneity to them. As a method it can assist children to develop a new response to an old situation and an adequate response to a new situation (Moreno 1994). For autistic children adequate responses to new situations can be a challenge, but it was something that Cole had to master if he were to manage school. Significant progress has been made in this area and I feel optimistic about his future.

Cole is a bright and happy little boy and as he approaches his sixth birthday, many of his cognitive skills are on a par with or better than other children of his age. While he is less spontaneous and more anxious than his peers, he is much more willing to risk co-operating with others than he was and his language and vocabulary continue to improve. He is very loving and wants a cuddle if he hurts himself or feels upset. When I first started working with him he could hurt himself quite badly and not react. He has far fewer tantrums nowadays, although they have not gone completely; he is after all, still a five-year-old boy.

Psychodrama with parents of autistic children

Cole's development has been remarkable and is a testament to his family, particularly, his mother. She has been tireless in her willingness to be with him, accept him, as he is and not for what he might become. My experience of working with Cole and other small children with autism confirms that their family is their only external resource of any significance. This mother learned how to just be with and enjoy her son. She has been able to grieve for the son she didn't have, in a way that enables her to marvel at the one she does have. Often in support meetings we used action methods as a means of deepening our understanding of Cole and his needs. By enacting a particular issue or incident in a session, she was able to experiment with the roles within herself which were helpful and unhelpful. The following story about bedtime, often cited as a challenge for parents of children with autism (Siegal 1996; Greenspan 1998; Wing 1996), may illustrate this.

Cole did not go to bed without a struggle, nor did he stay there all night. We talked about this, and agreed that what happened at bedtime might be one of Cole's 'distress rituals'. Steven Wertz (2000) of Growing Minds talks about distress rituals in children with autism as being their pattern of gaining a specific response, rather than authentic distress. Cole's mother told me how hard it was for her to hear him screaming (she got in touch with that part of herself that felt guilty and inadequate) and that often she surrendered and got into bed beside him. We agreed that we could address this issue the following evening. That evening she went out leaving me to take on her role and put Cole to bed. He was watching cartoons in his pyjamas. As he watched, I explained that when the cartoon was finished it would be time to brush his teeth and go to bed. He came and brushed his teeth, then started shouting 'no bed, no bed.' As I tucked him in, I explained that he could sleep now and get up in the morning. I asked if he wanted a story. He was really clear, looked straight at me and said 'no story'. When I left the room, he got up and came to the door, calling for Mummy. I went through and gently led him back to bed. He began to scream. I explained once again that it was bedtime, he was furious and puzzled by this unexpected response to his screams. I explained that I would be in the next room and that it was now time to sleep. When Mum came home he was asleep and slept all night.

The next night it was Mum's turn. She felt very anxious, and as she went through the same bedtime ritual as I had the night before, I doubled her and encouraged her. I was doubling the part of her that knew that this is what she needed to happen. He screamed when she left him and her distress was visible. Again I doubled and supported her to tell him what was going to happen. He slept all night. On the third night, she took him to bed without doubling and he looked up at her and said 'night night Mum'. He slept till morning and we were ecstatic. Brushing his teeth, going to bed and sleeping till morning is now his bedtime ritual, replacing the earlier distress ritual. So, by first me and then his mother playing out a different bedtime scenario, he developed a new response to this old situation. Of course, this could have been done psychodramatically, outside the real life scenario. However, with Cole and his mother, I have found that employing some action methods, notably doubling, mirroring and role reversal in real situations, to be more effective than classical psychodrama.

As all psychodramatists know, facilitating a shift in one person in a relationship, shifts the whole relationship. This is particularly important to remember in relation to children with autism. 'A disability related to communication and social interaction is not one-sided; it exists in the relationships between people' (Beyer and Gammeltoft 1998, p.16).

In terms of understanding and responding to the nuances of the social world, Cole still has a way to go, but he has come a long way from that lost little boy who was locked in his own world with only familiar patterns and rituals for company. The big difference is that now he is interested in other people and reaches out to them, free to cross the bridge and back, whenever he wants. He attends a local primary school and plays with other children, holds his own in squabbles with his older brother and spontaneously hugs his Mum, for whom he has a marked preference, when he is happy. He has moved from the little boy who was unable to connect to the little boy who bounced home after the school sports day to greet his father with a smile and a story: 'Look Dad, shorts on, Cole running.' He is beginning to want to share his experience with others.

Psychodrama with older autistic children (Sandra Grieve)

What I have learned from all of the children I have worked with is that they will reach out when they find a point of connection. I work with a 14-year-old boy called Ricky. He experienced a lot of abuse in his first few years of life and is also autistic. He is in a state of high anxiety most of the time and experiences the world as a very frightening place. He continually asks questions, usually, the same questions over and over again. Often the staff at his school and the other children experience him as irritating. He is completely baffled by this. Like Cole, he finds mind reading a challenge. The school that he attends operates a behaviour system based on points. Certain appropriate behaviour is rewarded by points each day. Ricky is obsessed with points. He is constantly calculating them or telling me about them or asking me about them. However, his connection between behaviour and points is both tentative and cast in stone. I have been working with him weekly for two years, both individually and in a group. In our individual sessions we usually act out a scenario from a classroom experience, often based on a situation where he didn't get his points! We use toys as auxiliaries and in this way we will explore what happened, with Ricky role reversing with his class teacher or one of his classmates. We always have some toys in the role of points and sometimes he or I will role reverse with some of them. Psychodramatic action has unlocked doors for him and made it possible for him to gain some insight into social and interpersonal situations, which were previously both terrifying and unpredictable.

Ricky's patterns are more fixed than Cole's. He did not have the advantages of a committed, secure, family unit, nor did he have any early intervention. Initially, it was believed that his anxiety and behaviour were a response to the early abuse; he was not diagnosed autistic until he was 11. So, for Ricky, action came late. The advantages of using psychodrama with him are many. For him, there is a system to it. He knows that when he asks a question, it is time to reverse roles. We are able to find ways of concretising abstract concepts – abstract is hard for him. He is able to experience the physical as well as the rational and emotional and, above all, we have a lot of fun.

Conclusion

We hope that what we have shared with you demonstrates that children with autism are primarily children. A growing body of research is strengthening the belief that the roots of autism are genetic and neurobiological, rather than psychological. Research at the University of Sunderland by Dr Paul Shattock, together with research at San Diego University and the work of an international network of physicians known as DAN (Defeat Autism Now) continue to support this belief. That does not diminish the impact of biology on psychological development; what is important to remember is that autism is a different way of being in and sensing the world. It is simply a part of a whole child who, in common with other children, is in the process of becoming. Despite the claims of some programmes, there is currently no 'cure' for autism, which is after all, a spectrum of disorders rather than one static condition. What *is* possible, is to facilitate a child's learning in the areas of social and communication skills, and to do some of the reparative work in the areas of developing imagination and pretend play that the condition has made so challenging for the child. In that way, we can support them to become more of themselves than they might otherwise manage. By carefully observing these children and taking our cues from them, in a way that honours their absolute right to be who they are, we can build on their actions and on the trust between us. When we find that point of contact with a child we must act. We must be brave, be bold and build that bridge together.

References

American Psychiatric Association (1994) *Diagnostic and Statistical Manual of Mental Disorders.* Washington DC: American Psychiatric Association.

Beyer, J. and Gammeltoft, L. (2000) *Autism and Play.* London: Jessica Kingsley Publishers.

Baron-Cohen, S. (1995) *Mindblindness.* Cambridge: MIT Press.

Daniel, S. Personal communication on 29 August 2001.

Dolto, F. (1994) 'Les étapes majeures de l' enfance.' *Articles et Conférences–1.* Paris: Gallimard.

Fein, G.G. (1981) 'Pretend play in childhood: an integrative review.' *Child Development 52,* 1095–1118.

Frith, U. (1989) *Autism: Explaining the Enigma.* Oxford UK and Cambridge USA: Blackwell.

Greenspan, S. I. and Weider, S. (1998) *The Child with Special Needs.* Reading MA: Addison Wesley Longman.

Janert, S. (2000) *Reaching the Young Autistic Child.* New York and London: Free Association Books.

Leslie, A.M. (1987) 'Pretense and representation: the origins of theory of mind.' *Psychological Review 94,* 412–426.

Moreno, J.L. (1994) *Psychodrama and Group Psychotherapy. First volume.* McLean, VA: American Society for Group Psychotherapy and Psychodrama (first published in 1946 by Beacon House Inc).

Parten, M. (1932) 'Social play among preschool children.' *Abnormal and Social Psychology 27,* 243–269.

Piaget, J. (1962) *Play, Dreams and Imitation in Childhood.* New York: W.W. Norton.

Randall, P. and Parker, J. (1999) *Supporting the Families of Children with Autism.* Chichester, England: John Wiley.

Siegel, B. (1996) *The World of the Autistic Child.* Oxford: Oxford University Press.

Sternberg, P. and Garcia, A. (2000) *Sociodrama. Who's in your Shoes?* Connecticut: Praeger.

Tiegerman, E. and Primavera, L. (1981) 'Object manipulation: an interactional strategy with autistic children.' *Journal of Autism and Developmental Disorders 11,* 4, 427–438.

Tustin, F. (1990) *The Protective Shell in Children and Adults.* London: Karnac Books.

Ungerer, J.A., and Sigman, M. (1981) 'Symbolic play and language comprehension in autistic children.' *Journal of the American Academy of Child Psychiatry 20,* 318–337.

Vygotsky, L.S. (1962) *Thought and Language.* Cambridge MA: MIT Press.

Williams, D. (1996) *Autism, An Inside-Out Approach.* London: Jessica Kingsley Publishers.

Wertz, S. (2000) *Distress Rituals in Children with Autism.* Unpublished.

Wing, L. (1996) *The Autistic Spectrum, a Guide for Parents and Professionals.* London: Constable.

Winnicott, D.W. (1971) *Playing and Reality.* London: Tavistock.

Wolfberg, P.J. (1999) *Play and Imagination in Children with Autism.* New York and London: Teachers College Press.

CHAPTER 8

Providing Dance Movement Therapy within a Mainstream School

Sue Curtis

Introduction

'I don't get it,' said Leah.

'What is it you don't get?' I asked. 'What we'll be doing, or why we're meeting?' She looked blankly at me again and replied, 'I just don't get it'.

Leah is nine years old and was one of three new members joining a dance movement therapy (DMT) group with two other children – two girls and three boys. We had all met for an initial briefing about the coming year's work together. She was referred to the group by her teacher, who was concerned about her poor self-esteem, lack of peer contact, low achievement and lack of self-confidence. In the classroom she mainly sat on her own, never initiated ideas and seemed aloof and withdrawn. Her peers perceived her as weird and stupid and generally she had few friends, spending most of her time alone.

'I just don't get it.' Her words stayed with me and her blank expression had a haunting quality. On reflection, I realised she literally doesn't get 'it' or anything. That is, she never gets picked for a group and that the idea of belonging to a group was a complete mystery to her. She had never belonged to any group before.

Leah is not alone in the mainstream setting, where large class sizes and the demands of the curriculum upon the teacher make it increasingly difficult to meet the child's emotional needs. Children and young people who are troubled and suffering emotional distress not only trouble others with whom they come into contact, but find it difficult to be available for learning, and often give the impression of being stuck, somehow frozen, in their difficulties (Greenhalgh 1994).

This chapter will describe how DMT can address children's emotional needs in an educational setting and help children like Leah to manage better within the classroom. It will illustrate this therapist's approach to exploring movement and imaginative play and the attention to non-verbal expressions of confusion, distress and anxiety displayed as difficult, challenging or withdrawn behaviour in the classroom. It will also illustrate this therapist's particular attention to the value of the multi-disciplinary team with examples of the effectiveness of the liaison between therapist and teacher.

Dance movement therapy works on a child's difficulties through body movement behaviour and non-verbal communication, providing a channel for the child to both express and work through emotional and cognitive difficulties. The sessions aim to promote and increase emotional, mental and physical integration. For example, a child who experiences difficulties in completing school tasks may not have a cognitive learning deficit, but emotional stress may be interfering with their ability to organise, think and attend. Success in movement tasks that use organisation, thinking and attention can help relieve the stress and improve school work (Leventhal 1980; North 1972).

In the mainstream setting, situations in which children are withdrawn from class can include learning support for cognitive skills, such as reading or writing, or they may be removed because their behaviour is unmanageable. Either way, children may be worried that they will be seen as a failure or stupid. The DMT sessions offer a modality where mixed groups can work together without the fear and pressure to 'get it right'. Difficult feelings can be safely expressed, and the child may be less compelled to act them out in the classroom. As the work progresses, the children in turn let other children know about their experiences. The sessions begin to be known as a place where you can have fun, move, and look after each other.

Referrals

Referrals for DMT groups or individual sessions are always in liaison with class teachers and other professionals. Some children are easy to identify – for example, those whose behaviour continually disrupts the routines of the class, through aggression or tantrums. Others are not so easy to identify. Often teachers will ask me to observe a child, saying there is something about the child that worries them, that they cannot quite put their finger on. Often it is not the child's behaviour that is of concern, but a pervading sense of sadness or anxiety. If left unattended, this may in turn lead to problems with coping with curriculum activities, and the child may become frustrated or despondent. In these instances they may resort to defensive tactics, and avoid situations that compound and highlight their difficulties.

In general a group will consist of between three to six children, depending on the reason for referral and individual needs. Some children cannot tolerate even a small group, and are therefore seen on an individual basis. As Payne (1992) explains, 'It seems the group experience brings out problems of adjustment not possible in individual sessions. The latter focus more sharply on the individual, providing for trust and security and eliminating the stimulus for activity received in the group situation' (p.65).

Setting

The sessions take place in a private space, free from interruptions. It is important to create the 'safe container' required for therapeutic work (Dale 1992). In the school presented in this paper, the work takes place in the library. Tables and chairs are pushed to the side, with one table available in a corner of the room, with paper and pencils on it. This is known as the 'time-out' table. This is not used as a behaviour control, but is a place that the children freely chose to go, in order to signal that they want some quiet time, undisturbed by others.

A large bag of props is placed in another corner of the room for the children to use if they wish. This consists of large coloured cloths, various soft balls, a long elastic stretch band, puppets, hoops, ribbons, a small parachute and a large body/physio ball. These props can be used practically of themselves or to projectively embody and identify children's feelings or feeling processes. Close to the 'time-out' table, a cassette player, tapes and blank tape for recording are placed.

Structure

Whilst the sessions are non-directive, they follow a simple structure modelled after the work of DMT pioneer Marian Chace (Chaiklin 1975). First we check in asking how individuals are today, how their week has been, and remember events and themes from the previous session.

Then we do a short warm-up to bring the group together physically, encourage vocalisation and imagination, and to gauge the group feeling in preparation for the middle section. This may develop into ritual 'beginning'. For example, one group chose a strong movement each and put them together in sequence, culminating in holding hands, jumping up and shouting out their group name. They called it their 'power' warm-up. If at any time during the rest of the session a member felt upset or low, someone would run over, put their hands on them and 'top up' their power.

The middle section is completely non-directive, allowing children some control over the process, 'with the encouragement and empathic support of the therapist' (Levy 1988, p.255). The group members decide how they want to spend the time. This may include, for example, the use of role-play, stories, drama or activity based games (Melville-Thomas 1991; Stanton-Jones 1992). This can also be a time when the connection between bodily feeling, sensations and affect can be transformed into images and thoughts (Dosamantes-Alperson 1983).

Finally, at the end of the session time is set by for closure to remember and reflect upon what has taken place. This may take the form of writing down thoughts, feelings and images in a group book. This book is confidential and kept safely by the therapist.

Case Studies

Finding an identity – Leah

In her initial sessions Leah stayed on the periphery of the group, often sighing and watching and passively sitting in a corner. Sometimes she would pick up a prop from the prop bag, as if waiting to see if anyone would notice, but rarely initiated any ideas. When she did begin to create things with the props, one of the others generally came and grabbed them. She never defended her creation or asked for her things back. The one time she did join in, she wrapped a cloth around her and became a monster. Whenever it was time for members to write what they liked, she would either say 'everything' (copying one of the others) or more often 'I don't know'. On many occasions Leah would watch the other female member interacting in the group. She would make comments like: 'She's a dancer', 'She's a gymnast', 'She's so good' and 'I can't do that'. She would look on with awe, laughing nervously. But for most of the sessions she remained quiet, in a corner.

During the third month of therapy, there began to be a shift in her ability to make a place for herself in the group. One session, the first back after Christmas, she sat in the corner and drew a picture. It was a picture of a house, with two bedrooms, two playrooms and an attic. Each room had brightly coloured curtains. Outside the house a smiling sun shone down, and a tree was growing. She said that one of the rooms was hers, with a playroom for friends to visit. At the top of the house she drew a plaque, which said '1991'. I asked her if she remembered something from that year – 'That was the year I had a birthday party.' She continued the whole session, colouring in carefully, but still watching the rest of the group's activities of play, dancing and football. Later on, one of the boys joined her (who himself is a very good artist), and he commented on how nice the house was. She carefully put a border around it and signed her name. For the first time it felt as if she had placed an important part of herself in the group and in the group book. However, at the end of the session, when asked what she had liked, again she replied, 'I don't know.'

The following week an argument broke out in the group. Everybody wanted to do different things, and moaned that there wasn't enough space. Markers were placed on the floor delineating one space from another, but then arguments ensued as to how to get to the props, without crossing someone else's space. Leah sat quietly in the corner watching. 'Why don't you move the bag?' she whispered. The argument continued. I asked if people had heard her and encouraged her to say it again. 'Why don't you move the bag?' she repeated in a loud voice. The others stood still, then one of the boys moved it, over to the 'time-out' table where she was sitting.

Two boys began a friendly football match, whilst the others continued to play 'holidays'. Slowly Leah got up from the table, wrapped a white cloth around her and placed a ring on her head. She moved steadily around the edge of the room – 'And who is this?' I asked. 'I'm an angel, looking down from heaven on everyone.' In the following sessions, Leah began to take on a more active role. Together with the other girl in the group, she joined in activities, such as parachute games, and helped the group to find solutions to problems.

In one session, the other girl, Helena, pretended to be a Queen who fainted and collapsed on the floor. The others watched, and called out suggestions to get her to stand up. 'She's got library sickness,' Leah said. 'I have to get her favourite book and wave it around her, with the flags.' Helena slowly came round and Leah helped her to a chair. 'She won't drop till much later now…she's safe here.' At the end Leah wrote in the book, 'I liked helping the Queen get over library sickness.'

Two weeks later the whole group decided to make houses. At first, Leah looked lost, as the other female wanted a house on her own. She sat at the side. One boy shouted out: 'You can make one with me!' Together they made a parachute house. Inside she said there were toys, with a window to look through. Outside she made a golden garden, with a porch for people to come and sit. In the area between the houses Leah suggested there could be a park, where everyone could meet and play whenever they wanted. At the end of the session she said, 'I liked being in the house.' This was the first time that Leah had worked with the whole group as a cohesive unit. The following week the group finally settled on its name: 'The Good Group'. During the next month Leah consistently named things she had enjoyed in the session.

Six months after the onset of therapy, Leah had managed to find a more solid presence in the group. She no longer sat at the side for long periods, stood up for herself when needed and protected her things. In one session she had a tug-of-war with the strongest of the boys and said, 'Never underestimate a girl!' In the class her teacher reported that she had now begun to join in with group 'circle time', and to actually tell others how she felt. On another occasion, the class were involved in a morning 'hello game' called 'Good morning, your majesty', which Leah had never before joined in. This time however, when asked 'Good morning', she sat pensively, sighing and putting her finger to her face, while the rest of the class waited for nearly two minutes. Finally, she replied, 'Good morning, your majesty' in a high and funny squeaky voice. For the first time ever the class had waited patiently for her contribution and Leah had had the courage to try something new openly in front of everyone. The teacher said it was a very moving moment.

Children need to develop a sense of emotional safety and trust in others for development and learning to proceed. If we do not sufficiently establish personal constructs which provide nourishing forms of meaning and identity, then we will find little meaning in learning, and we will resist it (Greenhalgh 1994).

COMMENTARY: TRUST

Establishing a safe and secure environment, where feelings, thoughts and ideas can be shared, without fear of reprimand, or the worry of 'getting it wrong', is vital for children to develop confidence and self-esteem. As Greenhalgh (1994, p.45) states: 'The more secure we feel, the more open we are to experience, so long as we believe it will enlarge rather than undermine our sense of self.' Learning to trust the therapist and other members of the group involves risking being vulnerable and being seen. For many children the opportunity to move and play together and express themselves non-verbally as well as verbally is a liberating experience. As one child put it, whilst trying out different postures to show his feelings, 'In here you don't feel embarrassed.' Greenhalgh (1994, p.28) asserts that, 'To experience the feeling of safety and acceptance, we have to allow ourselves to feel in some ways dependent upon significant other people in our lives. We cannot risk trust if we cannot risk some form of dependence on another person.'

Sometimes groups have supported each other through difficult and traumatic experiences. On one occasion, one girl came into the group and said that her dad had died. She sat nonchalantly, rocking on her chair, as if nothing different had happened. Later in the session she expressed her anger in movement. She threw all the props over the floor, stamped around, but said nothing. One boy said, 'She's upset and angry, because her Dad has died.' She went over to the table and drew a picture of herself crying. He joined her and drew a card, with tears on it, and addressed it to her. At the end of the session he said she was sad, and that made him sad too.

In one of their last sessions, the group built a group tent. Inside was a place for everyone, including me. In this scenario I was given the role of 'manager', whose job it was to look after and run the tent. Later in the session, the play changed and my role was to be the 'guide'. In both instances the group was able to show me that they needed me to be there to help look after them.

Many children need a lot of time to distinguish the role of the therapist. During the first month of one boy's therapy he constantly asked me if I was going to tell his teacher or the head about what he did and said. When I consistently said I wouldn't, he said, 'You're not normal, you're mad. Why aren't you like a teacher?' It took many weeks before he could trust me enough to show me and tell me about the painful events and experiences that constantly worried him and interfered with his behaviour.

When innate difficult feelings which are colouring children's view of their world are responded to with sympathy and understanding, their severity is mitigated, a more benign internal world begins to develop, and this in turn leads the children to view the (external) world as a more benign place, one peopled by loving and caring figures in whom they can afford to place their trust and from whom they can learn and take things in (Barrows 1996). Another child, at the end of two years' work said, 'What's your job? I know, you're the person people come to see when they've got a problem and things go wrong.'

The multi-disciplinary approach – William

William is a seven-year-old boy, with severe asthma. He was referred for individual DMT, because his teacher was concerned about his behaviour in class and that he was under-achieving. In class, when asked questions, he would stare into space and say nothing. It was difficult to assess whether he was deliberately obstinate or didn't know the answer. Other times he would be found sitting under the table. On the way to the sessions William would stretch out his arms, hold on to the wall or stair railings, and jump up the stairs, feet together, with his body held tensely. In our initial sessions together, William presented as a very anxious and self-contained child. He found it difficult to initiate ideas of his own, appearing to be constantly worried about what to do next. If I directly asked him what he wanted to do he would pause for a long time and then say 'don't know'. When I made a suggestion he seemed relieved to have an idea to work with and would then join in happily. When he did manage to initiate an activity he seemed to get 'stuck' or give up quickly and look to me to provide another suggestion. It was as if the smallest request was experienced as a big pressure, which he would then generally respond to by going 'blank'. This was reflected in his body movement behaviour, by tense, stiff movements, interspersed by long pauses or stops.

For weeks and months the pattern continued, with progress being painfully slow. Whenever he arrived he said he was OK, and at the end of the sessions, he always said he'd had fun. Although his classroom behaviour improved, he remained behind in his work, tense and withdrawn. After five months' work, the summer holidays arrived and William moved up a year, with a new teacher. He started coming late to school and I became more and more concerned. He continued to 'jump' up the stairs and wheeze through sessions. One day, I asked him to try and describe what happened in class, when he was working. He sat still, growing more tense and said, 'I get stuck.' I asked if his head went blank and he said, 'yes'. Gently I put my hand on his forehead and moved his head side to side. He laughed and smiled. He got up and took the big body ball and threw it to me. For the rest of the session we passed and caught the ball, playing with having 'stuck' and 'unstuck' bodies in as many ways as possible.

This continued for two more sessions, until the next week William ran up the stairs, one foot in front of the other. I said he'd come up in an 'unstuck' way, and asked about his week. 'It's been a little bit unstuck,' he replied. I asked him if his teacher knew when he got stuck in class; 'don't know,' he replied, so we role-played me as the teacher and William doing work. He sat fiddling with his paper and pen as if writing, while I pretended to look over and see him getting on with his work. We swapped roles and I role-played being stuck, gazing over and trying lots of non-verbal ways to let him know I needed help. William laughed. When I asked how he could let the teacher know he needed help, he again said, 'Don't know'. I suggested he might walk to the desk, so he tried it.

He moved tensely over towards me and froze. Later he said, 'It's OK in our session, but I can't do it in class in case I get ignored.' He did say, though, that I could tell this to his teacher.

When I first liaised with his teacher, he told me that William could ask for help at any time. I pointed out that William was terrified and couldn't do it, and that the teacher needed to ask. The next week William said he went to the desk but couldn't speak, so left. Over the next two months the teacher and I liaised over different ways of allowing William to practise coming to the desk – for example, giving out paper or rulers to the class. This had some success, but still William remained cautious and scared. His lateness to school continued and on many days he missed the whole day. He said he was scared to come in late in case he got told off. Again I liaised with his teacher, who began to talk with William so that he might feel secure and supported.

Although William still finds it difficult to initiate ideas, he can now run to the session and has developed his movement and memory skills. Last week he said that the week had been better – he'd played with friends. He'd managed to go to the teacher's desk, ask for help himself and get it. William and I are now discussing the possibility of him joining a group, where he can work with friends in developing his skills. He thinks it's a good idea!

The multi-disciplinary approach – Karl

Karl is a seven-year-old boy who was referred for individual DMT sessions because, despite being lively, bright and articulate, he could never complete his work, often writing only one line. In the sessions he quickly engaged in symbolic play, creating stories, making plays and using a rich and expansive vocabulary. However, bodily he remained narrow, small and precise, using very little space. He took great care to sit up straight and not make too much noise. Despite his vivid imagination and creative use of the sessions, I found that I always felt very sad when working with him. However, when asked he would always say, 'I'm fine'. One day, he began kicking the big ball around with great force. I asked what feelings the ball might have. 'Flipping, freaking ones', he said, and when exploring other possible feelings of the ball he named happy 'Jamaica' feelings and sad 'Niagara' feelings. The magnitude of his sadness resonated within me.

I asked his teacher if Karl had ever cried in class, and was told he hadn't, though he always looked sad. I told her that I thought when he did, it would probably go on for a long time. A month later, when I arrived for work, I was met by his teacher. She told me that Karl had been bursting into tears all week.

In his session that day he drew a pencil case. With every line he drew, he would then correct it, until finally he had a beautiful picture of a pencil case, with 'Sonic the Hedgehog' on the front. He wanted to draw things to put inside. We looked at the pencil case, which was zipped up, and I said it reminded me of him, with lots of feelings zipped up inside. He looked and smiled. He said, 'The sad feelings are stuck inside.'

The following session, he took out the pencil case, and said, 'It's wrong.' Slowly, and with great control, he coloured over Sonic the Hedgehog, obliterating every trace. I found it excruciatingly painful to watch him destroy the picture. I asked him what Sonic would say if he could talk. 'I want to come out,' Karl said sadly. After a few moments he added, 'There's a happy bit that wants to come out.' As we talked together about the sad 'stuff', Karl said that he'd like his teacher to know, but was worried that the other children might laugh in case he cried. He agreed that I could ask the teacher to find some private time with him, to help him with what makes him sad in the classroom.

The next week he came in and said that some happy feelings had come out, because he'd played with friends. He said the sad feelings were still stuck inside – 'They're stuck inside my head.' He went and got the big ball and we played 'Let's try and find the sad feelings in Karl's head.' He laughed and ran around, as I tried to catch his head with the ball. He jumped on tables, made leaps onto the floor, and rolled and ducked and dived. For the first time his body found new and large shapes and he giggled and giggled and giggled.

In the work with Karl and following his lead, we moved between exploring his symbolism on a body-movement level, together with those he presented through drawings and projected onto props. Karl seemed to actively enjoy this interplay of the non-verbal, DMT medium, whereby he could work through problems on a purely symbolic level (Chaiklin and Schmais 1979; Dosamantes-Alperson 1983) alongside verbally interpreting his drawings and play (Dale 1992).

The following week his teacher told me that Karl had been fighting in class over the past few days. When he came to the session he kicked and punched and threw the ball to show me what all the different feelings looked like. He raced around the room and then grabbed the ribbons and started to wave them wildly. Within seconds the ribbons became tangled up. He pulled them apart saying, 'Angry ones! sad ones! scary ones! happy ones!', throwing and tossing them in the air. He gathered them together and again they got tangled up. I said they looked all muddled up and that maybe they were like his feelings, all mixed up and then bursting out. He nodded his head and smiled. Slowly he began to untie them. I said that maybe together we could unmuddle his feelings so that they didn't all burst out in class. 'Yes,' he replied quietly.

I explained to his teacher that it seemed that Karl was moving between two extremes – being neat, controlled and holding himself in, or having all his feelings rush out at once. We discussed ways in the classroom that he could find a transition between the two, by having clear step-by-step instructions. She said that he was currently really interested in doing work from 'life cycle' books, showing the step-by-step development of newts and dragonflies. It has enabled him to produce his best ever written work. Nearly a whole page!

Critical moments: endings

Four of the five children in one of the groups are leaving this year to go to secondary school. Since the beginning of the year, the theme of the sessions has been about worries of new situations, whether they will cope and what will they remember and take with them. Initially fear and anger became inter-twined, and were manifest by characterisations. Two boys would often collect vast amounts of props and tie them onto their backs and set out on a journey. When asked where they were going, one said 'I have to go my own way', and they journeyed round the room, pulling the heavy props with them. I said it reminded me of when they go on their own way to secondary school; 'Yeah,' came the reply. Sometimes, when the feelings became too much, characters like 'messy man' would emerge, who would throw everything around the room and hurl sponge balls at others.

Endings of individual sessions became frenetic and chaotic and nobody wanted to write in the book. In their final term, they had to face examinations. One boy came in telling the group of a nightmare he'd had. I asked if the exams felt like a nightmare and leaving school very frightening. 'Yeah, it's scary!' Again balls and props were tossed and 'messy man' erupted in a violent rage. When it got too much, I held onto 'messy man's' arms. He leant against me then collapsed, and hid his head in the prop bag. I sat on the floor next to him, cradling his shoulders, whilst the others stood looking on. I said maybe he'd like to stay inside the bag and not think about secondary school. 'I wish we could skip it,' said one boy. 'Stay in the juniors forever,' said another. 'In the infants,' whispered 'messy man'.

The group continued to use their sessions to think about and play out their fears. Towards the end, the group began to make folders, to put memories and drawings in, so that they could take them with them when they left. As they sat calmly, sticking and drawing, one boy asked, 'Why do we come to this group?' 'Messy man' looked at him and said, 'So that we can understand each other and our feelings.' 'To help us feel better about how we feel about each other,' said another. 'It's just like food on a plate – write that in the book, Sue.'

When children face the transition from junior school to secondary school there are inevitably many worries and concerns for teachers to contain. The emotional preparation needed to deal with such a major life event takes time and understanding. The sadness, fear and anger that many children experience at the prospect of moving on can be overshadowed by other events such as exams, clearing classrooms, trips out and the end of year party. Sometimes the acknowledgement of this process is left till the last few weeks of term, often out of concern that the children 'are not upset' too soon.

After liaison between the DMT therapist and the teacher about the impor-tance of early preparation for this transition, one teacher spent the whole of the last term of the year helping her class to find creative ways to express their concerns and experiences. They wrote poems and stories and drew pictures of their memories of junior school and their hopes and fears for secondary school. As she herself was also leaving the school to go and teach abroad, she did the same. Every child's work, as well as her own, was then mounted and photocop-ied along with two pages of all their signatures and a photograph of the whole class and made into a book. On the last day of the year, she sat the class down and played a tape of the song 'Memories'. Whilst it was playing she gave each child a copy of the class book to take home with them: 'Memories of School'. Inside was an individual and personalised message from the teacher, saying why she would always remember them. Communication of this kind, in which another person feels understood, 'held' in someone else's thoughts, where experiences of an intimate nature are shared and acknowledged, is a transform-ing experience. It moves one from relating 'on the outside' to relating 'on the inside' (Dale 1992, p.185).

The process of ending requires emotional preparation, allowing for feelings of loss, anger, grief and sadness. When children recognise and integrate their experiences, they themselves may signal to the therapist that they are ready to end and separate and say goodbye. However, emotional change cannot merely be willed to happen. Development is helped by providing appropriate opportunities to work on issues at an inner level and to find personally mean-ingful resolutions (Greenhalgh 1994). On the last day of one boy's therapy, he went to the prop bag and took out the long tube of lycra cloth. During our work together he had often used it as a kind of umbilical cord, whereby he would lie in one end and get me to tie the other end around my waist and pull him around the room. This time he asked me to hold one end and then he crawled in the other. 'Hold it so that you can see me through it,' he said. He crawled closer to me until we were only a few feet apart and then he stopped. Silently we gazed at each other. Then quietly he said, 'You can let go now.'

Leah – moving on

One session the boys played football whilst Leah and Helena became cheer-leaders, shouting their support. The game progressed until near the end, an argument broke out over the score, and two of the boys became upset and started shouting abuse at each other. Leah suggested that they go to the 'time-out' corner, as they were angry. The argument raged, and one boy began shouting personal insults to the other. Leah stood up, moved over to him and stood in front. 'You shouldn't say things like that, because if he's like that, then I'm even worse.' For the first time she had confronted another member (the most aggressive) as well as protecting another.

Towards the end of the therapy there was a month where many members were absent. The group struggled to keep going. One session, as we did our warm-up, the boys all fell to the floor, pretending to be weak and stuck. Again Leah came up with suggestions but this time also joined the play, allowing herself to be 'stuck' and helped by others. Later she again dressed as an angel, but had her halo stolen. She played being angry and got her halo back. The following week the 'stuck' theme continued. Monsters populated the room – having babies and eating people's heads. Leah danced around the room, moving in and out of the others, in large smiling movements, jumping and turning as she went. She challenged the monster, saying she was a ghost, who would get revenge for being eaten. At the end of the session, Leah sat quietly, and reflected on the events. When I asked what she had liked, she said, 'I liked nearly becoming.' 'Nearly becoming what?' said one of the boys. She didn't move or answer. 'Maybe we'll have to wait and see,' I answered.

Until this point, although Leah had been able to consistently join in the groups and speak up for herself, all her characters had had an ethereal quality, disembodied and hazy, e.g. ghosts, angels, monsters. The following week, after the warm-up, she went to the prop bag and pulled out a cloth, she rolled it up and wrapped it across her body, like a uniform. She took a pencil and notebook from her bag. 'I'm a reporter,' she said, 'I'm going to interview people and find out about their history. I'm going to make a book of people's stories, for the future.' At the end of the session she wrote, 'I liked finding out about people's stories and writing them down.'

Acknowledgements

'Providing Dance Movement Therapy Within a Mainstream School' by Sue Curtis. Part of this chapter first appeared in *Focus on Dance Movement Therapy 2*, 4 (1997). Published by daCi UK, London.

References

Barrows, P. (1996) 'Individual psychotherapy for children in foster care: possibilities and limitations.' *Clinical Child Psychology and Psychiatry, 1*, 3.

Chaiklin, H. (ed) (1975) *Marian Chace: Her Papers.* Columbia: ADTA.

Chaiklin, S. and Schmais, C. (1979) 'The Chace Approach to Dance Therapy.' In P.L. Bernstein (ed) *Eight Theoretical Approaches to Dance Movement Therapy.* Iowa: Kendall/Hunt.

Dale, F. (1992) 'The Art of Communicating with Vulnerable Children.' In V. P. Varma (ed) *The Secret Life of Vulnerable Children.* London: Routledge.

Dosamantes-Alperson, E. (1983) 'Working with internalized relationships through a kinesthetic and kinetic imagery process.' *Imagination, Cognition and Personality 2*, 4, 1982–83.

Greenhalgh, P. (1994) *Emotional Growth and Learning.* London: Routledge.

Leventhal, M. (1980) 'Dance Therapy as a Treatment for the Emotionally Disturbed and Learning Disabled Child.' In A. Riordan and S. Fitt (eds) *Dance Therapy for the Handicapped.* Reston, Va: American Alliance for Health, Physical Education and Recreation and Dance.

Levy, F.J. (1988) *Dance Movement Therapy – A Healing Art.* Reston, Va: American Alliance for Health, Physical Education and Recreation and Dance.

Melville-Thomas, R. (1991) 'Come dancing.' *Special Children*, (October).

North, M. (1972) *Personality Assessment through Movement.* London: Macdonald & Evans Ltd.

Payne, H. (1992) 'Shut In, Shut Out: Dance Movement Therapy with Children and Adolescents.' In H. Payne (ed) *Dance Movement Therapy, Theory and Practice.* London: Routledge.

Stanton-Jones, K. (1992) *Dance Movement Therapy in Psychiatry.* London: Routledge.

CHAPTER 9

Psychodramas with 'At Risk' Youth
A Means of Active Engagement

Erica Hollander

Introduction to the work

Some months ago, as both a trial lawyer and a certified psychodramatist, I was asked to help teach conflict resolution for peer counsellors at a coffee house set up for students from Columbine High School after the shootings. When I met with the prospective peer counsellors I quickly saw that what they had in mind for conflict resolution was more accurately described as conflict aversion. They thought that, if a conflict surfaced, that would mean that they as peer counsellors had failed in some respect. I sought to persuade them that the worst thing they could do with conflict was to try to avoid it or ignore it. As I did so I realised that my own attitudes regarding conflict resolution arise from the idea that communicating the truth is key to resolving conflicts of all kinds, and that, for me, that idea is deeply embedded in the practice of psychodrama as I know it.

With that in mind I want to describe in this chapter some of the psychodramatic work I have done with adolescents in a youthful offender diversion program run by the Denver, Colorado District Attorney's Office and in other settings. My purpose is to encourage others to use psychodrama and enactments of all kinds, including playback theatre, with teenagers. Psychodrama is particularly well suited to working with adolescents and their issues. Reasons for using psychodrama with this age group are many: it is vivid, quick and potent, it keeps active and energetic young people engaged in its process, it does not depend on books and lectures or adults in authority issuing rules or proscriptions, yet it teaches or can teach important lessons, so that the material for the dramas is created by the young people themselves and the lessons can emerge from the group process following the dramas. Consequently such lessons are not likely to be seen as that most dreaded enemy of the adolescent, an invasion of autonomy.

Also, psychodrama can be fun, very playful, entertaining, creative, and humorous. Dr J.L. Moreno, its founder, said that he brought the laughter back into psychotherapy with psychodrama. Laughter makes palatable what will be resisted if offered with greater solemnity (Hughey and Stietzel 1994). Humour is often a very useful tool in work with adolescents (Willis1991). Moreno also liked to claim that psychoanalysis allowed the dreamer to analyse his dreams, while psychodrama allowed the dreamer to resume dreaming (Moreno and Moreno 1959; Moreno 1964; Yablonsky 1987). Working with young people in the sad and difficult period of their lives in which they pass from childhood into adulthood, I think it immensely important that dreaming be kept alive. In addition, the psychodrama process is flexible. It can be readily adapted to differing cultural backgrounds or learning styles or predilections such as musical or dance or artistic abilities. In fact, almost any metaphor can be used creatively in psychodrama, so that a drama can be played in the symbolic terms most meaningful to the individual protagonist. In the accounts which follow I hope some of the range of its possibilities will be demonstrated. I will describe some of my work with families, some with individuals, some with youthful offenders in family settings in the juvenile justice system, some at home in *in situ* dramas, and the use of warm-ups and the 'Behind the Back' technique. There are many other exercises we might add to this discussion: for example, uses of psychodrama and sociodrama to deal with ethnic, racial, and class conflicts; exploring the subject of school and family violence and when to turn to adults for help; gender roles and their import. The uses of the psychodrama are only limited by the creativity and skills of the director.

Families

First, let me tell you about an instance in which I used psychodrama instead of talk to make getting to know the families of other group members more active and engaging. Some familiarity with the families of all group members can be acquired quickly and vividly via enactment rather than talking about them or description. For example, in a mixed gender group of a dozen adolescents meeting with a counsellor on an outpatient basis to learn social skills, we used psychodrama to allow each member to introduce their family members to the others in the group. I suggested that each group member think of a time when they were at some kind of family gathering – be it a picnic, holiday dinner, bowling game, day at the beach, or whatever they thought of on the spur of the moment. I encouraged them each to choose a family event with a lot of characters so members of the group could be included in playing the necessary roles.

Then, instead of having the family member describe the scene, the family member-protagonist cast the other members of the group into the parts of mother, grandmother, brother, father, cousin, even an hallucinating dog in one instance. For each character, the protagonist gave a short self-presentation and one line of text about how he or she felt about the protagonist or the family. The group member proceeded to sculpt the pose, for example, of the uncle at the barbecue and say the line the way the uncle would actually deliver it, then would go on to choose another person from the group to play the uncle's role. The protagonist continued in this fashion till all the family members were in place and cast in their roles. Roles could also be assigned to inanimate objects such as the picnic table or tree in the backyard which had seen many such barbecues and could comment on the family practices or history. Finally the group members and protagonist were allowed to play their roles, interacting with one another, checking with the protagonist to see if they were remaining on target or astray.

This exercise worked very well to give the group a greater sense of cohesion, and it allowed some members who were ordinarily quite reticent to fully participate. One boy who was very afraid to play a role at the start was allowed to choose if he wanted to try it, summoned his courage, and did fine. The opportunity to serve a purpose in another's drama successfully touched him and helped bring him into a more active role in the group.

Individuals

In another outpatient group with adolescents unfamiliar with psychodrama, I began with a list of a number of topics they could choose from for enactment. They chose to dramatise their hopes and dreams and what a great show they put on! They enacted singing at famous concert halls, running winning touchdowns at the Super Bowl, and other feats of fame and grandeur. They sang songs to the rest of the group who acted as their audiences, as they envisioned doing at their dreamed of days of triumph. It was all very grand and expansive except for one boy who quietly said he felt like he had nothing to offer of that kind. His dream, it turned out, was not about fame or celebrity but about a family outing on a Saturday to the park with his wife and the two children he wanted to have. Since he had such a different order of dream, and since he felt quite shy about it, we chose to present his dream via playback theatre – that is, as if he were looking into a mirror. He told the story and the rest of the group served as actors to act out his dream drama, with me as director. He felt fully supported by the others who played out his dream picnic and family. It worked beautifully.

Youthful offenders

On one occasion the Denver District Attorney's Office Youthful Offenders Diversion Program scheduled a full day of psychodrama for four families. Each family had a teenager who had been encountered by the justice system as a perpetrator of a family assault. Candidates for the diversion program were youthful offenders considered to be good candidates for correction outside more restrictive juvenile detention. The youthful offenders in the diversion program were largely first time offenders or, perhaps they had been in some minor trouble before, but they were still seen as redeemable, and accessible to teaching and therapy. It was a requirement of the day that all members of the family had to commit to do the whole day of psychodrama work. This was a fascinating day. They did not know one another before coming to the day of psychodrama and they had never met me before. So we had to begin with some getting acquainted and relevant warming-up.

Warm-up

I began by telling some stories about my own family and how we often failed to communicate with one another. For example, I told how one year I had bought a subscription to a beautiful and rather expensive undersea photographic magazine as a present for my father, based on how much I knew he loved the sea, swimming and snorkelling. He had done these things with me many times. I had never heard anything from him about the magazine till years later when I saw a copy on his coffee table. I asked him if he liked the magazine and he said, yes, it was very fine, but he did not know where it had come from. For a long time, he had been getting the magazine and enjoying it, while I had thought he did not like it. Nor had he known that it had been sent to him as a gift from his daughter, so he had missed some of the joy it represented. I offered the story to the families who had come to do psychodrama without fully knowing what was in store for them. I wanted my self disclosure to help them see that they were not alone with their issues of difficulty in communication. I also wanted to stress that we could learn from one another.

We then moved into an exercise with double circles (Hollander and Hollander 1998). There was an inner circle of chairs facing out, and an outer circle of chairs facing in and each participant had an initial partner to speak with. We began a series of exercises based on the *sociogenetic* law, in which we move from simple to complex systems of relationships (Moreno 1953). This particular arrangement was based on the idea that it would be easier for them to speak to one other person at first than to address the whole group. So they began with the first partner, saying hello, and then 'telling a favourite family memory' they had. First the member of the inner circle would talk and the outer circle listen, then they would reverse and the outer circle member would tell his/her favourite family memory and the inner circle member listen. They would take a few minutes each and then they would take a little time to compare their favourite memories. I chose favourite fond memories because I wanted to spend part of the day's energy building up the positive side of their feelings toward their family.

Next they shifted partners by the inner circle moving one space to the left so each person had a new partner to greet. This time I asked them to tell their partners 'who in the family they would go to if they had a problem and needed help.' The inner circle spoke first and then the outer. Again, they took a little time to compare notes at the end. Then they switched places by the inner circle again moving one space to the left to a new partner. This time I asked them to tell their partner 'who in the family they trust the most and what is it about that person that makes him/her trustworthy.' Again, after each had told his/her individual tale, they compared their stories and choices.

Next, they shifted partners again, and this time I asked them to act the part of the most trusted person in their family, 'becoming' that person, and tell something about themselves to their new partner from their position in role. The listener could interview the trusted person being role played and try to see what was to be learned about the trusted person's relationship with the protagonist. This allowed each of them to identify with a trusted family member and play his or her role; it allowed them to feel the admirable traits of the trusted members in their own families, and to play with being that trusted other.

When they shifted partners yet again, this time they were asked to tell about 'the best holiday memory they had from their families.' Finally, the whole circle had been completed, so that each person in the inner circle had had a chance to speak one to one with each in the outer circle. After some general sharing about how those present found the exercise of the double circles, we were ready to move on.[19]

Thereafter, I broke the group down into the component families and sent each family off to its own space for a quarter of an hour with instructions to design a way to enact, in a family sculpture or in presentation of some other kind, and by enacting to introduce the family as a family with its own character to the others present. They had to work together as a family to reach consensus on this, and to co-operate with one another in making a family identity presentation. At the conclusion of their preparations, they all came together to see each other's presentations and skits. Questions were lively after each presentation.

Enactment

After the families had each made presentations and had seen the others, there was quite a lot of talk and energy in the group. The group seemed to me to be warmed up to do a full psychodrama, and knowing this is a matter of experience in directing the enactment process (Levy 1969). We were then ready to choose a protagonist, or principle actor, for that psychodrama, whose story would be enacted by the group as a whole. Each person other than the director was allowed to say what he or she would work on in a drama if chosen as protagonist. Virtually all the topics were around the assaults which had brought the teenagers into the juvenile justice system. Once everyone had offered a theme to work on, a protagonist was chosen by action sociogram (Moreno 1953). The group was asked to focus on one criterion – that was, whose work would best represent the common theme. They all went simultaneously to put their hands on the shoulders of the person whose work they felt most interested in other than their own.

The group chose a particularly quiet and reserved young man to be its protagonist. His drama concerned how he had gotten out of control and had become violent and struck his mother. His mother and sisters played themselves and some of the other families' members played roles as friends and so on. The most salient aspect of the drama that emerged in the enactment was that everyone in the family had known that he was becoming increasingly frustrated and angry and isolated well before the violence erupted and yet no one had known what to do to avert the outbreak. Nor had they spoken about it aloud. Sisters and mother all said now, in the 'after the fact' account that they all had known that the tension was building to an impossible level before the violent assault occurred.

The boy's enactment revealed a family assault in the sense of a failure of the family system to offer alternatives. The mother was able to speak about her difficulties as a single mother, with more to do than she could handle, feeling unappreciated and alone. The son was able to speak about how isolated he had felt both before and after his attack on his mother. The catharsis of abreaction was about his guilty feelings and remorse (Hollander 1969, Fox 1987). The catharsis of integration at the end of the drama was about how things might have gone differently if only someone had spoken up, said that they felt the tension, tried to break out of the pattern of being trapped in dysfunctional habits (Hollander 1969; Hughey and Steitzel 1994).

In the group therapy session that follows the drama, the director's instructions are to tell one's own story that relates to the drama – what came to mind for those in the audience or in auxiliary roles that was similar to their own lives. The group members are told not to judge or analyse, or make suggestions. The sharing after this particular drama emphasised the prologue to violence as identified and identifiable in each different family setting. The idea of breaking out of the silence and 'tagging' what had been going on was talked about by all those present. This lesson alone made the day worthwhile: that if everyone knows what is going to happen and no one acts to avert the tragedy, then it is their failure as a family and not just the one perpetrator's failure that is in issue. We tried to discuss fully what other options might be available if tension built up again, and how to make some better use of the fact of prologue once it is seen for what it is. We discussed talking about the building of tension, trying to get help with it from other family members or professionals or both.

'Behind the Back' technique

Finally, we used a technique called 'Behind the Back' designed to encourage people to say the positive things they may feel and be unwilling or unaccustomed to saying to the faces of others (Haskell 1975). We set up the room with the perpetrators seated in front of the rest of those present but with their backs to the others. The perpetrators were told not to say anything until all the others from their families had spoken fully and completely about how they felt about the perpetrators in positive terms. The sisters and brothers and parents, without identifying themselves, in fact told the violent ones how much they were loved, how sad their assaults had made the others, how worried they were about whether the ones who acted out would be able to get themselves back onto track or not, how frightened the others were for the perpetrators.

The perpetrators were plainly deeply touched by what was said to them. Each of them had tears in his eyes as he listened to the love of the family members being expressed. Some of the comments also came from those who had just met that very day – concern and hope for the violent ones from new acquaintances. At last, the perpetrators were permitted to speak in reply, and to turn and face their families. Everyone was moved by what was being said and struggled with. Commitments were made to try 'to get things straightened out' and to deal with one another with more care and awareness in future.

The 'Behind the Back' exercise is one well worth using with 'at risk' adolescents. At the end of the day, the families present were intrigued with what we had done. Parents were rethinking their own contributions to the atmosphere of violence and everyone present had had to face the fact that they had all known the tension was building to the breaking point before it broke without doing anything to avert it. One father present at our session had an 'ah-hah' experience. He said he supposed that he should stop talking about violent actions he might take if he wanted his son to get the message that violence is not to be condoned. He said, 'I guess that if I want to stop his violence, it is not a really good idea for me to tell him that, if he comes home with a ring in his eyebrow, I am going to pull the thing out with pliers.'

Female teen offenders

On one other occasion I visited a teenaged girls' group in the youth diversion program for young offenders. This group was composed mainly of girls who had stolen from department stores and been caught and also included a few girls who had been involved in family assaults. The entire group was on a kind of probation status with definite curfews and rules about where they could be and with whom they could associate as a result of their involvement in the youth diversion program. They were working through some substantive learning and family strategies, and they also came to associate with one another in forming a group during the program with the help of a case worker.

On the day before I came to visit some of the girls in the group had been picked up for breaking the curfew rules, being out too late, and had been caught by the police. As a consequence, they were facing a hearing regarding what would become of them – whether they would be 'bounced out' of the youth diversion program and then placed back into juvenile detention with the mainstream youthful offenders – or have extended probation, or what disposition might be made. We role played the scene of the police bust – where they were and what they were doing when the police came and took them to the station – full of excuses and rationales. Then we 'went' to the hearing room, set the scene there, and role played what they intended to say to the hearing officer who was going to have to make the dispositive decisions in their cases.

The most important piece of this enactment was for the girls to feel what the judge or hearing officer was going to want to hear and understand. It was important therefore to allow the girls to reverse roles with the hearing officer and try to feel what she would be interested in hearing. It was plain from that perspective that most of the excuses they were offering moments before would have little bearing on the outcome and, once they tried reversing roles with the judge, they knew that.

In situ drama

In one other family, I was asked to come to the actual home where the family assault had occurred between older son and mother and enact the assault on site with the whole family present. We did a bit of preparation with the parents first, asking them to each remember and talk to us all about how they had had some difficulties getting along with their own parents as teens. They did recall aloud some serious disagreements and wounds they felt they had received at the hands of their parents. The children were listening avidly to all this, and it was going to be more difficult for the parents to be dogmatic afterward once they acknowledged that they might not have been perfect as adolescents themselves.

Then we did the assault drama, *in situ*, but the protagonist was not comfortable being in his own role. He was, he said, afraid he would be violent again, and did not want to get into the provocative situation. So his therapist played his role, and he acted as an assistant director to me. All others in the family were situated at their usual stations, mother in the kitchen, father coming in from work, good little brother at his computer. Again it was apparent that everyone knew the script completely and that these events had happened not once but many times. Once it had become violent, and often before that it had been near the edge of violence. It was important for the perpetrator to step into his mother's role in the kitchen, trying to get his therapist, playing him, to help with setting the table for dinner, which he was ignoring until she in frustration turned off the TV to get his attention. That is when he hit her in the actual history, but what we did with it in enactment was not to re-enact the assault but just to let him feel her frustration and to say something about how the situation felt from within her role.

Again, there was the sense of needing to do something different to avert the crisis, and the sense that it might be possible to do it otherwise if the building up of tension was identified and addressed. There was a palpable sense of how much they all wanted their family to improve and to get better at handling its inevitable stresses. There was also the beginning of an insight into how to avoid going down the same path again: by 'tagging' what they saw and felt, by calling it as they saw it and identifying what they knew it to be, by trying to work together to avert the violence, by seeking help from one another and from trained outsiders, by not hiding from the fact that the tensions were increasing, by not avoiding one another and the facts of their lives. At the end of this session, the patterns were evident and the perpetrator had had a chance to see them and to feel his mother's frustrations as well. The potential for real growth and understanding was created.

Summary

In summary, I hope you can see from these brief illustrative examples what a versatile tool psychodrama can be in working with 'at risk' adolescents. It is unusually useful in reaching teenagers preoccupied with their own emancipation because it allows them to choose their own material and metaphors. Reluctance to engage in more traditional learning settings can be overcome with creativity and humour. Acquaintance with others who are important in the lives of group members is much more fun if acted out than talked about, and, while the enactment is occurring, group cohesion is being increased. Family communication and awareness can be increased dramatically in only a short time. Whatever the substance of concern, whether it is violence or confrontations with authority or hopes and dreams, it is wonderful to have a means which can accommodate the truth of a youthful outlook with humour and spirit. These examples are only a small sample of what is possible when a trained psychodrama director meets an energetic and creative youthful population.

References

Fox, J. (ed) (1987) *The Essential Moreno: Writings on Psychodrama, Group Method, and Spontaneity by J.L. Moreno*. New York: Springer.

Haskell, M. (1975) *Socioanalysis: Self Direction via Sociometry and Psychodrama*. Long Beach, CA: Role Training Associates of California.

Hollander, C.E. (1969) *The Hollander Curve*. Littleton, CO: Evergreen Institute Press.

Hollander, C. and Hollander, E. (1998) *The Warm Up Box*, 3rd edn. Denver, CO: Wandell Press.

Hughey, A.R. and Stietzel, L. (1994) *Empowerment through Spontaneity.* San Jose, CA: Associates for Community Interaction Press.

Levy, R. (1969) *Human Relations–A Conceptual Approach.* Scranton, PA: International Textbook Company.

Moreno, J.L. (1953) *Who Shall Survive? Foundations of Sociometry, Group Psychotherapy and Sociodrama.* Beacon, NY: Beacon House.

Moreno, J.L. (1964) *Psychodrama, Volume I.* Beacon, NY: Beacon House.

Moreno, J.L. and Moreno, Z. T. (1959) *Psychodrama, Volume II.* Beacon, NY: Beacon House.

Willis, S. T. (1991) 'Who Goes There? Group Analytic Drama for Disturbed Adolescents.' In P. Holmes and M. Karp (eds) *Psychodrama: Inspiration and Technique.* London and New York: Tavistock Routledge.

Yablonsky, L. (1987) *Psychodrama: Resolving Emotional Problems through Role-playing.* New York: Brunner Mazel.

CHAPTER 10

DRAGO-DRAMA™
Archetypal Sociodrama with Adolescents

Mario Cossa

Introduction

Something that inspires me about working with teens is that adolescence is a unique time of restoration, reparation, and re-creation. From a developmental perspective, tasks and challenges that might not have been met fully or at all in infancy get a chance to be worked on and worked through again. This time it is the social network, rather than the family, that may serve the function of the 'good-enough parent' (Winnicott 1965).

For twelve years, I have worked as the founder/director of a youth program that combines expressive arts therapies, improvisational theatre, and peer theatre/education. This programme, ACTINGOUT™, also employs other modalities as appropriate in both therapeutic and educational settings. Over the years, through the spontaneity and creativity of staff and many interns, we have created an invigorating, 'good-enough parent' for a lot of kids. One special approach that is original with us, and which we use in many forms, is DRAGO-DRAMA™.

In 1989, when ACTINGOUT (AO) was in its first year of operation, a stuffed animal (a dragon created by my friend, Katie) sparked my thinking, and the first DRAGO-DRAMA was created. In its current form, DRAGO-DRAMA offers participants a 'quest' experience in which an individual or group of 'Seekers' encounter their Dragon (a life obstacle) to reclaim their Jewel of Great Worth (a life victory or goal).

An outline of DRAGO-DRAMA™ scenes

1. Select and develop characters.

2. Explore, in action, the characters' lives within their village.

3. Experience the moment of the Dragon's passing over and stealing each person's Jewel of Great Worth.

4. The townspeople sleep and dream of a Dragon and a Jewel.

5. Townspeople share dreams in the Town Common.

6. The Wizard appears and Seekers are selected.

7. The Seeker(s) earn three gifts: the Shield of Self-Confidence, the Wand of Whimsy, and the Cloak of Courage.

8. Journey through the Sea of Shoulds, and encounter the voices of morality, obligation, compulsivity, and shame.

9. Encounter the Sirens of Self-Doubt.

10. Journey in the Dreary Downs and encounter the Goblins of Gloom.

11. Encounter the Ogres of Oblivion.

12. Encounter the Duchess of Depression.

13. Journey through the Forest of Fears, Poltergeists of Paranoia, and the Gnomes of Gnightmare.

14. Encounter the Mage of Malice.

15. Encounter the Dragon and reclaim the Jewel.

16. Return to the village for celebration and sharing.

When employed therapeutically, DRAGO-DRAMA allows sufficient distance for youth to explore their personal material safely, by providing a metaphoric and archetypal structure. When employed educationally it generates interest and excitement through role playing.

The activity is structured so that each group member may elect to be in the role of 'Seeker' at the same time, operating from a 'character' that each member creates. Even within this group form, the process includes 'member-specific moments', which occur as each individual within the group encounters challenges and characters, which become specific to each of them.

DRAGO-DRAMA combines elements of psychodrama, the action method for enactment of specific personal material by an individual (called the 'protagonist'); and sociodrama, the action method focused on the group or issue rather than the individual. Both were developed from the work of J.L. Moreno (1980). In some respects it can also be considered drama therapy: it is a dramatic-action approach utilised for therapeutic ends, and in which the group members are operating within character roles.

The director/therapist also operates from role, as the Wizard. When working with a leadership team, as we generally do, there may be several Wizards, co-directing, and other trained leaders who play roles to facilitate and deepen the experience. Throughout this chapter, I will refer to the group leader in the singular, with the understanding that, in practice, there may be a leadership team.

In our years of questing for Dragons, we have also developed an original, musical play: *What the Dragon Stole* (Cossa and Goodman 1999). Those AO group members who have participated in both the play and in their own DRAGO-DRAMAs have experienced different levels of learning in each venue. One AO group member was more able to access personal material from within a role in the show than from participating in DRAGO-DRAMA as a client-centred therapeutic experience.

Theory

DRAGO-DRAMA incorporates archetypal encounters (Jung 1965) with metaphoric psychodrama. It operates within what J.L. Moreno called 'surplus reality' (Moreno 1944), and what some call the 'imaginal realm' (Lewis 1993). DRAGO-DRAMA offers the protagonist (the client participating in the primary role of the drama) and the group members a 'screen' upon which to project an examination of their strengths and strategies for encountering life obstacles.

Although developed independently from the Therapeutic Spiral Model™ (TSM), a psychodramatic model for working safely with trauma survivors, developed by Dr Kate Hudgins (2000) and her colleagues, language from this model describes the theoretical basis for the therapeutic application of DRAGO-DRAMA quite well.

Protagonists are first armed with 'prescriptive roles' of *restoration* (personal, interpersonal and transpersonal strengths), *observation* (the ability to witness without judgement or being caught up in affect), and *containment* (the ability to remain 'present' despite having strong feelings). As the drama unfolds, protagonists develop or strengthen 'transformative roles' (those that support healthy life choices and transformation of negative patterns of behaviour), while encountering their 'trauma-based roles' (maladaptive responses and defences as well as the internalised *victim, perpetrator*, and *abandoning parent* voices).

DRAGO-DRAMA operates metaphorically, and works from a foundation of restoration. Utilised similarly to the first stages of TSM trauma work, DRAGO-DRAMA is well suited to adolescent trauma survivors who are not yet ready for psychodramas of *conscious re-experiencing* (Hudgins 2000). As this chapter develops, I will occasionally reference TSM connections. For readers interested in a more detailed description of the TSM, references cited in this chapter will provide additional information.

Technique and clinical examples

Warm-up

When beginning the DRAGO-DRAMA process, group members are asked to consider which 'victories' and 'obstacles' may be important to explore at this point in their personal work. We relate each 'victory' to the 'Jewel of Great Worth', and each 'obstacle' to the 'Dragon guarding the Jewel'. We recognise the 'obstacles' can also be 'opportunities' and that not all Dragons are necessarily bad. Through movement or graphic arts participants may explore what kind of Dragon they may encounter, or what this Jewel might be like (both the Dragon and the Jewel can change or evolve in the course of the drama). Sometimes a group works with graphic images that focus on dragons as a theme. These images may be very rich and symbolic, allowing our members to project their personal material onto the images, regardless of their previous knowledge of or experience with dragon legends and myths.

Group members create characters through whose experience they will encounter the Dragon. Together, each group begins to form their collection of characters into their 'village'. Some of this is done in advance of the action, and some becomes more richly described during the early stages of the dramatic action. Many of our AO members have prior experience with various 'role-playing games' which enhances the process of character creation. Each participant also maintains a 'Dragon journal' within which to record their experiences in words and pictures. Whenever they are needed, the Wizard/director can make the journals and writing/drawing implements 'appear' so that members may access this material or add to it.

It is possible to move through all the elements of DRAGO-DRAMA in about an hour (a very surface exploration), or in one three-hour or full-day workshop within which the goal is to provide insight and information, or to evaluate areas for further work. With more time available, therapeutic goals may also be set. Because we generally apply DRAGO-DRAMA therapeutically we only go as far in any given session as seems appropriate for that situation. The full quest takes as long as it takes. This chapter is presented from the therapeutic perspective, with the understanding that the educational process follows the same form, but does not go deeply into personal material.

The Action

SELECTING PROTAGONIST(S)

In this and future sections, I am offering a narrative to suggest the type of language that helps set the mood for the drama. As the chapter progresses, I will switch to a descriptive form, leaving to the potential director the task of creating the actual words.

> Once upon a time, there was a village nestled in the foothills of a mountain overlooking the sea. The people there were a lot like people everywhere.

During the next section the group enacts the narration and characters and their relationships to one another become more clearly defined. Sometimes additional narration emerges in response to the actions and words of the group members, so there is interplay between actors and the director, which is unique to each group: 'Sometimes they laughed…sometimes they cried…they worked…they played…' and so on. 'One afternoon, they gathered in the town common for a shared lunch.' (Each character might name the dish they bring to share.)

> As they ate, it seemed as though a dark cloud had passed over the sun, though when they looked up, the sky was clear. They felt a coldness in their hearts, as if something vital were suddenly missing. Without speaking, they took their belongings and headed home. They each spent a troubled evening, not knowing what was wrong. A strange feeling came over them as they drifted off to sleep.

Once the group leader has ascertained, through prior assessment and knowledge of each group member's material, that guided visualisation is appropriate and safe (it can trigger dissociation in some trauma survivors, and so would be contraindicated in those instances), a 'dream' is directed. In the dream/visualisation, each townsperson views their 'Jewel of Great Worth' shining in the distance. As they approach it, the sky darkens. The darkness becomes the Dragon, an obstacle blocking them from the Jewel.

> The next morning, they all rushed to the Town Common to share their wondrous and frightening dreams. They discovered that each of them had dreamed the same dream, although the appearances of the Jewel and the Dragon had been very different for each of them. Suddenly, they noticed a figure approaching from the hills (*the director*). As s/he drew near, they saw it was the Wizard of Wisdom, and they grew silent. They knew the Wizard only ventured out in times of great trouble or great joy, so they gathered round to see which it was. 'People of the village, I bring a warning. A terrible Dragon is roaming the countryside, and you are in danger. The Dragon must be overcome. The task is dangerous, but the reward is great, for the Dragon hoards within its lair the Jewels of Great Worth that it has stolen from you. I will guide you on your quest, if you are ready.'

The Wizard then invites those who feel most ready to encounter the Dragon to step forward. The protagonist(s) may be chosen 'sociometrically' (a selection process by which group members support a particular member to work because this person's issues will best serve the group), or by the 'luck of the draw' (using playing cards or other tokens) that will decide who assumes which role. A single protagonist may be chosen, or a protagonist and a 'sidekick' (double). It is our general practice that all those wishing to participate as protagonists embark on this quest as a group of Seekers. If costumes are to be used, the protagonists may select their garb at this point.

The various options offer different types of experiences. The reader is encouraged to view each section of the DRAGO-DRAMA from various perspectives, recognising the different ways the action might play out if there were a single protagonist, a pair, or a group.

THE JEWELS AND THE GIFTS

At this point, the Wizard may ask questions to clarify for the protagonist(s) the nature of the Jewels they seek. The protagonist(s) may define their Jewels in personal and specific terms: 'My Jewel is my self-esteem and my ability to stand up for myself.' The Jewel may also be described in more general or poetic terms: 'My Jewel shines with a fierce inner light and reflects all the colours of the rainbow.' The Wizard then has three gifts to offer the Seekers, but each must be earned. The process of earning each gift allows each protagonist to assess and become more aware of the strengths and abilities that they already possess. The group members can also realise that as a collective they have a great number of strengths and abilities at their disposal.

The protagonist(s) give a personal affirmation related to their readiness to do the work of encountering the Dragon, thus earning the first gift, the 'Shield of Self-Confidence', which includes personal, interpersonal, and transpersonal strengths. The second gift is the 'Wand of Whimsy', which holds both the power of humour and the ability to step back and view situations and the self from a distance. To earn this gift, each Seeker tells a joke or does something silly. In the midst of the laughter, we introduce the concept of the 'observing ego', which is the part of self that does not get caught in the affect of the moment, but can observe without judging. For many, the development of this role is the major focus of a year's work. The final gift is the 'Cloak of Courage.' From *What the Dragon Stole* (Cossa and Goodman 1999, p.12) come the following line: 'Remember, courage is not the absence of fear. The absence of fear is stupidity. Courage is our ability to act in spite of our fears.'

To earn the Cloak, each Seeker relates a time in which s/he was able to take effective action about something in spite of fear about it. It is important at this point to note that the boundary between the Seeker/character and the protagonist/participant must remain flexible. Acts of courage that are named may be those of the character or of the individual playing the character, or, perhaps, of the individual as translated through the experience of the character. For group members for whom the formation of the Dragon is related to childhood trauma, the cloaks provide support to stay present by recognising the safety of the group while experiencing the possibly intense affect of trauma memories. Upon bestowing all three gifts (and it may take several sessions to get this far), the Seekers are bid farewell and informed that the Wizard's voice will go with them as a guide on their journey. S/he then stands them in a circle and transports them to the Dragon's dimension, perhaps with a chant. This sends them on their way, to the edge of the Sea where the journey will begin.

THE QUEST, DAY ONE

The first leg of the journey takes the Seekers over the 'Sea of Shoulds'. The group creates the Sea through movement and sound. The Wizard/director checks that the group has voiced the appropriate 'shoulds' that apply for these protagonists. If not, 'role reversal' with the Sea can be used (the protagonist moves into the role of the Sea for a time to speak the needed lines). The goal at this stage is to focus on societal norms and community values through global statements, such as 'Boys must be tough', 'Girls should sacrifice for their relationships', or 'You should floss your teeth regularly.' However, some statements more specific to the protagonist(s) are also useful, such as: 'You should be more like your sister.'

The Seekers need not overcome the Sea, but are directed to observe which messages lift them up and which threaten to drown them, and which obscure vision and which enhance it (for example, a 'should' about regular flossing lifts them up, because it is a 'good' thing). If time allows, the Seekers may meet various creatures: 'Murray' and 'Mary', the 'Morays of Mustn'ts and Morality'; 'Christy', the 'Crab of Compulsivity'; 'Otto', the 'Octopus of Obligation'; and 'Shalimar', the 'Shark of Shame'. The protagonists then can become more aware of the inner and outer voices that make up their mental/emotional seascapes.

As this scene is played out, the director is assessing the degree to which the protagonists are ready to move beyond these generic messages to encounter their personal voices more fully and completely. It may be that time should be spent on supporting the group members in freeing themselves from the 'cultural conserves' (Moreno 1980) that define their generation. If the protagonists are able to move past these conserves, they, in their role as Seekers, arrive at their first destination, the 'Isle of the Sirens of Self-Doubt'.

Group and/or team members are invited to be the Sirens who voice doubts that plague each protagonist. Here we are focused on material that is more personal to the protagonist(s), even if the originator and/or current holders of these undermining attitudes and statements are never named specifically. Again, role reversal can be used to deepen the experience. In some instances, the messages conveyed by the Sirens remain generic, such as, 'You are not good enough or smart enough.' In many instances, they become quite specific to the individuals involved, so we hear statements such as, 'You are such a slut, no one could ever love you', or 'You are so stupid; sixteen years old and still in the ninth grade.' The Seekers must face and overcome the doubts voiced by the Sirens, perhaps by using ideas from sidekicks or other group members, and also by employing the Shield of Self-Confidence to reconnect with personal, interpersonal and transpersonal strengths. After overcoming the Sirens, the first 'day' of the quest is over, and the Seekers rest.

ONGOING ASSESSMENT AND TRANSITION ONE

The group leader must make an assessment at this point. Unless the Sirens have been defeated or transformed, or at least toned down significantly, the protagonists may not be ready to face some of the other characters within

DRAGO-DRAMA, and need to do more work in the area of 'restoration', as defined by the TSM (Toscani and Hudgins 1996). Indeed, for many teens new to therapy and new to action approaches, an extended period may be required before successfully overcoming the Sirens. Moving past them without having achieved a real victory not only seems 'bogus' to the participants, it can lead to retraumatisation by moving too quickly into deeper levels of work. (Although metaphoric work is less likely to retraumatise, the possibility still exists.)

This does not mean that each protagonist must have fully claimed a complete sense of self-esteem before moving on. However, an authentic sense of positive change felt to be occurring or able to occur soon for each participant is ideal, so that each is able to believe in this process enough to continue with appropriate personal investment.

THE QUEST, DAY TWO

When the Seekers are ready to move on, either the scene mysteriously changes, or group members can create a 'tunnel' which leads to the second destination, the 'Dreary Downs', realm of the 'Duchess of Depression'. Within this realm there are two challenges to face before meeting the Duchess.

The first is presented by the 'Goblins of Gloom', who, literally, weigh the Seekers down with discouraging messages, such as: 'The task is impossible', and, 'Any effort to defeat the Dragon is doomed to failure.' If time has elapsed since encountering the Sirens, emerging victorious from this conflict allows each Seeker to reconnect to the victories experienced in the Sirens' realm. In addition, the Seekers learn that brute force is of no use in trying to move out from under the weight of these creatures. As they explore various tactics, with coaching from the Wizard's voice, they discover that in letting go of the need to push back, they are able to move out from under the Goblins' oppressive weight. This lesson is symbolic of letting go of affect and moving into the 'observing ego role'.

The next challenge is offered by the 'Ogres of Oblivion', who entice the Seekers with distractions, like food, alcohol, tobacco, drugs, and sex. This is an opportunity for the protagonist(s) to explore ways they avoid or try to deny feelings through self-indulgence. The Ogres provide a very serious challenge. Even with adult groups, it has often taken quite some time before the Seekers are ready to move away from this encounter. Depending on the needs of the group, we may spend a number of sessions here, or move on while recognising that there may still be unfinished business here with the Ogres.

Through encounters with the Goblins and Ogres, group members have been exploring maladaptive responses and defence mechanisms, which, in TSM language, are 'trauma-based roles' (Hudgins 2000). As the Seekers move on to face the Duchess of Depression, the drama moves into the role of the 'abandoning parent/caregiver'. The Seekers' and other group members' meta-phoric/sociodramatic encounters with these roles in DRAGO-DRAMA may serve as warm-ups to future psychodramatic work. The message of the Duchess is one of hopelessness and despair. Like the ineffective parent, she expresses the belief that there is nothing that can be done to make things different. Played by a member of the leadership team, she may intone:

> It is hopeless. There is no way you can defeat the dragon and reclaim the Jewel. Even if you could, the victory would be short-lived, because you would soon discover that there are other stolen Jewels and other Dragons who guard them.

The Goblins encourage the Seekers to get so caught up in struggle that they cannot move. The Ogres then entice them to escape into sweet oblivion. The Duchess continues these seductions, entreating the Seekers to give up the quest, to dwell with her in despair, depression, and inaction. Role reversal and interview within role can be used to establish the protagonists' specific inter-pretations of the Duchess' challenge. The Wand of Whimsy is often a helpful tool for handling this situation, not so much by encouraging the Seekers to 'laugh it off' (depression is not funny), but by reframing reality in a broader perspective. The quest may be difficult or even terrifying, but that does not make it impossible. True, there may be new Dragons to encounter and new Jewels to reclaim, but that is part of the adventure of life. By employing the Wand's true function, that of observation without judgement (observing ego), the Seekers can overcome the Duchess successfully and, once again, earn a moment of rest.

The location is once again transformed, into the 'Forest of Fear'. Group members become the trees and inhabitants of the Forest, such as the 'Polter-geists of Paranoia' and the 'Gnomes of Gnightmare'. Against this backdrop, the 'Mage of Malice' appears. The Mage is a 'shadow' figure, the one who provides the final challenges before the actual encounter with the Dragon.

One aspect of the Mage's challenges is to be able to face up to fear, contain it appropriately, and move forward in spite of it. The Cloak of Courage becomes important at this point. Role reversals by the protagonist(s) with the Mage and with the Cloak are important in assessing the ability of the protagonist(s) to contain the affect associated with the fear. Development of these realisations may take some time, and, when employing DRAGO-DRAMA as a tool of therapeutic transformation (as compared to its use as a tool for supporting greater understanding), this step cannot be rushed. Concurrent exploration of the second aspect of the Mage's challenges may offer additional support in meeting the first challenge.

Just as the Duchess represents the 'abandoning parent/caregiver', so the Mage represents the entangled 'victim/internalized perpetrator'. 'I see the evil within your heart,' declares the Mage:

> and I see that it is because of your own wickedness that you have deserved your lot in life. This evil allows me to claim you as my own. Here with me you shall abide forever.

This is another crucial moment of awareness for the protagonist(s). It is an opportunity to let go of self-blame and be able to affirm:

> I may behave in ways that are foolish, or destructive, or even hurtful, but I am not evil. Above all, I was not responsible for what was done to me as a child. I can become responsible for reclaiming my life now.

After both challenges have been met, the Seekers may overcome the Mage or, perhaps, transform this character into the 'Sage of Support', as a way of encountering the 'shadow self' and incorporating it into one's repertoire of response. The Mage's challenges are then met, and the Seekers rest once again.

ONGOING ASSESSMENT AND TRANSITION TWO

These moments of 'rest', noted here and previously, are natural stopping points if the DRAGO-DRAMA is to be enacted over a number of sessions. They also serve as periods in which the leader and group members may assess their readiness to move on to the next level of work. The assessment, indeed, must be made for both group members and leader. Both must feel sufficient completion with the previous material as well as a readiness to continue. There is no shame in deciding to halt the drama, or postponing its continuation. 'Discretion is the better part of valour.'

THE QUEST, FINAL DAY

The protagonist(s) are now ready to enter the final stage of dramatic action. Since the Dragon can represent a wide range of life obstacles, not necessarily related to previous trauma, the form and intensity of the encounter can vary greatly from drama to drama, or even from one protagonist to another within the group. Even with the entire group acting as protagonists, unless it is clear that the Dragon represents an obstacle to the group itself, we have each member encounter the Dragon individually. This encounter is the climax of DRAGO-DRAMA and needs to be given the time it requires so that group members may most fully benefit from their own as well as each other's experiences.

In dramas with a single protagonist, the entire group, part of the group, or members of the leadership team may enact the Dragon. This enactment can be quite imaginative, utilising costume and props. In one instance, in which the Dragon represented the protagonist's compulsive overeating, group members created the terrible beast from food, dinnerware, and cutlery.

In dramas in which there are multiple Dragons to encounter, a team member or even the director may give voice to the Dragon. If there are group members who have elected not to encounter their own Dragons at that time, they may also be employed for this role. It is important, however, that whoever plays the Dragon is able to do so in a manner that will maximise the experience for the protagonist.

In cases in which the Dragon represents the 'perpetrator', we recommend having this role played by a member of the leadership team, or represented by an object and voiced by the director. Encountering a perpetrator metaphorically is intrinsically safer than in conventional, interpersonal, or scene-based action therapy. However, it still has the potential to retraumatise the protagonist, or set back the work if the role is not enacted appropriately.

One cannot anticipate the way the encounter with the Dragon will proceed. Protagonist soliloquy (the speaking aloud of inner thoughts) and role reversals by the protagonist with the Dragon may all come into play. Clinical judgment must be employed in role reversing a protagonist into the role of the Dragon if it is a representative of the perpetrator.

At some point in the process, a role reversal with the Jewel of Great Worth may help protagonists focus on what they are reclaiming, and provide support for the encounter with the Dragon or insight into the type of tactic to be employed. It may be necessary to bring in the sidekick to help a protagonist stay present in the moment and succeed in the encounter. This scene is the climax of the drama, and it requires the judgment and spontaneity of the director, protagonist, and group to find the resolution that best serves the needs of protagonist and group. Over the years, some of the Dragons that our protagonists have encountered have been slain. Others have been banished, or been relegated to a position of lesser power. With some, it has been a matter of renegotiating the relationship. With others, the Dragon has been befriended and enlisted as an ally. The honesty of the encounter is more important than the outcome, and so not all Dragons can be overcome in the moment. With some, the protagonist gains a better understanding of the work to be done, and commits to doing that work on another occasion.

When the Dragon is appropriately encountered, protagonists should again spend time with their Jewel, using soliloquy and role reversal as needed to understand and reclaim more fully that part of self that the Dragon has been holding. Once the Jewel has been fully identified and claimed, the drama can move into a final celebration, with music, dance and any other elements created by the group.

Sharing

The drama may end at this point, and a traditional type of psychodramatic sharing among protagonist, auxiliaries and group may occur. It is also possible to stage the sharing as part of the play, in the form of 'tales told around the campfire' by the Seekers returned from their quest.

Discussion

DRAGO-DRAMA is always a work in progress, and no two dramas have ever been the same. The framework we have created is a container for moving the action through certain archetypal explorations, but the real key to the mystery of the form is discovered through the spontaneity and creativity of the director and each group member.

When employed as an experience to gain insight and information, and conducted in a relatively short period of time, it is better to focus on the main characters at each site (the Sea, the Sirens, the Duchess, the Mage, the Dragon) than in moving in and out of encounters with all the supporting characters (the Octopus of Obligation, the Ogres of Oblivion, the Gnomes of Gnightmare, and so on). As a therapeutic encounter, DRAGO-DRAMA can still cover a wide range of issues, and can be utilised in varying amounts of available time. As is true with most psychodramatic work, it will always take more time than you think it will. When I first started directing DRAGO-DRAMAs, I was likely to complete each in one session, start to finish. As it has developed, and as more elements have been included, I have allowed more time for in-depth utilisation of the form.

Over the years at ACTINGOUT, our Dragon quests have become a time of new beginnings, joy, and a fertile period for ideas. May DRAGO-DRAMA be all these things for you and those you serve.

References

Cossa, M. and Goodman, T. (1999) *What the Dragon Stole.* Keene, NH: ACTINGOUT.

Hudgins, M.K. (2000) 'The Therapeutic Spiral Model: Treating PTSD in Action.' In P.F. Kellermann and M.K. Hudgins (eds) *Psychodrama with Trauma Survivors: Acting Out your Pain.* London and Philadelphia: Jessica Kingsley Publishers.

Hudgins, M.K., Drucker, K. and Metcalf, K. (2000) 'The containing double to prevent uncontrolled regression with PTSD: A preliminary report.' *The British Journal of Psychodrama and Sociodrama 15*, 1, 58–77.

Jung, C.G. (1965) *Memories, Dreams, Reflection.* London: Collins and Routledge and Kegan Paul.

Lewis, P. (1993) *Creative Transformation: The Healing Power of the Arts.* Wilmette, IL: Chiron Publications.

Moreno, J. L. (1944) *The Theatre for Spontaneity, Psychodrama Monograph, No.4.* New York: Beacon House.

Moreno, J. L. (1980) *Psychodrama: First Volume, 6th edn. New York: Beacon House.*

Toscani, M.F. and Hudgins, M.K. (1996) *Trauma Survivors Intrapsychic Role Atom* (monograph). Charlottesville, VA: Therapeutic Spiral International Charity.

Winnicott, D.W. (1965) *Maturational Process and the Facilitating Environment: Studies in the Theory of Emotional Development.* New York: International Universities Press.

Part III
Action Methods
and Child Maltreatment

The Use of Action Methods in the Treatment of the Attachment Difficulties of Long-Term Fostered and Adopted Children

Paul Holmes

Introduction

Sarah and David had always wanted a family but the doctors had told them, after a number of years of treatment, that they would never have their own, natural, children. The social worker was very encouraging and said that Jenny and Roy (by now aged eleven and six) had been very well behaved in their present foster family (the fourth since they were removed three years previously from their mother's care as the result of her chronic neglect). The social worker said that he was sure that both the children would settle well and thrive in the care of Sarah and David.

Initially life appeared fairly calm in the household but, after a year or so, Jenny's increasingly demanding behaviour (associated with stealing from her parents) became very trying. The problems were made worse by Jenny's inability to accept any responsibility for the tensions at home and the war of attrition she seemed always to be fighting with Sarah. Life at home was always dramatic and full of action; one row led to the next. Jenny slammed doors and shouted. At night she appeared to suffer nightmares, talking in her sleep or lying awake huddled under the duvet. However, much to Sarah's frustration, Jenny would not be comforted and always denied that she had bad dreams.

To add to the stresses on this family Roy was suspended from school on several occasions because of his aggressive behaviour in the playground. Roy however would accept physical comfort from Sarah and David but Jenny never allowed either of her adoptive parents to touch her even when she was upset or distressed. Sarah and David felt very dispirited and undermined by their children. They knew that, for all their good intentions and hard work, they were failing to successfully parent Jenny and Roy. After one particularly stormy (and at times violent) weekend they felt at their wits' end and thought; 'so maybe our love isn't enough'. Sarah found her feelings towards Jenny turning to dislike and almost hate. On Sunday afternoon, after yet another of Jenny's tantrums, Sarah knew she was very close to hitting her daughter. On Monday morning she contacted the local social services' duty team. The meeting with the social worker resulted in the referral to the Attachment Project.

Is love enough?

Is the straightforward love and care of dedicated new parents such as David and Sarah (be they adoptive or long-term carers) enough to help troubled children such as Jenny and Roy? The experiences of many of these parents showed them that, however hard they tried, their children remained both disturbed and disturbing.

As long ago as 1950 the American psychologist Bruno Bettelheim published a book which addressed the fact that 'love is not enough' (Bettleheim 1950). His therapeutic regime provided help for emotionally damaged children within a residential setting. However, increasingly, the use of such resources has been frowned upon by child care experts. Indeed many very emotionally disturbed children, who had been taken into the care system, are now placed with parents such as Sarah and David. Until very recently, individuals or couples who offered to look after children were often told that the quality of their parenting and positive regard would be sufficient to heal the emotional wounds carried by these sad and often misused and abused young people. However these children continued to be distressed and very disruptive and many turned out almost to be 'home-breakers' as they behaved in ways that put their placement within their new family at risk.

Over the years this population of children have been offered therapeutic help through the use of various treatment techniques such as systemic family therapy and individual psychoanalytic or play therapy. However, the reports of their new parents have frequently indicated that these children remained as unhappy and difficult to live with as ever, any improvement in the therapy situation not generalising to home life. This chapter will discuss the use of therapeutic interventions using action methods with children living with either long-term foster parents or within adoptive families in order to attempt to resolve some of the underlying psychological and inter-personal difficulties that may exist in these placements.

Theoretical underpinnings

It has long been recognised that children whose earliest relationships were disrupted (and who may have been through the care system) often show a much greater level of emotional and behavioural disturbance than do their peers (Richardson and Joughin 2000). This, of course, is not surprising as (more often than not) these children have been removed from their birth families because of the high levels of neglect and abuse they suffered at the hands of their parents. John Bowlby (a psychoanalyst working in London after the second world war) wrote cogently about the consequence on a child's development, and their ability to attach to other people, if there were difficulties in the relationship with their mother when they were an infant (see, for example, Bowlby 1979 and 1998). It is now recognised that such problems with their original care takers (usually their birth parents) may result in the child suffering long-term emotional damage which may significantly impact upon their ability to form secure and trusting relationships with other people in later life.

More recently a population of children have been identified who have significant problems in settling with their new parents *however positive the quality of care offered to them in their new families.* Such children are described as having 'attachment' difficulties or, if the problems are sufficiently severe, an attachment disorder (see for example Goldberg 2000).

It is a truism to say that every individual exists in relationship with other people (albeit, for some, these interactions may be distant and unsatisfactory and, for an unfortunate few, tormented and dangerous). From birth infants seek closeness (instigated through behaviours such as crying or smiling) with a care taker (usually initially the mother although fathers are also crucially important) in order to have their basic needs for food, warmth and protection met.

It is well known that these earliest relationships have a powerful formative consequence on the infant's developing psyche or inner psychological world and the style of their subsequent relationships (or attachments) to other people. Each individual produces their own 'internal working model' (see Jeremy Holmes 1993 for a discussion) which determines their patterns of relating throughout their life. In addition to physical behaviours (such as holding or feeding their child) the mother has, as an adult, complex emotions, reactions and thoughts about their child. It has also been shown that a mother's own style of attachment will influence the subsequent attachment style of her infant.

The infant however is perhaps much more overtly a being of action with alternating periods of activity (crying, feeding, shitting) and, when distressed, may reach high levels of physiological arousal (turning bright red with a fast beating heart). It is now argued that these physical states impact on the infant's still developing brain, physiological and emotional states being closely inter-linked.

The mother's response to the infant in a state of high arousal and distress will vary; most mothers will react to their baby with intuitive warmth and appropriate behaviours (such as holding and cuddling their child and making comforting and soothing noises). Other mothers, unfortunately, may be less attuned to their baby's complex needs. They might be physically or emotionally absent or (worse still) might actively intrude emotionally upon their child or even assault it. Children with such experiences will fail to develop an internal working model in their mind in which physical and emotional distress can be resolved in the context of an intimate relationship (or bond) with another person. Indeed their inner world of object relationships will be full of danger and tantalising excitement (see, for example, Paul Holmes 1992).

Authors from the psychoanalytic tradition (in which historically the focus was on the inner world of the individual patient rather than their external, social, context) describe in their literature how such experiences in infancy lead to potentially life-long difficulties in an adult's style of relating to other people. Such disturbances in relating, if the level of dysfunction is severe enough, may result in an individual as being diagnosed (by psychiatrist and therapists) as suffering from a condition such as a borderline or narcissistic personality disorder (see Fonagy *et al.* 1995).

Attachment theorists have taken a somewhat different line and have focused more on the manner in which an individual (be this a child or an adult) relates to other people. There is, however, a clear relationship between the 'inner world' described by psychoanalysts and the individual's consequent style of relating to other people. Those who research into the nature of relationships have observed that a number of different attachment patterns exist in children (each a consequence of the different ways in which care-takers may respond and interact with the infant). Four clear categories have been described (see Howe *et al.* 1999). The first three result in fairly stable styles of relating to other people (which continue into adult life as an individual's 'personality'). These are:

Secure attachments

Children with secure attachments know that their care-takers will recognise their needs and distress and will respond to them unconditionally and appropriately. These children grow up to be adults who can form secure and stable relationships with their partners and other people. Such individuals are also able to act in a reflective and autonomous manner in the world.

Avoidant attachments

Children with avoidant attachments experienced as infants that their relationship and intimacy seeking behaviours (crying, demanding, smiling) resulted in the care-taker becoming agitated or less emotionally available to them. These children thus began to develop strategies and emotional defence systems in which they withdrew and found ways to look after their own emotional needs. As adults such individuals may tend to dismiss the importance of intimate and trusting relationships and may be resistant to experiencing strong emotions. However, once stirred, very powerful feelings may emerge. In psychoanalytic terms individuals at the extreme of this personality type might be considered to have narcissistic difficulties.

Ambivalent attachments

Children with ambivalent attachments had care takers who were unreliable, inconsistent or insensitive to their child's needs. As infants they developed maladaptive strategies to gain the attention from their carers needed to secure their fundamental survival. These children's behaviour became suffused with anger and was often very demanding and whinging. Such strategies may be successful in gaining the attention of parents but often resulted in the child having a low sense of self-worth and an inability to develop a fully autonomous sense of self. In adult life this group of people will seek relationships but will remain uncertain and confused about intimacy and remain preoccupied and emotionally entangled with other people (having failed to achieve secure, trusting autonomy). It is likely that, in severe cases, such individuals might be considered to have rather neurotic personalities as adults.

The children in the fourth category of attachment style have suffered much more distress as infants and often more overt neglect and abuse.

Disorganised attachments

Children with disorganised attachments have had even more confused and traumatic experiences as infants and have failed to make any consistent relationships with their primary care taker who (in addition to being unable to calm and reassure their child) may have been the actual perpetrator of terrifying experiences. As adults these individuals remain distressed and often overtly disturbed having a significantly higher level of psychiatric problems (especially those associated with anxiety) and significant disturbances of their personality structure such that a diagnosis of a borderline personality disorder might be appropriate. This group of individuals also show, as adults, an increase in delinquent, violent and criminal behaviour.

Reactive Attachment Disorders

It is the population of children with disorganised patterns of attachment who most commonly become the focus of concern when they are placed in new families. I should stress, however, that similar problems may also be exhibited by a child who remains within its birth family if its earliest experiences were sufficiently negative. Such children, as I have indicated, may now be described as suffering from a reactive attachment disorder. Their behaviour is categorised by an inability to trust others (with resulting constant battles for control). The underlying anger of these individuals is often expressed through violent or destructive behaviour and difficulties in developing intimacy (demonstrated by features such as poor eye contact, lying and a willingness only to be touched on their terms). Living with these children is a very challenging experience as the child's provocative behaviour may uncover and release long-standing, but normally controlled, difficulties both within the carers' own personalities and in their relationship with each other.

Classical therapeutic interventions with attachment-disturbed children

The parents of these children often (not surprisingly) go to professionals seeking help for their children and some respite from the day to day trauma of living with a child (or sometimes more children) who will not accept normal parenting or intimacy. For reasons, not fully understood, it is often the adoptive mother, rather than the father, who suffers most from the child's provocative and ambivalent attacks on their parenting. Indeed, in my clinical experience, women in this situation often present in the clinic as distraught, full of rage and apparently incompetent in the role of a parent. It would seem that, at times, living with a child with an attachment disorder is, almost literally, maddening. Therapeutic approaches for children with attachment difficulties have involved individual, often psychoanalytic therapy for the child or family, usually systemic, therapy for all those currently living at home.

The parents' accounts of their reception by therapeutic teams (from child and adolescent mental health services) vary. Sometimes, no doubt following the theoretical underpinning of systemic family therapy, the problems are attributed to the quality of parenting offered by the adoptive couple. They are given the message that dysfunctional families (by implication 'poor parenting in the here-and-now') result in troubled and 'symptomatic' children. Understandably the parents tend to feel very undermined by such an assessment: after all, they are doing their best to care for these difficult children.

Other therapists, perhaps following a more psychoanalytic model, do understand that the child's problems related to dynamics within the child's own psyche and the 'emotional baggage' they have brought with them into their new family. However the individual therapy provided (with its emphasis on the child-therapist relationship) often leaves the adoptive parents feeling very cut-off from the therapeutic process, the more so if the child begins to form a good relationship with the therapist but remains a nightmare to live with at home.

Action methods with attachment disordered children

Whilst these interventions may sometimes be efficacious, the new parents of this population of children often report little change in the child's behaviour or relationships. It is also now clear that, especially for abuse or neglect in infancy, the psychic 'record' of these events are held in the child as a 'body memory' in which words cannot be used to describe the history. These past experiences, nonetheless, still strongly influence the individual's behaviour. Such memories cannot be easily accessed through 'talking therapies' but may reach consciousness and be explored through the use of action methods. Such therapeutic interventions also facilitate the exploration of 'iconic' and 'echoic' memories in which complex traumatic events, occurring over time, are recalled by the individual as a *single* image or sound rather than by a more factual recall of events (see van der Kolk *et al.* 1996).

Therapeutic methods have therefore been developed (initially in the United States and subsequently here) that attempt, in a much more active and action orientated way, to address the underlying difficulties within these children and their families. Such therapy focuses on the issues of the child's style of attachment and history of trauma in the context of their present important relationships; i.e. within the context of their present, new, family (Welch 1989 or Hughes 1998). These methods became known to British parents with attachment disturbed adopted children who began to look for such help from therapists in this country. The approach I have been involved in developing (initially with my colleagues at Family Futures in London and more recently with the staff of the Attachment Project in Brighton) represents a response to the needs of these families.

Multi-systemic attachment focused therapy

It has become clear however that the problems that occur in families with long-term fostered or adoptive children cannot be attributed entirely to the 'emotional baggage' brought into the family by these children. Indeed the psychological problems within an individual can be seen as having their aetiology in one (or more) inter-connecting systems. These can be conceptualised as existing within the organic substrate (e.g. genetic or biochemical disorders), via intra-psychic and inter-psychic (family) systemic dysfunctions, to problems in social systems. These may include organisational and financial difficulties that may exist in schools or the wider community (Holmes 1989). In summary the areas of concern involved in a multi-systemic attachment assessment are:

- Factors within the child (often 'emotional baggage' brought into the new family but also problems associated with constitutional or genetic conditions such as ADHD, Attention Deficit Hyperactivity Disorder).

- Factors in the carers (both as individuals and as a parenting couple). Issues such as the quality and style of the parents' own childhood and their experiences of loss (such as infertility) will impact on their relationships with their adopted child.

- Factors in the 'here-and-now' relationships between the members of the family. Such factors will involve the ability to set caring and appropriate boundaries on the child's behaviour and conflict resolution skills.

- External contextual factors (such as the dynamics within the child's school or the local social services department).

Assessment

The Attachment Project initially undertakes an assessment on children referred for treatment that looks at all these areas, as therapeutic interventions may need to be made in more than one of these systems (see Holmes 1989). The team, together with the family, agree a treatment plan in hope that some of the areas of concern highlighted in the assessment can be addressed in therapy.

Treatment

The treatment process attempts to address issues at different systemic levels ranging from the social (by, for example, attempting to improve the child's support systems in school) to the intra-psychic with the family experiencing intense cathartic moments which will perhaps make shifts in the child's psycho-physiological systems. Therapy may (over a period of time) involve offering the parents individual or marital therapy sessions (to address problems conceived as lying, mostly, within the carers or their relationship with each other). Further, the psychiatrist in the team might recommend (for a child with ADHD) that there be a trial of a drug such as methylphenidate (Ritalin). The therapeutic components of these styles of treatment are well described in an extensive literature and I will not expand upon them in this chapter.

Action methods in intensive attachment focused therapy

In this chapter I will focus on two areas of intervention, which might be categorised as the 'narrative' and 'cathartic' components of the treatment, in which action techniques are used to address the child's history and emotional difficulties in the context of their present family relationships. The therapeutic work described in this account took place over two days (each of about five hours) of 'intensive' treatment two weeks apart. In addition Sarah and David had meetings with the members of the team. There were also three further days of 'intensive' treatment spread over a total of three months. Thereafter the family were offered a few shorter meetings to provide a degree of on-going support and follow-up.

First action-orientated session

Sarah and David and their children, Jenny and Roy arrived at the clinic for their first day of intensive therapy in a rather stressed state. Jenny had been very difficult that morning and had said that 'no way' was she coming to the session (although she had agreed to do so during the Project's initial assessment period with the family). Sarah had tried to encourage Jenny but had been kicked and punched. Meanwhile Roy had locked himself in the bathroom and initially refused to come out.

The Attachment Project team (on that day consisting of Barbara, Larry and Sheila) welcomed the family, provided them with coffee and soft drinks and sat down to talk about how life had been in the family over the three weeks since they had last met. David started by describing the problems the family had experienced that morning. Jenny cut across her father's account and said that she had been in a fight at school. Roy sat and sulked. The team felt rather dispirited but reminded the family that it had been agreed that, during the day's session, they would work on the children's time-line.

The team then laid out on the floor of the large group room a large U of plain paper three foot wide and almost thirty foot long. The family assisted with the task (or to be more accurate the parents did whilst the children sat and watched). Sheila explained that the aim was to use the paper to record the important events in the children's lives. She suggested that to start with the children might draw pictures on the paper of all the various houses they had lived in during their lives; Jenny's first home being at one end of the sheet and their present home at the other end.

Roy said, 'We live with Sarah and David now. Can I put our house on?' 'Yes, of course,' said Barbara. Roy then knelt on the floor and drew a picture of his home. Larry marked a date, 2001, by the house. He said, 'So this point is now, 2001, but where should we start this line?' There was silence, then Sarah said, 'Well why not with Jenny's birth, that's one place to start.' Barbara, who was sitting close to Jenny on cushions, said, 'Well Jenny, do you know where you were born?' Jenny looked rather tense but muttered under her breath, 'Hastings.' Sheila asked, 'In a hospital or at home?' Jenny replied, 'I don't know.'

Larry then consulted the detailed chronology the team had prepared before the session from the children's old case notes (which had been borrowed from the social services department in Hastings). 'It says here that you were born in a hospital, perhaps you could draw a picture of the hospital at one end of the paper.' Jenny, encouraged by Sarah, got down onto the floor and drew a sketch of a building on one end of the paper. Larry went over and added a date, 1990, the year Jenny was born.

Barbara asked, 'Roy, do you know where you were born?' Jenny answered, 'I know, he was born at home, I remember Mum saying that he came so quickly, they couldn't get an ambulance. So he was born on Mum's bed.' Barbara said,

'So, Jenny, could you draw a picture of that house?' Jenny looked tense and moved to sit by the wall of the room. Roy jumped up, 'I'll draw it.' Jenny looked on, her face was clouded and she began to suck her thumb. Sarah went to sit next to her and was pushed away. Sarah let her be as she knew from experience that, when in this sort of mood, Jenny would always rebuff support and could become very angry if any attempt was made to touch or cuddle her.

It was clear that something about that house distressed Jenny, indeed both her parents and the team knew that it was there that she had been abused by Roy's father, Don. However the details of her experiences were unknown. Over the next two hours the family, assisted and encouraged by the team, were able to draw pictures on the time-line of the various places the children had lived from their births to the present day. The houses included the three homes Jenny had lived in with her mother. In the last of these houses they had been joined by Don, Jenny's new step-father. It was in this house that her brother was born and it was from this home that the children were removed by the police and the social workers and taken into care.

The children were also able to draw pictures of the four foster homes they had been placed in before they were adopted by Sarah and David. There was an argument over the details of the foster homes. Sarah thought that the children had been in only two foster placements. Jenny was adamant, 'No, it was four. We've forgotten Debby and Matt. It was Matt who thumped me. He got into trouble with the social. Good, I didn't like him.' The parents looked surprised, they had never been told about this episode by their social worker. However Jenny was clearly upset by it. Roy added, 'I liked Debby, she had a nice dog, Rover. I was fed up with Jenny when we had to move. I missed Rover. It was all Jenny's fault.' Slowly, as the day progressed, the family were able to create a clear account of the children's lives from birth to the present, each home (eight in all) being named and added to the time-line.

The family looked pleased (if a bit tired). It had not been an easy day. The team and the family agreed to meet the family again for another day in order to explore further the children's time-lines.

NARRATIVE ISSUES

It is now clear that having a well-formed 'narrative coherence' of one's life is an important factor in psychological well-being and stability. Indeed the Adult Attachment Interview developed by Mary Main (Main 1995) uses an individual's style of telling their story (their personal narrative) as a key indicator to their style of attachment in relationships.

One of the tasks of an individual therapist is to bring some coherence to a patient's understanding of their past. Jeremy Holmes (2001) argues that there is a 'factual' version of one's life story (which he likens to 'prose') and a more 'poetic' account which can be, it may be argued, changed during therapy in a way that can empower the individual and resolve some emotional problems. Such a process occurs, for example, when a psychodrama moves from a protagonist's sense of factual reality into the realms of 'surplus reality' during a therapeutic session (Moreno, Blomkvist and Rutzel 2000). Michael White describes a similar creative use of narrative in his style of family therapy (White and Epston 1990). However it is important to note that a narrative of an individual's life is also held within the social context. For many of us knowledge of our past is shared with family members (parents, aunts, uncles, siblings and our own children) and recorded in family photo albums and videos. Such shared knowledge is used to re-enforce, support (or at times correct) the more personal 'narrative' held within an individual's mind.

Children living in substitute families often have a confused and incoherent memory of their own histories, in part because the trauma may have occurred when they were very young or because they have repressed or 'forgotten' crucial aspects or events in their lives. This problem, common for many adopted children, is beautifully described in P. D. James' novel *Innocent Blood*. The author describes the painful attempt of a young woman, adopted in childhood, to discover and unravel the facts of her past and make sense of its impact on her present life. Adopted children often do not have a shared understanding of their complicated personal histories with their new family (and in particular with their adoptive parents). Indeed there may not even be a common narrative of the family's history shared between their birth siblings.

Action attachment therapy addresses the issue of a child's (or children's) history both within their family of origin and subsequently. The staff of the Attachment Project make, often heroic, efforts to obtain the old social services files for the period prior to the child's reception into care and adoption. This therapeutic work is undertaken in the context of family sessions with their new parents.

The next session

The mood was lighter when the team met the family again (about two weeks later). Somehow the effort of drawing the various homes and naming the people (birth family and foster carers) with whom they had lived seemed to have calmed the children. Barbara then started the session by saying, 'Let's get your time-lines out again and visit some of these houses.' The paper record was carefully unfolded and laid out on the floor of the therapy room. The children looked at it and Jenny started to suck her thumb.

Barbara suggested, to start with, that the children walked from house to house, along the paper time-line, accompanied by their parents. Clearly, Roy was not present in the first two homes. However he watched as Jenny stood on the drawing and Larry said, 'This is the hospital you were born in.' Jenny looked at her mother. Sarah said, 'I wish I'd been there when you were born.' Jenny smiled for almost the first time that day and allowed Sarah to approach and to put her arm around her. This positive moment didn't last long and Jenny pulled herself away from her adoptive mother's arm.

Sheila then said, 'Let's move onto your first home.' Jenny then moved on to her first real 'home' drawn on the time-line. Sheila added (having checked the chronology), 'The papers say you lived here with your Mum and her boyfriend, Bob, for about a year, then you and your Mum moved to stay with your Nan when you were four.' Jenny moved across to the drawing of her next home and said, without prompting, 'I miss my Nan, she was nice, but she died.' Sheila then asked Jenny if she would like to select one of the soft toys in the room to represent her Nan. Jenny chose a cuddly brown teddy bear and placed it, on the time-line, in her Nan's home. Roy then said, 'Can I get Rover?' Larry said he could and Roy selected a toy dog from the pile of soft animals and puppets and placed it in the house drawn on the line to represent the home of their foster carers, Matt and Debby.

Sheila then suggested that the children should name the people with whom they had lived in each of the homes. As they listed the people Sheila wrote the names on pieces of paper and placed them by each drawing of a house on the time-line. The children were then asked to select more toys or puppets to represent the most important of these people. Jenny selected a dragon for Roy's father, Don, and a rather battered rag doll for her mother. Roy agreed, when asked, that the dragon could be used to represent his father and the doll their mother. Slowly the dramatis personae of the drama of these children's lives were being brought into the room and placed in the right place on the time-line. Sheila asked Jenny about her own father. She said, 'I don't know. I knew Mum's boyfriend before Don, he was Jerry, but he wasn't my dad. Jerry used to hit my Mum when he was drunk.'

The team knew, from the social work notes, that Jenny had been conceived when her mother, still a teenager at school, was raped by a casual friend. Until the Attachment Project became involved with this family, Sarah and David had only been told that Jenny's father was 'unknown'. The true facts had been discussed with them in one of the preparatory meetings with Larry and Barbara. It had been agreed, amongst the adults, that Jenny was too young and her emotional state too fragile, for her to be told the true story. The adults decided that, when doing the life-line, Jenny would be told that her mother 'didn't know her father very well' and that 'he had not been nice' to her mother.

Jenny selected a small wire figure to represent her birth father. She placed it on the drawing of the hospital. Suddenly, without warning, she jumped on the figure saying, 'I hate you, you weren't nice to my Mum. I hate you!' Sarah and David looked on in amazement. They had never heard Jenny mention her birth father let alone express any feelings about him. Sarah approached Jenny again and once more the child allowed her adoptive mother to hold her briefly.

Sheila then asked the children, accompanied by their adoptive parents Sarah and David, to walk along the time-line and to stand for a moment in each house. They started at the hospital and Roy joined them when they reached the house in which he had been born. They continued through the four foster placements until they all stood on the drawing of the family's present home. Barbara then said, 'Now do that again and see if you can find, in your mind's eye, one nice object or memory you can take from each of these places.' Jenny said, 'But I can't remember the hospital.' 'Well,' said Barbara, 'Just imagine what nice object you might take from a hospital.' Jenny smiled and said, 'I'll take a baby's dummy.' With this she stuck her thumb in her mouth. Jenny then moved onto her Nan's home where she decided to take her Nan's cat, Fluffy. Jenny was then asked to move onto the drawing of the house her mother had shared with Don and where Roy had been born. Jenny suddenly looked very tense and said, 'I don't like this house. It scares me.' Barbara asked her why. Jenny replied, 'I hated Don…he…' She then stepped off the time-line and sat against the wall. She allowed her mother to move close to her but refused to be touched. Sheila asked Jenny why she was so fearful of that house. Jenny didn't respond but Sarah said, 'We all know, Jenny, Don wasn't very nice to you.' Jenny added with passion, 'And Mum was always drunk. I hated that house.'

Children are often 'haunted' by their memories of abusive experiences which reappear in their dreams and nightmares. Further, the dramas of their past are often re-enacted (usually without any conscious planning) in their relationships with those who care for them. 'Ghost busting' is one way to explain the tasks of therapy to a fearful and traumatised child.

Larry then suggested that Roy should step onto the house on the time-line as he had been born there. Roy did as he was asked but looked rather confused.

Larry said, 'I know it's difficult, you were only a baby then.' Roy nodded in agreement and looked at his adoptive father. Larry continued, 'Do you know why Jenny was so upset in this house?' Roy nodded but still looked and then said, 'The social worker came and took us away, Mum was always drunk.' Jenny then added from her seat against the wall, 'And Don abused me.' The children were then supported to continue the exercise, moving from house to house, until they reached the drawing of their present home with Sarah and David. They were asked again to think of one positive object associated with this home. Jenny mentioned her duvet cover adding, 'It's warm under that. I feel safe.' Roy said he liked the family's dog.

It was apparent to the team that there was real emotional energy associated with two of the houses drawn on the time-line: the home the children had lived in with their mother and Don, and the foster home with Debby and Matt. There was a discussion about which of these two periods of time to explore further in the session. The family agreed that it perhaps made more sense to focus on the home with the children's birth mother and Don.

Jenny and Roy were asked if they could draw a large image of their Mum and Don. Jenny looked worried, but with the help of Barbara she drew a large outline of her mother whilst Roy looked on. She said she couldn't draw Don, but was able to tell Barbara that Don was 'Big and ugly, he had big hands and spots. I hate him.' Barbara drew a large image with these characteristics. The family were then asked if they would like to write letters to these two people expressing their thoughts and feelings about what had gone on in that house. Sarah and David settled down to this task with Larry whilst Barbara worked with Jenny and Sheila supported Roy. After 20 minutes each of these three groups had prepared their letters.

The figures of Mum and Don were then stuck up on the wall of the therapy room and the family prepared (with the help of the team) to read their letters to the figures on the wall. Sarah and David's letters were straightforward. They expressed their anger with Don for abusing the children and their frustration towards Mum for not protecting her children from abuse. They also thanked Mum for giving them the opportunity to have two such nice children as Jenny and Roy as part of their family. Jenny looked bemused. She had never imagined that Sarah might be angry with Don on her behalf. She always feared that Sarah would blame her, Jenny, for the problems in the family. Roy's letters were very also clear. He said that he missed his Mum but that he didn't like it when she had been drunk. He said that he would like to see Don again.

Jenny said she couldn't read her letters out loud in the session but agreed, after some coaxing, that Barbara could read them out on her behalf. Her letter to Don stated that she hoped that he would 'really suffer' for what he had done to her and expressed frustration and anger to her mother at her inability to protect her. Larry noted Jenny's high level of tension and asked her if she would like to say more to Don about what he had done to her. Jenny agreed, rather to the surprise of her adoptive parents. 'Well,' said Larry. 'What about putting Don on trial for what he did?' 'How?' said Jenny. 'Well, we could make a court here, you'd be the judge, supported by Sarah and David, and Roy would get his say too.' Jenny looked a bit lost. Larry said, 'As judge you sit up high. Don's in the dock over there.' Larry pointed at Don's image stuck to the wall. 'And your parents and Roy are here to help you.'

Jenny, supported by Sarah, got onto a chair placed on a table facing Don's image on the wall. She sat there, a parent standing on either side of her and Roy sitting below her on the table swinging his legs. 'So,' said Larry, 'Let the trial begin. Usher, bring the prisoner up from the cells and read the charge sheet.' Sheila became the court usher. 'The court will stand for Judge Jenny.' Everyone in the room stood as Jenny adjusted her position on her chair. The court usher continued: 'Don, you are charged with upsetting and abusing your young step-daughter Jenny. What do you say?' There was no response from Don's image on the wall. Sheila continued, 'Well, perhaps Judge Jenny, you should tell Don exactly what he did to you.'

Jenny looked a bit confused and worried but eventually said, 'You shouldn't have done that to me!' She then went on to detail some of the things her step-father had done to her. Sarah and David, standing close on either side of her, were amazed. They had often experienced Jenny's temper tantrums but they had never seen such focused rage. The team looked on. When Jenny paused Sheila said, 'And is there more?' Jenny said, 'Yes' and began to make disclosures of abuse that (as far as the team knew from the social services records) had never been made before. Suddenly Jenny burst into tears and jumped off the table. Sarah moved to comfort her. Jenny initially allowed her adoptive mother to comfort her but soon tried to push her away. 'Stay with it,' Barbara whispered into Sarah's ear. 'Move in closer,' Larry said to David, encouraging him to support his wife's attempt to comfort Jenny who was, by now, beginning to shake Sarah off. 'Leave me alone. I don't want you. I don't trust you. I don't need you.'

Larry encouraged Sarah to stay close to her daughter. Jenny struggled but Sarah put her arms around Jenny and said, 'I'm here, I'm not leaving you. I love you.' As Jenny continued to struggle David moved closer to support his wife whilst Barbara sat with Roy. 'Stay with her,' said David. Jenny tried to push her mother away but Sarah held on, trying to maintain eye contact with her child. David gently put his arm across Jenny's legs to stop her kicking her mother. Slowly Jenny calmed down and she allowed her father to wipe her forehead which had become hot and sweaty. 'That's good,' said Sarah, 'You don't have to fight us all the time. We love you and we know that really awful things have happened to you in the past. Now you are safe.'

It took time for Jenny to calm to a stage when Sarah felt she could let go of her daughter. The team watched, giving emotional (and if required) physical support to Sarah and David. They had been here before with other families and they knew how draining it was to attempt to allow a child a different resolution to an emotional crisis. In the past Jenny would have broken free, stormed and raged and (just as she had as a much smaller child) found her own, isolated, way to produce a fragile equilibrium. It was time she did it in the arms of adults who treated her with respect and whose trust she might (over time) begin to believe in.

Roy looked on in amazement. He snuggled up to Barbara. When it was clear that Sarah no longer needed her husband's support in holding Jenny, Sheila indicated that it might be an appropriate moment for David to hold and cuddle his son. So, tempers cooled and intimacy increased, the session came to a close. Eventually, after a final round of coffee and soft drinks, the family left the clinic. The team collapsed in the next room. Tomorrow they would be working with another family. However they knew that they would need to phone Sarah and David to find out how the day after this session had gone and to give the support the parents needed to care for their delightful but demanding (and controlling) children.

CATHARSIS

I have already described how, normally, a highly aroused infant (distressed, screaming, with an increased heart rate and flushed skin) may be calmed by the care and concern of an adult (usually a parent). Through a combination of touch (holding and rocking) and sound (soothing noises and talking) the mother is able to assist the child to reach a psycho-physiological equilibrium. During this time it is important that the mother makes eye contact with the child, thereby increasing the intimacy between them.

It seems probable that, as infants, children with a disorganised style of attachment never experienced this process. Indeed the adult who might have been expected to provide a relationship that would allow the child to calm down may often have been the same person who was actively causing the child to be fearful and distressed. Further trauma can be caused to the child's psyche when, perhaps later in their childhood, adults who are supposed to care and protect them, were actively abusive. The use of catharsis (or abreaction) in psychotherapy has often been seen as controversial and its use has been debated in psychotherapy since the beginning of the last century (see van der Kolk, McFarlane and Weisaeth 1996). Certainly the simple re-enactment of a traumatic event in therapy may simply retraumatise an individual leading to further psychological harm rather than relief.

In the session Jenny was clearly (and understandably) very distressed as the therapeutic process facilitated her ability to reconnect with memories of abuse (both cognitive and body) from her past. As Jenny made emotional contact with her past trauma she fell back into her well practised defence mechanisms, used since earliest childhood, of fighting off any support from the outside world. Such 'support' within her birth family had only resulted in further negative experiences. Initially Sarah's attempts to be close to her and calm her were unsuccessful as Jenny attempted, once more, to be 'alone'. However the session gave Jenny the possibility to resolve her high levels of psycho-physiological arousal (i.e. episodes of extreme rage or distress) within the context of a safe and caring relationship with her new parents.

The next day the team rang Sarah and David who said that, rather to their surprise, Jenny had been calm after the session and had even accepted a warm hug and a kiss before bed. Barbara warned Sarah that Jenny would become distressed again and would revert to her old methods of 'keeping herself safe'. Sarah said she knew this all too well adding that the family were looking forward to their next day of intensive therapy with the project.

Conclusions

In this chapter I hope that I have been able to give the reader the feel of how action methods may be used to work with children with disorganised attachments. Jenny (and to a lesser degree Roy) had developed a style of relating, which whilst understandable in the context of their history of neglect and abuse, was now deeply dysfunctional and cut across the attempts of their new parents to provide them with a trusting, creative and enjoyable family life.

I have only been able to touch upon the complex nature of this therapeutic work (with the associated issues of psychological theory and good clinical practice). However I trust that any reader inspired by this work will seek to make contact with and training from those teams, in this country and abroad, willing to take the emotional risks to develop this style of treatment.

Acknowledgements

The therapy described in this chapter is based upon the clinical work of the Attachment Project in Brighton and Hove. The Project is managed and funded by the three local statutory agencies (Health, Social Care, and Health and Education) with additional, time-limited, funding from the Department of Health.

I would like to thank the various families on whose real therapeutic journeys this imaginary account is based. The therapists too are a creation of my imagination. I would, however, like to thank my very real colleagues in the Attachment Project (Charlotte Savins, Felicity Aldridge, Kathy McCabe, Leslie Philbrick, Louise Bomber, Steve Warlow and Yvonne Black) for their dedication to developing action-orientated treatment for long-term fostered and adopted children and their families. The work of the Attachment Project is based on the work of our own therapeutic family of origin, the Family Futures Consortium in London (Alan Burnel, Christine Gordon and Jay Vaughan).

References

Bettelheim, B. (1950) *Love is not Enough.* New York: Avon Books.

Bowlby, J. (1979) *The Making and Breaking of Affectional Bonds.* London: Tavistock/Routledge.

Bowlby, J. (1998) *A Secure Base. Clinical Applications of Attachment Theory.* London: Routledge.

Cline, F.W. (1991) *Hope for High Risk and Rage Filled Children.* Evergreen, CO: PO Box 2380.

Cline, F.W. and Fay, J. (1990) *Parenting with Love and Logic.* Colorado Springs, CO: Pinon Press.

Fonagy, P., Steele, M., Steele, H. and Leigh, T. (1995) 'Maternal representations of attachment during pregnancy predict the organisation of infant-mother attachment at one year of age.' *Child Development 62,* 891–905.

Fonagy, P., Steele, M., Steele, H. and Leigh, T. (1995) 'Attachment, the Reflective Self and Borderline States: The Predictive Specificity of the Adult Attachment Interview and Pathological Development.' In S. Goldberg, R. Muir and J. Kerr (eds) *Attachment Theory: Social Developmental and Clinical Significance.* Hillsdale, NJ: Analytic Press.

Goldberg, S. (2000) *Attachment and Development.* London: Arnold.

Holmes, J. (1993) *John Bowlby and Attachment Theory.* London: Routledge.

Holmes, J. (2001) *The Search for the Secure Base. Attachment Theory and Psychotherapy.* London: Brunner-Routledge.

Holmes, P. (1989) 'Wheels within wheels and systems within systems. The assessment process.' *Children & Society 3:3,* 237–254.

Holmes, P. (1992) *The Inner World Outside. Object Relations Theory and Psychodrama.* London: Routledge.

Howe, D., Brandon, M., Hinings, D. and Schofield, G. (1999) *Attachment Theory, Child Maltreatment and Family Support.* London: Macmillan.

Hughes, D. (1998) *Building the Bonds of Attachment. Awakening Love in Deeply Troubled Children.* Northvale, NJ: Jason Aronson Inc.

James, P.D. (1980) *Innocent Blood.* London: Faber & Faber.

Main, M. (1995) 'Recent Studies in Attachment: Overview with Selected Implications for Clinical Work.' In S. Goldberg, R. Muir and J. Kerr (eds) *Attachment Theory: Social Developmental and Clinical Significance.* Hillsdale, NJ: Analytic Press.

Moreno, Z., Blomkvist, L. D. and Rutzel, R. (2000) *Psychodrama, Surplus Reality and the Art of Healing.* London: Routledge.

National Institute of Clinical Excellence (2000) *Technology Appraisal Guidance No. 13. Guidance on the Use of Methylphenidate for Attention Deficit/Hyperactivity Disorder (ADHD) in Childhood.* London: National Institute of Clinical Excellence.

Richardson, J. and Joughin, C. (2000) *The Mental Health of Looked After Children.* London: Gaskell (The Royal College of Psychiatrists).

Van der Kolk, B.A., McFarlane, A.C. and Weisaeth, L. (1996) *Traumatic Stress. The Effects of Overwhelming Experience on Mind, Body and Society.* London and New York: The Guildford Press.

Welch, M.G. (1989) *Holding Time.* New York: Fireside Books.

White, M. and Epston, D. (1990) *Narrative Means to Therapeutic Ends.* New York: Norton.

CHAPTER 12

The Yellow Brick Road

Helping Children and Adolescents to Recover a Coherent Story following Abusive Family Experiences. Facilitated Contact with Birth Parents using the Therapeutic Spiral Model™

Chip Chimera

The universal desire for home was famously expressed in Frank L. Baum's *The Wizard of Oz*. The scarecrow with no brains could not understand why Dorothy would want to return to dull Kansas – but as she memorably explained to him, however attractive the rest of the world might seem, 'There is no place like home.'

Introduction

Professionals working to help children heal in the aftermath of abusive family experiences face a number of paradoxes. Frequently children believe that professionals can have no brain at all if they do not understand how good it was at home and how much they long to go back. This chapter addresses work with children who have been severely traumatised by the abusive behaviour of their parents towards them, then removed from those parents into substitute care. It considers the issues surrounding decisions regarding contact with birth parents where there is no plan for reunification. Facilitated contact is used for this. Facilitated contact is distinguished from observed contact in that it requires direct and active therapeutic involvement with the family. Clear aims and objectives are set out for facilitation. It is child-centred. Parents and other adults must be made aware of the purposes of the contact and it is always undertaken with the consent of the parties.

A broad systemic framework is adopted within which attachment theory informs practice. The use of action methods, particularly the Therapeutic Spiral

Model™ (TSM) (Hudgins 1999 and 2000) enables children to reconnect with past experiences in a way that corrects past wrongs and enables the growth of self-worth and self-esteem within a safe environment. This model enhances the healing process and guards against retraumatisation. The contact is facilitated by a therapist who is active and directive whilst allowing conscious choice for the participants at each step of the process.

The nature of the issue

As a professional working with children separated from their families of origin, I am often struck by the degree of loyalty that exists from the children to those families. Even where children have undergone terrible and destructive attacks and acts of abuse, they frequently long to return to 'that grey place' hoping the family they left has magically transformed and will be a good and nurturing place for them. Children may express anger with their parents and state that they wish never to return to them. However, this anger is often found to mask a deeper longing for the same parents to rescue them and return them to an idealised future. This was the case with five-year-old Tony who consistently stated he never wanted to go back to his drug abusing and suicidal mother. When he saw her after a gap of five months however, Tony was full of questions as to where she lived, what it was like, who else was there, how had she got here, etc. Such questions indicate the child's preoccupation with the parent. Although they may be angry, they are anything but disengaged.

Separated children often find it difficult to accept alternative parenting (Department of Health 1991). Child care professionals are all too familiar with children who have experienced multiple breakdowns of adoption and fostering placements. Often the remedy is 'more of the same failed solution' (Watzlawick *et al.* 1964, p.32). Another family is found, contact with the birth family is further reduced because the child is upset by it. There is a belief that the child should be kept as far from the parent as possible.

In many of the situations in which I am asked to intervene, parents and social workers have become polarised. Frequently parents carry the diagnosis of personality disorder and are therefore considered by mainstream mental health professionals as incapable of change. Often there have been months and years of battle. Nevertheless the child remains attached to their parent. It can be difficult for child care workers to understand that even where the attachment is anxious, it is still an attachment (for a more detailed discussion of patterns of attachment see Holmes, this volume). In these situations facilitated therapeutic contact can help the child to a more positive relationship with their parent, whilst at the same time promoting a realistic experience of the parent's limitations and strengths.

Research on contact following separation and long-term alternative placement is somewhat sparse and inconclusive. Quinton *et al.* (1997) have reviewed the research available. They conclude that:

> The data from samples of children in long-term foster or residential care show no systematic relationships between contact and placement breakdown, children's emotional or behavioural development or their intellectual attainment. The evidence suggests that contact arrangements can work amicably in the placement of younger children, but there are no studies of contact and its effects in adolescence. (p.402–403)

This research also indicates that whether or not contact takes place seems to be more dependent on the beliefs of the workers involved with the child as to whether or not it is advisable (Quinton *et al.* 1997).

The purpose of facilitated therapeutic contact

Facilitated contact is only undertaken with the agreement of all parties. In order for facilitated contact to be effective, the contact facilitator should gain a thorough understanding of the quality of the child's attachments to his or her original significant carers. This information is gained from the historical record, from conversations with the parent, with the child's current carers, and if appropriate, with the child himself or herself.

It is also essential to understand the child's current social, emotional, educational and developmental functioning. The child's current context must be supportive. The support of current carers and other professionals who understand the importance of the original relationship to the child and the potential impact on the child of facilitated contact being established is essential.

Dimensions of facilitated contact

A number of writers have suggested frameworks for assessing whether or not contact is viable (see for example, Baker 1995; Black 1995). I have found the following five dimensions of contact are helpful in assessing appropriateness or not of undertaking this work. They overlap each other and have issues in common. Each will be examined in turn:

1.   continuity of relationships that are important to the child

2.   providing experiences that extend the child

3.   improving self-worth and self-esteem

4.   re-evaluating information and correcting distortions in the child's perception

5.   reparation of past harmful events.

1. Continuity of relationships that are important to the child

Research (Quinton *et al.* 1997) has shown consistently that children's relationships with significant family members endure in the mind of the child. Where attachments have been made the significance endures for the child, even in anxious attachments of all categories: ambivalent, avoidant and disorganised (Howe 1995). It is rare that a child has made no attachment to at least one of its parents or parental figures. Sometimes an older sibling or another member of the family or network fulfils the parental function and is the child's primary attachment figure.

Narrative approaches (Byng-Hall 1995; White 1989) indicate that we all make sense of the world through the stories that develop from our experience in relationship with others. Human beings are concerned with ascribing meanings to events. Understanding and making sense of where one comes from has an impact on the person's sense of themselves in the world in relation to others and to their continuing sense of personal history. It is through relationships that our sense of ourselves in the world becomes established. Some child care professionals operate the 'begonia theory' of child placement (Paul Holmes, personal communication). That is that children can, like house plants, be transplanted from one pot (family) to another and, given the right soil conditions and temperature, will thrive and grow regardless of the pot they have come from. In fact, the opposite is true and family of origin material is carried with the child internally into their new placement. Where possible the continuity of important relationships should be encouraged where it is of value to the child.

2. Providing experiences that extend the child

Children who are removed under conflictual conditions are often stuck in the past. Positive 'here and now' experiences can enable the child to begin to move forward again. Therapeutic contact can enable more developmentally and age appropriate relationships to begin to take shape with the original attachment figure. It is important to understand the parents' own experience of being parented and their attitude to the parenting they received. The attitude will indicate whether a replicative or a reparative script is in operation (Byng-Hall 1995). Each will require a different approach by the contact facilitator.

In a replicative script the same pattern of interaction is carried down through the generations. For instance, 'my father used to give us a good hiding and it did me good.' Here the parent has internalised the belief system of the previous generation and therefore feels justified in perpetuating abusive practices. A great deal of work needs to be done with these parents to examine the belief system and raise consciousness as to the harm the experiences actually did cause the parents as children. Where replicative scripts are in operation parents have usually identified with their own abuser(s).

A reparative script is the opposite: 'It was awful being hit every night and I'm going to make sure that doesn't happen to my children.' Such parents are caught up in their own experience and may not see the needs of the child. Boundaries are often very blurred and the abuse that occurs is more likely to be emotional than physical. Readers are encouraged to see Byng-Hall (1995) for a full discussion of these patterns and their connection with attachment theory.

3. Improving self-worth and self-esteem

There are at least three elements to this. First, it is common for children to believe that somehow they deserved the ill treatment they received from their parent, that somehow they were just too bad, too sexy or too stupid. Therefore, the parents had no choice but to abuse them. Professional healers need to be very careful here about the attributions of blame to the abusers. It can be important just to sit with the child's discomfort in feeling that they are a bad object and deserving of abuse. If the corrective message 'it is not your fault' is offered too early the child may form the opinion that the helper does not understand. This can shut down the telling of the story. Sometimes the child believes that they have sacrificed themselves to protect other children in the family. The facilitator and other professionals may be holding information about abuse of other children that is not known to the child.

Facilitated contact with a parent who has been a perpetrator of abuse or acted as an 'abandoning authority' (Hudgins 1999) who can begin to take responsibility for their actions, conveys the message to the child that they are seen as having value and are worthy of care. This in itself contributes to the child forming a different more positive picture of himself or herself.

A second aspect of this increase in self-worth could be the process involved in the parents' efforts to achieve contact with the child. Where parents have had to use legal processes and have persevered, often over a period of years, to gain contact, the child can begin to see themselves as a valued person in the eyes of the parent.

There is of course the opposite side to such perseverance. Sometimes parents' efforts are in order to retain control over the child or to ensure their continued silence or for some other reason that primarily meets the need of the parent. This underlines the need for a thorough assessment prior to beginning this task. Third, the provision of 'quality time' with a significant attachment figure can in itself promote and enhance self-esteem.

4. Re-evaluating information and correcting distortions in the child's perception

This includes the child's view of the parent as well as their view of themselves in the abusive system. There is a significant overlap with the previous category. The accurate labelling (Hudgins 1999 and 2000) of abusive experiences and the explanation of the parent regarding how they could fail to protect the child is a significant part of the healing process. In these situations, facilitated contact can become highly therapeutic for both the child and the parent, bearing in mind that the child is always the primary focus for therapeutic input. This is illustrated in the case below where Karen's mother's main motivation was to apologise to her daughter for not believing her older sibling who said that sexual abuse was taking place.

As stated above, children often internalise responsibility for the abuse and view themselves as unlovable and unworthy of protection. Facilitated contact can expand the picture and widen the focus to other aspects of the family functioning. This can relieve the child of the responsibility for their own abuse and allow them to develop a more realistic picture. Here is where the change in meaning takes place regarding what happened and how harmful events could develop.

5. Reparation of past harmful events

Where conditions are favourable and the parent has been able to acknowledge their responsibility, skilled facilitation can help with healing hurts from the past and righting the wrongs to the child. If parents are able to support the child to examine the painful and almost unsayable experiences that they have endured and help them to understand that what happened was wrong, a number of therapeutic effects can follow.

First, fear can be transformed into righteous anger. Often children feel angry but also believe they are not entitled to their anger. As stated earlier they may believe that they caused the abuse. In these situations anger may be acted out through delinquency, aggression, self-harm, addictions, etc. Allowing the child to express righteous anger involves the following:

- The acknowledgement that one has been wronged, incorporating an acceptance of this on a deep level, sometimes for the first time.

- The acceptance of one's right to be angry about the abuse. Abused children are frequently additionally punished for showing angry feelings. Therefore angry feelings can be suppressed, leading to depression, or acting out in a generalised, almost habitual way. The child may acquire the label of having 'behavioural difficulties.'

- The acknowledgement by significant others of the child's right to be angry. Often it is the acceptance by the parent of the child's righteous anger that can begin to free the child from the trap of destructive behaviour.

- Additionally, the witnessing of the child's pain and the recognition of the child's truth by the parent enhances the healing process and can strengthen the positive aspects of the bond between them. Indeed, narrative approaches privilege the importance of witnessing by significant others as a crucial part of the change process (Freeman *et al.* 1997).

- Finally, the taking of appropriate authority by the parent and the *genuine* apology to the child for the hurt they have suffered can be therapeutic for both the parent and the child. Often the parent is able to voice previously unacknowledged guilt.

It is predictable that old patterns of responsibility for the parent by the child can reappear at this stage. The contact facilitator must keep awareness of the need to keep the best interests of the child as paramount at all times. It may be that the process motivates the parents to seek therapeutic help in their own right. However, clear boundaries must be maintained and the process must privilege the therapeutic needs of the child.

The approach

A framework guided by a systemic family therapy approach allows the whole picture and multiple perspectives to be taken into account. In what follows the TSM is applied to specific case material. The narratives of each of the protagonists, and the beliefs and meanings they have attached to events, is identified and explored. The TSM is used to provide a safe method in which a story can be explored and changed.

Background

The family members' names and significant details have been changed to protect confidentiality. Karen was 12 when I was asked to undertake an assessment for the court regarding the mother's application for contact. There had been a gap of five years since the last parental contact. Karen had been removed from her mother's care along with her younger sister Gloria and older sister Sammy when Karen was just four years old. When Karen was four years old Sammy disclosed sexual abuse perpetrated by Luke, mother's partner of two years and Gloria's father. At the time of the abuse Karen was four, Gloria six months, Sammy and Gerry were 10 years old. Gerry and Sammy are dizygotic twins who were 10 when Sammy disclosed Luke was abusing her. Gerry was received into care briefly during the original crisis. He was returned home after several weeks in care and remained there with his mother.

The mother, Charlotte, did not believe Sammy's disclosure. She made and broke agreements with the social services department regarding Luke's contact with the children and visits to the home. There were numerous child protection conferences and family assessments. Still the mother allowed Luke back into the household against the advice and knowledge of the social worker. Eventually the local authority decided to apply to the courts for care orders on the children. These were granted and the children were permanently removed. Because of the ages of Karen and Gloria it was decided that adoption was the most appropriate course of action.

The two girls had different characters. During the time they were in foster care Karen displayed 'disturbed behaviour.' She was withdrawn, seemed unhappy, became easily angered and lashed out. She engaged in some sexually explicit behaviour. Although she never made a disclosure, professionals assumed that she, like Sammy, had been sexually abused. Karen's last contact with her mother was at age five. A meeting was arranged at which the mother said her final goodbyes to Karen and Gloria. Karen and Gloria were then also

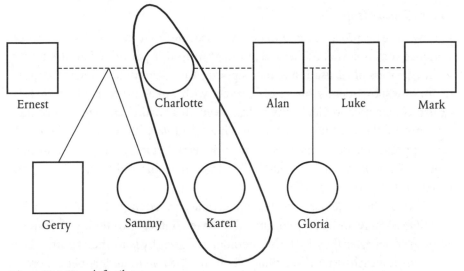

Figure 12.1 Karen's family tree

separated. Gloria was considered the more 'adoptable' child. Karen remained in a foster placement for further assessment and preparation for a permanent family.

Unfortunately this placement broke down. I discovered during the assessment that Karen's experience in placement was that she felt blamed by the carers and continually compared to other children in the family in a negative way. She acquired the role of scapegoat. This was significant as Karen, while she had no memory of it, carried the role of scapegoat in her family of origin. In systemic terms this emphasises how disturbed patterns of attachment can accompany children and may be repeated in their new environments.

Eventually Karen was placed in a specialist unit that dealt specifically with children with disturbed behaviour. This was a therapeutic unit where a high proportion of the children were known to have been sexually abused. Sadly, this unit closed precipitately after several months for reasons that had nothing to do with Karen. However, it was another disruption and a third severance from care figures, further confirming Karen's view of herself as bad and undeserving of love. Fortunately for Karen, she found herself in the care of highly skilled foster carers. This couple was able to understand Karen's complicated behaviour as an expression of her early experience and were able to help her manage her difficult and confused feelings. After many difficulties the placement settled and remained stable for two and a half years before the assessment.

Wider Systems Issues

Following care proceedings Luke was prosecuted. He received a seven-year sentence for his sexual abuse of Sammy. During this period, Charlotte underwent a process of realisation and acceptance that Sammy had been telling the truth. She subsequently broke off contact with Luke and formed a new relationship. Sammy and Gerry, the twins, meanwhile had been placed with their biological father and his new family. They lived very close to the mother. As they approached adolescence Sammy and Gerry began to drift home to their mother. Eventually the local authority sanctioned this and their return to the maternal home became official.

This is where the narrative becomes somewhat strange. Throughout all of this time Sammy and Gerry continued to have contact with their two younger siblings, even after they had said 'permanent' goodbyes to their mother. The twins visited each sister three times per year. They were under specific orders from the social worker as to what they could and could not say regarding the mother and what they could bring from home. Whilst it was possible to regulate presents and photographs from home, the rule about what could be said was, of course, unenforceable and uncontrollable. Like the 'Good Witch of the North' the twins kept the idea of home alive just by their presence, and kept the connection, although tenuously, between Karen and her mother.

Over the years the social worker became the 'Wicked Witch of the West' in the mind of the family. The family saw her as putting continual obstacles in the way of direct contact. Every Christmas card and every birthday card from the mother or other family members was opened and vetted by the social worker. She decided unilaterally what presents were appropriate and inappropriate. Unlike the Wicked Witch of the West in Dorothy's story, the social worker had the best of intentions, the protection of Karen.

The social services department had formed such a negative view of the mother, based on their dealings with her at the time of care proceedings, that they mistrusted all of her motives. They were mindful that Karen had not yet told her story of abuse, in spite of many hours of therapy during her placements. They saw the mother's attempt at contact as an attempt to continue Karen's silence and to further control her. The social worker wanted to hide the fact of the mother's application for contact from Karen for fear it would unsettle her and undermine her placement. Eventually the mother heard from the twins that Karen had expressed a wish to see her. This motivated Charlotte to apply for contact. Her contact application was opposed by the local authority. I was asked to undertake an independent assessment, the result of which was a court order for three facilitated contact sessions per year for two years.

Getting ready for the journey

When planning the sessions the current context of both Karen and her mother needed to be considered. Contextual issues included the mother's current situation and readiness to do the work, the foster carers' attitude and approach, and the influence of the other professionals via the statutory child care review. Charlotte's narrative at this time in her life contained a strong description of herself as a bad mother. She had long concluded that she should have believed Sammy about the abuse and that Luke had fooled her. She blamed herself for the break-up of the family. She felt the strong wish to apologise to Karen: 'I just want to tell her I'm sorry.' She was not exactly sure what she was sorry for, or where her responsibility began and ended. She did not know what, if anything, had happened to Karen. She both feared that Karen had suffered abuse and wanted her to tell her story and at the same time dreaded hearing her fears confirmed. She wanted to reconnect with her daughter.

Karen's narrative contained a great deal of confusion. She was unsure about why things happened when they did. Her story lacked coherence and was full of 'don't knows' and uncertainties. Karen had blocked out most memories of her early childhood, even positive ones. Karen's one certainty was that she wanted to see her mother and for them to be able to talk. She wanted her mother to accept her but feared what the mother would think of her. This meant she was hesitant in openly expressing or exploring her feelings. She tended to hide her feelings, even from herself. She was at once protective of and angry with her mother. The combination of fear and concern on both their parts led to therapeutic impasse. Neither of them could progress for fear of what the other would think or do.

Karen and Charlotte shared a family characteristic of having few words for feelings (McDougall 1986). They were strikingly similar in this respect in spite of being separated for most of Karen's life and Karen having been with highly articulate carers. 'Good', 'bad', 'sad', 'angry', and 'weird' were the extent of their feeling vocabulary. Action techniques are used with people functioning within a wide range of intellectual ability. For this family the visual images involved at each step of the way through the action expanded their understanding and deepened their experience.

Along the Yellow Brick Road – the clinical structure of the Therapeutic Spiral Model™ (TSM) and the progress of therapeutic contact

Sessions occurred at approximately four-monthly intervals. Before each session the therapist contacted the foster carer, with Karen's knowledge, to discuss how Karen had prepared for the session and what the current issues in her life might be. Karen was fortunate in that her foster carers were supportive of contact and saw it as part of their role to help Karen prepare for and debrief from the sessions. It is essential that someone known and trusted by the child takes on this role. Charlotte was also contacted. For the first sessions this took the form of a telephone call. Later, it became important for the therapist and the mother to meet before the contact. The preparation of Karen, Charlotte and the therapist is the equivalent of the warm-up in psychodrama. It is an essential part of the process and took place not more than 24 hours before the session itself. The TSM typically uses coloured scarves and decorated cards to concretise strengths, defences and traumas. The model was developed specifically to work with trauma material in a safe manner and prevent uncontrolled regression. This was a response to traditional psychodrama practices that can take people into their trauma material without having previously identified the protagonist's positive coping skills. The concretisation of strengths and their actual physical presence in the therapeutic space is crucial to this method as it increases protagonist safety and gives the therapist very powerful tools to help when the trauma material becomes active.

Session one – reconnecting

Karen had very few childhood memories. Action techniques were used to help recover positive and neutral/non-abusive memories. This was a gentle session exploring shared memories of place and time: a cloud motif carpet, a disabled and kind neighbour, a memory of a picnic with grandfather. Both mother and daughter chose coloured scarves that represented different family members. They explained their choice of colour to each other, enabling them to deepen their understanding of a shared past and recover buried memories.

Both were able to choose scarves to represent themselves and identify their own feelings. The session contained many moments of fun and laughter. Toward the end of the session the mother and daughter were able to identify their mutual wish for the whole story to unfold. Karen agreed she would write down as much of her story as she could remember. This would form the basis of our work in the next session.

This session had been a positive one for Karen. It reawakened hope that issues could be resolved. Previously Karen had been in individual therapy with another therapist. She had not discussed her abuse and had stopped the therapy a few months prior to this session saying that although she liked the therapist she 'just sat there and didn't do anything.' Following this session Karen decided to recommence her individual therapy. She had started on her journey to find 'home' and, like Dorothy, was collecting allies on the way.

Session two — four months later

This session was anticlimactic. Unfortunately, in the intervening months, the mother's life underwent huge turmoil. The second session was spent processing this with Karen and her mother. Karen had been warmed up to exploring her story further with her mother and was clearly disappointed at the change in emphasis. Karen had fulfilled her commitment to prepare a written account of her memories specifically for this session. Due to the change in emphasis these notes were not used but were marked for use in the next session. Although she was angry with her mother for the change in focus, she was unable to express the anger. True to the family script, she put her needs aside to accommodate her mother. As we were to discover later, Karen had no belief that her needs would be met or even acknowledged. Following the session she destroyed the notes she had carefully prepared for it. She continued to use her individual therapy and her carers for support, but was unable fully to share her experience.

The family and Karen's carers agreed to allow a maximum of four hours for the third session. Given the family's style of communicating, this time was necessary to ensure they could end with their strengths intact, a basic tenet of the TSM. Before the session I met with the mother to ensure her support for Karen. I also liaised with Karen's carers and made telephone contact with Karen herself. This warm-up became the pattern for subsequent sessions.

Session three — clinical structure of the TSM

The third session followed the three distinct parts of the TSM. Stage one is the identification of strengths. The mother and daughter chose cards to represent an inner strength they could acknowledge in themselves. This made it possible for them to enter different and more positive self-descriptions. Often at this stage clients report they have never been asked concretely to think about how their inner qualities have helped them. The concretisation of strengths is an essential part of doing this work in a safe and non-retraumatising way. This family had been saturated with negative self-descriptions for many years.

To represent their inner strengths the mother chose a dolphin, the daughter a horse. They were then asked to choose different cards to represent their healthy selves, the part that brought them to the session and wanted to heal. The mother chose the eagle goddess, representing renewal and accuracy of sight. The daughter chose the winged horse, Pegasus, representing instinct, wisdom and imagination. As the therapist, I also chose cards to represent these two aspects, so that my strength and positive wish to do the work were concretely represented in the room.

The identification of strengths is essential for the work to proceed. Clients who are stuck in negative self-descriptions may need a number of sessions before they are ready to confront traumatic material. In this method, trauma material is not entered into until strengths are identified and concretised. They placed the cards in the room as observers. The strengths they represent are thus available as needed during the session. Fears were also concretised in a mountain lion (mother) and a snake (daughter). Clinical judgement deemed it inappropriate for the therapist to concretise fear on this occasion.

Stage two continues to build safety. The family and therapist form a circle of coloured scarves to represent the strengths and safety needed to support the work. The emphasis is on externalisation of three sources of strength: intra-personal (inner qualities), inter-personal (important relationships) and transpersonal (those that connect the client with a higher power, or nature – something experienced as larger than themselves). Scarves lend themselves to this activity because they are pliant and colourful. However, other materials can be used, e.g. soft toys or drawings.

The strengths present for Karen and Charlotte were commitment, determination, confidentiality, righteous anger, seriousness, humour, love, courage, trust and relationship with carers. When the circle is complete the action can commence within it.

In the third stage the story is enacted. This can take many forms. Karen and her mother constructed a time-line, using cards depicting scenes from childhood and fairy tales. The first step is to create the whole of the line. Karen and Charlotte were able to work together to construct Karen's time-line from her birth to the present day. It is essential that the session ends in the present, where strengths and coping mechanisms are at their most powerful. Karen's time-line included the following significant events: birth; moving house; father leaving; the birth of the younger sibling; moving again; Sammy's disclosure;

Karen's abuse; social workers coming; investigations, chaos and confusion; the children going into care; the move to foster care; the move to the adoptive placement; adoptive placement breakdown; move to current foster placement; reconnecting with mother and birth family; present day.

Mother and daughter began to 'walk through' and put details into their under-developed story. Revisiting ordinary events of everyday life before the abuse was in itself a healing experience. Karen learned that she was a wanted child and that the pregnancy and her birth had been planned. The backdrop to the abuse was Karen's definition as a 'naughty' child, always in trouble. During the early part of the session, the mother was able to reframe Karen's behaviour as cheeky, mischievous and inquisitive, rather than 'bad'. Charlotte was able to help Karen remember several incidents with warmth, affection and humour. Karen also learned of her part in Sammy's disclosure. Unfortunately, it was following Sammy's disclosure that Karen experienced her own abuse. She was able to begin to talk about the circumstances that led to her abuse, which had occurred when her mother was in the house. She explained through her tears how the abuser silenced her.

Charlotte was able to express appropriate anger and was supportive to Karen, relieving Karen of guilt and expressing her own regret and sadness for not believing. The subsequent traumas of removal, foster care and adoptive placement were also visited and marked for further work. The session ended in the present. Karen chose a card showing children dancing around a maypole, representing the family being back in touch with each other and a significant emotional contact having been re-established. As the relationship between the two strengthened, ordinary contact, unsupervised, was reinstated. Planned facilitated contact continued during the two years and gave space for the two to work on their relationship, deepen mutual understanding and acceptance.

Conclusion

Over the months Karen came to develop a more realistic view of her mother. Karen's earlier ideas about going home to live gave way to a deeper appreciation for her foster home as a place where her needs were being met and would continue to be met. During the course of the facilitated contact, she was able to reconnect with the past in a positive and supportive way that enabled continued growth. Some of the damage done in the mother: daughter relationship through the mother's failure to protect her daughter was rectified. A deeper understanding and better bond was established between the two of them. At the final session both acknowledged the journey they had made together and that there was further work to do in the future. For the present they were simply able to enjoy each other's company, go shopping, exchange gossip and generally get on with real life, and for that they no longer had need of a facilitator.

To continue the *Wizard of Oz* metaphor, Dorothy was able to return to Kansas, not to stay, but as a visitor with a more realistic view of her previously idealised homelife. She was able to salvage something of the relationship with her mother that had been so devastated by sexual abuse. The work did not solve everything and both acknowledged a need for future work. It did enable Karen to live more fully in the present and use the resources available to her whilst connecting her to a wider context of family life. The work offered the mother and daughter a safe way to explore traumatic stories, regain lost parts of the family narrative and begin to create new stories of connection, survival and mutual concern.

References

Baker, T. (1995) 'What Constitutes Reasonable Contact?' In P. Reder and C. Lucey (eds) *Assessment of Parenting: Psychiatric and Psychological Contributions.* London: Routledge.

Baum, Frank L. (1994) (first published 1900) *The Wizard of Oz.* Harmondsworth, Middlesex: Puffin Books.

Black, D. (1995) 'Parents who have Killed their Partner.' In P. Reder and C. Lucey (eds) *Assessment of Parenting: Psychiatric and Psychological Contributions.* London: Routledge.

Byng-Hall, J. (1995) *Rewriting Family Scripts: Improvisation and Systems Change.* New York: The Guilford Press.

Department of Health (1991) *Patterns and Outcomes in Child Placement: Messages from Current Research and their Implications.* London: HMSO.

Freeman, J., Epston, D. and Lobovits, D. (1997) *Playful Approaches to Serious Problems: Narrative Therapy with Children and their Families.* New York and London: W.W. Norton.

Howe, D. (1995) *Attachment Theory for Social Work Practice.* London: Macmillan Press.

Hudgins, M.K. (1999) 'Experiential Psychodrama with Sexual Trauma.' In L.S. Greenberg, J.C. Watson and G. Leisure, (eds) *Handbook of Experiential Psychotherapy.* New York: Guilford Press.

Hudgins, M.K. (2000) 'The Therapeutic Spiral Model™: Clinical Psychodrama with Trauma.' In M.K. Hudgins and P.F. Kellerman (eds) *Psychodrama with Trauma Survivors: Acting Out Your Pain.* London: Jessica Kingsley Publishers.

McDougall, J. (1986) *Theatres of the Mind: Illusion and Truth on the Psychoanalytic Stage.* London: Free Association Books.

Quinton, D., Rushton, A., Dance, C. and Mayes, D. (1997) 'Contact between children placed away from home and their birth parents: research issues and evidence.' *Clinical Child Psychology and Psychiatry, 2*, 3, 393–413.

Watzlawick, P., Weakland, J.H. and Fisch, R. (1964) *Change: Principles of Problem Formation and Problem Resolution.* New York and London: W.W. Norton.

White, M. (1989) *Selected Papers.* Adelaide, Australia: Dulwich Centre Publications.

CHAPTER 13

Touch Me – No!

Creative Therapies with Young Sexually Abused Children

Christina Citron

Introduction

I am a child psychiatrist who uses action methods, including psychodrama, at a special Outpatient Child Psychiatric Clinic, Vasa, in Stockholm, Sweden. At the clinic we only treat children under the age of 18, and their families, who are in some way affected by child sexual abuse. I came across psychodrama by chance in 1976 when I attended a family therapy course at the Centre for Therapeutic Communication in London where psychodrama was also introduced. I felt that it was right for me and have since trained in psychodrama. At first I practised it with adult patients only, but from 1985 I led therapy groups with sexually abused teenage girls and did some small psychodrama vignettes with them. In time I developed it further and in recent years I have been encouraged by the Norwegian psychotherapist Aud Steinsbekk, who invited me to one of her psychodrama workshops with women who were sexually abused as children.

I found psychodrama increasingly useful in my groups with sexually abused teenage girls. Psychodrama gives them the opportunity to share the abusive situation in a very realistic but still safe and controlled way. We can work in the 'here and now' with what happened 'there and then' and help the victims to see the difference. Whilst in the drama the protagonist, the one whose drama is being enacted, works partly from her unconscious, which can help her come in contact with how it really was. The risk, however, is that she becomes overwhelmed and starts to dissociate. I have found it especially useful to let the protagonist mirror the scene. That means that she can look on while others are performing it for her. In that position it is usually much easier to come in contact with denied and repressed feelings and thoughts. She can also be empowered to say what she wishes would have happened in the re-enactment. This usually ends up with some kind of rescue scene that can be played out with the protagonist in different roles, sometimes as an adult helping herself as a child (with another group member playing the child). She may then replay this, with herself in the child role and another group member playing the rescuer. To be rescued by some important person in the child's life seems to be very healing. As director I take the action slowly, frequently checking with the protagonist in order not to lead her in a direction she is not ready for, and making sure that I respect her boundaries. These ideas fit very well with the theory of trauma therapy by the Norwegian psychologist Helen Johnsen Christie (1999). She underlines the importance of working with four key factors: reality, autonomy/control, affect and cognition.

Reality

The therapeutic intervention is to be a witness to the abuse. Having a whole group as witnesses is very powerful. The therapeutic effect is to remove the dreamlike, unrealistic sense of the abuse, which is so common amongst those who have been abused.

Autonomy/control

The therapeutic aim is to re-establish autonomy and sense of self and that is achieved by focusing on coping behaviours.

Affect

Trauma, and that includes most sexual abuse, causes the afflicted person to become overwhelmed by feelings that cannot be expressed at the time of the abuse. In therapy these sentiments can be recognised and expressed. Johnsen Christie states that therapy is to admit, share and contain feelings and the therapeutic effect is a broader affect tolerance. The group is of great help also in this respect. Usually the participants can help themselves by empathising with others and, eventually, with themselves.

Cognition

The fourth factor involves working on the understanding of abuse. The goal is to help the victim to think in a different way about the abuse. Usually the abused person has to realise how small and helpless she was at the time and how cheated and deceived she was by the calculating perpetrator.

The structure of the creative therapy groups

We have an increasing problem in Sweden with very young children who are suspected of having been sexually abused by their fathers. It is difficult for them to get any help. Since people usually benefit from meeting others who have experienced something difficult and similar I felt that it might be favourable to put these children together and let them share the pain and help one another in a structured way.

I use psychodrama as a model but instead of using personal role play I encourage the children to play through puppets. I feel that this gives them enough control to be able to work with their pain. It acts as a mirror or projection and is, therefore, an additional safety factor (Bannister 1997). I think that psychodrama is similar to child play therapy and it also has similarities to 'play together' therapy that is often practised with children and their care takers.

We started the first child group in the spring of 1995 and the last one ended in the spring of 2000. Altogether we have had four groups during these years each with four to six participants, in total 20 children. If the children had not had any individual therapy earlier they were given a short individual intervention at our clinic, usually by one of the group therapists. In all cases we had a meeting with each child and mother before the group started, usually by both psychotherapists. The aims and goals of the group were:

- to avoid future stigmatisation
- to counteract helplessness
- to counteract deviant sexual behaviour
- to encourage the expression of feelings, including feelings of betrayal by the abuser
- to give the children an opportunity to show or tell what happened to them
- to counteract secrecy, denial and repression
- to minimise the risk of further abuse.

It will be seen that these goals are compatible with the theory of Johnsen Christie. Reality is stressed as the children aim to 'show and tell' and to counteract secrecy. Autonomy and self-control are gained as they combat helplessness and abusive behaviour. Their affect is changed as they are enabled to express feelings, and their cognition is increased as they learn about important features in sexual abuse. For example they understand it was not their fault.

Therapists

My co-therapist in these groups for small children has always been a psychologist, although there have been two at different times.[20] There are several advantages in working with two therapists in the groups. With these small children it is even more important that there are two leaders in order to keep everything in frame. I have found it especially useful for there to be one male and one female therapist to give the children a good model of two adults of different sex working together in a safe atmosphere. Usually there has also been a concurrent group for the mothers. The therapists of the two groups have had close contact, exchanging information to be able to meet the needs of the children in a flexible way.

Group format

Each group met once a week, for 12 sessions. The first group had sessions lasting 90 minutes, which fitted in with the concurrent group for the mothers, but we found this to be too long for these small children and accordingly we changed it to 75 minutes in the subsequent groups. However, in our final group the children were only around four years old so we thought that 60 minutes would be more appropriate. The children in the other groups were five to seven years old (one had become eight years) with an age-span of not more than 13 months in each group. The groups were open to both boys and girls but we had wanted at least two of the same sex in every group. The first groups ended up with only girls but in the last group, with the smallest children, there were three boys and one girl. One more girl was prepared to participate but unfortunately her father, who also was her care taker, would not allow her to.

The room

The group room was quite big and had a large table with chairs for art work. A big basketwork chest served as a setting for dramas with dolls. The room was further equipped with mattresses, pillows, a boxing-ball, stuffed animals, puppets and anatomical dolls. We also introduced a group box in which the children's folders, story books and other group material could be stored.

The first group meeting
Gathering
We sat on cushions in a ring on the floor and at the first group meeting we presented ourselves by our first names. We rolled a ball or sent a stuffed animal chosen as a group mascot and the one who had the item said his or her name and sent it to someone else until we all knew the names. This was repeated at later meetings until we were familiar with the names. We asked if anyone knew why he or she was in the group. Nobody was able to answer. The therapist said that we have heard that everyone has been touched by an adult in an inappropriate way, for example in the bottom.

Recognition of feelings
We designed cards with faces expressing four basic emotions: angry, happy, sad and afraid-anxious. Every child took a card to show his or her current feeling.

Individual folders
The children were given folders in which to store therapeutic material, for example, art work and working sheets. At this first meeting they signed and decorated them using different pencils and crayons. Pens with glittering ink were very popular in one group.

Snacks
We usually served fruit syrup with biscuits or buns.

Rules
These were discussed during snack time and we reminded the group how many times we were going to meet. We talked about confidentiality – everyone was allowed to speak about him or herself but not about the others, outside the group. We asked that shoes were removed during group time and emphasised that no one was allowed to hurt anyone else.

Fairy tales
We talked about fairy tales and introduced the story of Nono, see below. If we had time we started reading this story.

Rhyme
A rhyme was presented at the end, see below.

The subsequent meetings

We always began by checking up on the situation of each child. The group mascot was passed to the child who was to speak next. We asked if something special had happened, if they were preoccupied by something and so forth. Then we brought out the 'feeling' cards and asked how the children were. This was followed by focused activity, for example, drama and drawing, and then there was a period of free play. We followed the snack break by a calm activity, which included drawing, or simply relaxation. The fairy tale came next and finally we had the rhyme.

After some experimenting we have found the above programme useful for the five to seven-year-old children. The younger ones were more anxious and needed to play and feel comfortable before the focused activity could start. With them we also introduced a 'No corner' where they could go if they did not want to participate in an activity. At the final group meeting we had a more elaborate snack that the children chose. They also received a written card with the group rhyme. One group finished just before Christmas and each child got a gift: a little ceramic seal looking like Nono in the fairy tale.

It will be seen that the structure of the group deliberately echoed not only our own aims and goals but also the therapeutic aims outlined by Johnsen Christie. The reality of the children's experiences was always kept in mind, and opportunities for giving them control were seized. We paid attention to their affect and tried to ensure that their cognition was increased.

Creative methods that we have used

Rhyme

I have written a simple rhyme, in Swedish of course, to strengthen the sense of the body and the boundaries of the child. Roughly translated this is:

> My body belongs to me
> Your body belongs to you
> If someone touches me
> When I don't want it
> I have the right to say
> NO!

It is performed with simple movements to emphasise the message. The children accepted it at once and they soon took turns in leading it. We encouraged the children to shout out the final 'NO'. They have also presented the rhyme outside the group in a creative way. One of the mothers, however, told us that her daughter was anxious because she could not say no. After hearing this we did a drama dealing with how difficult it can be to say no, although you have the right to do so. We stressed that you are always allowed to tell someone afterwards when you have been abused.

Fairy tales

We have used an American story about a little seal, Nono, whose babysitting uncle touched Nono's private parts, and how Nono reacted to that and finally solved the situation in a happy way. This story is written in English and comes with a tape with songs that makes it very useful for English-speaking children. (Patterson and Needham Krupp 1993). The story presents many opportunities for dealing with difficulties arising when a child is sexually abused. While we were reading, a little soft toy seal that looks just like Nono was passed around. It was interesting to see how the children treat the victim. Mostly they were very caring. We have also read a short version of *The Invisible Child* by Tove Jansson (1973). It is about a little girl, Nini, who has become invisible because of emotional abuse. Being recognised by the Mumin family, she becomes visible step by step as she shows her feelings and stands up for herself.

Drama

I am inspired by psychodrama, a well-known method invented by Dr J.L. Moreno early in the twentieth century. However I have adapted his work to make it more suitable for use with these very small children, so I just call it drama. As I have explained, instead of acting with people we used puppets, dolls and stuffed animals. To make it easier to show sexual assault some dolls are anatomical dolls.

The children sat in front of the chest that we used for the play and I, as the director, knelt down behind the chest. As the director I talked directly to the children or through a doll or puppet. I often chose a puppet called the 'secrecy bird', who has a big beak that can open widely saying something like: 'I love secrets. I eat them all up. Some secrets may give you tummy-ache but my stomach can stand it without any pain so you can give me your bad secrets.' The children are in general familiar with the secrecy bird after having met him at the assessment interview, but they are in this way reminded of the secrets he can handle. They often have ambivalent feelings towards the secrecy bird. Sometimes they are angry with him, tear him and even bite him and sometimes they just love him and caress him. One girl wanted to brush 'his teeth' after the bird had swallowed her story about oral insult.

The first time we introduce drama to the group we may start with me doing a scene with a child doll talking with the secrecy bird and wondering about something that has made him or her feel uncomfortable. I ask, 'What has happened to the doll?' We change the story according to the response from the group but we always underline the right to tell. After that we invite the children to show us their own dramas about what has happened to them.

Every participant of the group is given an opportunity of re-enacting a drama about the abuse to which he or she has been exposed. The child who is chosen to do a drama goes behind the chest, picks the dolls and sets the scene. The child describes the room or place and everyone can imagine it. The child decides what is going to happen and gets assistance from me, my co-therapist and the other children to perform the drama. As a director I am active in promoting the drama, asking questions and providing ideas.

Most of the children in the groups have done a drama about their abuse, but in the group with the smallest children only one managed to do it. This one boy climbed onto the chest himself and sat, like a little doll, telling us what his father had done to him. Children who did not tell their own stories took part in the enactments of others but did not perform themselves.

Examples of dramas

Example 1

A five-year-old girl, who was said to be abused by her father before the age of three, insisted that she wanted to do a drama. She had not spoken about it for a very long time but was acting out sexually. We were unsure about how much she remembered. She was also still seeing her father who denied any abuse. She chose animal puppets: a duck and a fox. I had the fox. The girl told me in the role of the fox to kiss the duck in the bottom several times. The girl was handling the duck and she said 'no' and insisted that despite this the act was repeated many times. As the fox, I added that the girl must not tell anyone. As a director, I then asked what the duck should do. The girl asked for the 'secrecy bird' (handled by my co-therapist) to help her. She told the bird what had happened and wanted him to tell the police, who should capture the fox. As the fox, I said to the police (played by a monkey puppet, in uniform, handled by another child) that I had not done anything, but the group audience supported the story of the duck. The police took the fox away and the girl was very pleased with the ending.

It is possible that this drama could have been a fantasy version of the mother's story of the abuse. That is contradicted, however, by the way the girl shows how useless it is to say no. Furthermore it is peculiar that the girl in a later meeting with her mother and ourselves could not even remember that she had done the drama. My opinion is that the girl worked from her unconscious and was in close contact with her trauma. It is likely that she had only iconic memories of the abuse because it was committed at such an early age (Schore 1994). In fact this is very similar to a case described by Terr (1988) where a four-year-old boy, who apparently had no memory of early documented sexual abuse, played out a scene from a pornographic video, which he had been shown by the perpetrator.

The question is, how can the girl benefit from the drama? If there is a risk of dissociation it is very important to allow the protagonist to remove herself from the play and let her mirror the scene, to look at it while others present it. She is then aware of what happens, can have control and direct the drama from a distance. However, at that time I did not realise that the girl was dissociated.

Example 2

A girl in another group demonstrated with the anatomical dolls how she had a bath at her father's home. Her father helped her and nothing untoward happened during the bath. Afterwards she sat naked under a cover in a bed and watched the television. She showed with the 'daddy doll' how the father, who was dressed, laid down beside her. He put his hand under the cover up along her legs to her sexual parts where he moved his fingers up and down. She said 'no' without any effect. I asked her what the 'little girl' did then. She said she concentrated on the children's programme on the television. I confirmed how difficult it was for the little girl and suggested that she should change the ending of the story to something that she wished had happened. The girl finished the drama by letting her mother come to take care of the 'little girl'. She showed the mother and the little girl, now dressed, walking away holding hands. Then the little girl asked the mother to promise that the father should never have the opportunity to touch her like that again.

Commentary

We used 'surplus reality' scenes (Moreno 1993) frequently in the dramas, allowing protagonists to complete these in ways that reflected their wishes about how things should have been. This gives hope, shows that children have rights and strengthens the child. They often showed themselves being comforted by a supportive person, usually the mother.

The children also benefit from playing the mother's role and develop their own comforting competence by taking care of the hurt one. During enactments the other children usually became very involved, said what they thought and sometimes involved themselves in the drama that the director structured according to the therapeutic goals and the protagonist's wishes. We avoided having the children in abuser roles except, perhaps, for a short time to show what had happened. Very often the child chose to put the perpetrator in jail and made sure he was watched carefully as he was keen on cheating. The 'police doll' was of great help in many dramas.

We have also performed dramas of more pedagogic value. A group leader played a scene to which all children could contribute their comments and ideas. For example, we did a scene about a girl meeting her father because we had been told that one of the girls was worried about that. I just presented a basic scene and put a lot of questions to the audience and then demonstrated different situations according to the responses. Does the girl want to see her father alone and if so where? Does she want to be hugged or kissed? Does she want to sit in his lap? If a touch feels wrong, can the child say or do anything? It is important to emphasise the right to say 'no' but also to remind children that it sometimes does not work. We always remind children that they are allowed to say something afterwards if something untoward has happened. A very effective intervention is to allow the daddy doll to whisper something inaudibly and ask what he might be saying. The girl who was worried about seeing her father suggested: 'Don't call mammy!' and 'Make sure that no other person will be with us!'

Other themes have been brought in by the group directly or have been addressed because they are well-known dilemmas. The leader can, for example, with the help of a puppet, ask the group if it is apparent that he/she has been molested and whether there is something wrong with him/her and whether it is his/her fault. We also distinguish between disgusting actions and the self being disgusting. Drama is also well adapted for sexual education. For example it is much easier to allow a doll to talk about masturbation and to explain that sexual touch can also feel good.

The dramatisation facilitates the expression of thoughts and feelings and the children often say spontaneously what has happened to them, or say 'My father didn't do that.' The children seem to feel very relieved after the catharsis of their own drama. I think, though, that it is important not only to repeat what has happened but also to put another dimension to it. The surplus reality scene gives some kind of resolution, and makes for a satisfactory closure. It gives a child some control; they understand that they are allowed to speak about it. That gives them hope for the future. We have not seen any contamination between the children, either in the stories of sexual abuse or in the way they wish to have contact with their fathers. The 'resolutions' are, however, more alike.

Play

We use ordinary children's games to allow the children to move around when they need that. In one group we moved like trolls and fairies to music from *Peer Gynt* by Grieg. We developed an ordinary 'catch' game into a 'wolf game', where one member chases and catches the others, the lambs. The wolf can have a 'wolf puppet' to accentuate the role and when the nose of the wolf touches a lamb it 'freezes' with the legs a little apart. The lamb comes to life again if another child manages to creep between her feet. While doing this, the wolf must not attack. At the beginning we had just one free zone but the children developed two free zones where the lambs could rest. The children may be very cautious, at first, but in time they become brave and dare to tease the wolf or find many ways to cheat and escape. Usually one of the group leaders starts off being the wolf. With the smallest children we had to be very careful, even making the wolf go to sleep, so as not to frighten them. All but the smallest children enjoyed being the wolf. We have seen many wolf styles! One girl seemed to be intoxicated just like her father was when abusing her. The relevance of the metaphor had not escaped her.

On one occasion the wolf play developed into a spontaneous drama about a wolf mother and her cubs. They arranged a den and the whole group curled up there. I covered myself in a piece of cloth, and presented myself as the 'monster wolf father' and tip-toed around the den, now and then touching the legs of the young ones. The children were told to shout 'no' to the monster who then withdrew for a while. Also the wolf mother was encouraged to help. The children were enthusiastic about this improvised drama and after that the therapists initiated the play and asked the children to lie on the floor in a star form with their heads in the centre and the wolf circling round, now and then touching someone's legs. How the children react to this helps us to understand how each child reacts differently. It has been evident that the children are very different in their ability to say or shout 'no' but in the group they can practise using their voices.

We have also actively asked the children to fantasise about being an animal and to play out that animal's characteristics so the others can guess who they are. We ask the child what enemies does the animal have and how can she escape them? One therapist plays the enemy and the child develops her tactics against the dangerous animal. We also made some time for free play. Some children enjoyed boxing with a boxing ball. They expressed anger by putting significant animals or dolls on the top of the boxing ball and hitting it until they fell down. By playing and moving around they felt the joy of involving the whole body, which I also think is important for children, especially if they have been abused.

Art

The children's capacity and wish to draw and paint have differed greatly. Except for the very small children most of them have depicted their families in their drawings. They are encouraged to paint whatever they want. They have never been asked to draw the abuse but two have done so spontaneously. In one group we made a composite group painting where everyone, including the therapists, made a self-portrait. The group also added a picture of the secrecy bird and the group mascot spontaneously. The group painting was put up on the wall at every meeting.

With the smallest children we made a group painting by drawing the contours of their hands and then everyone painted the hands with patterns and colours. In the group with the oldest children we had them relax and imagine where in the body they felt sorrow, happiness, anger, fear and disgust. We then helped them to do a contour of their bodies on a large sheet of paper and then they filled in the feelings in the colours they wanted. This exercise should be done with care so that no child feels violated by the person who is drawing round her. To help the smallest children to understand that the group therapy was about to end, we made a calendar when there were four meetings remaining to the closure. Every group meeting was represented by an empty square where the therapists drew what had happened during the group meeting. This can, of course, be done from the beginning and with older children, who also can help to decorate the calendar.

Discussion

The girls in one of our groups took part in a large investigation carried out at the University of Linköping, where a researcher examined the effects of psychotherapy on sexually abused children but the results are not yet forthcoming. The children have been very keen to attend the meetings and their attendance has been very high, over 90 per cent, although two girls had to end the group prematurely because they moved from the Stockholm area.

According to the mothers the children enjoyed the group therapy and they have, in general, reported a decrease in the symptoms of the children. We ourselves have also seen favourable development in most of the children. Sometimes a symptom has returned or become worse during the therapy. Usually we have understood the reason and have been able to deal with it in the group. For instance, some of the children have, against their will, been made to see their fathers and this has caused some problems.

The mothers have also told us that the children have become more frank and happy. Many children have dared to tell others what has happened to them. We think that is a good sign that the children do not feel so helpless and that we have managed to counteract secrecy, denial and repression according to our goals. Furthermore the sexual acting out has diminished. Some of the children have needed more individual psychotherapy or some other kind of support even after the group.

Finkelhor and Browne (1985) have pointed out four factors which may lead to negative psychosocial effects on the child after sexual abuse: betrayal, stigmatisation, powerlessness and traumatic sexualisation. We used these factors to assist us in formulating our goals for the group and we feel that the goals were achieved, as discussed below.

Betrayal

Of course these small children are betrayed by their fathers whom they assume will protect them but who in fact abuse them. They are seldom betrayed directly by their mothers and other adults to the same extent that abused teenagers often are. In our groups all mothers but one have believed their children and fought for them. Nevertheless the children have probably missed a protecting mother during the abuse. In the rescue scenes they have played out their indignation about the betrayal by their fathers, by punishing them. They have also played out the wish for an ever understanding and protecting mother.

Stigmatisation

This seems to diminish simply by meeting others who have been abused. Already after the first meeting one girl told her mother in the waiting room: 'Mama, they all looked normal!' The feelings of difference had gone. The feeling of isolation is also removed and this is a well known effect in all group psychotherapy (Yalom 1975). We have directly addressed questions about guilt and shame in the dramas and in the fairy tales. We have also emphasised self-esteem and the recognition of different feelings, especially the right to be angry with the abuser. This may help to remove feelings of guilt.

Powerlessness

This has been counteracted as we have underlined each child's right to his/her own body and to his/her own feelings. The child has the right to say 'no' and to tell if someone has in any way hurt the child or not respected him/her. The secrecy looses its grip. The rhyme, which is repeated at each session, also has the effect of increasing personal power and control.

Traumatic sexualisation

Many of the children have shown signs of traumatic sexualisation by overtly sexualised behaviour but that has vanished or diminished during the therapy. They have been able to deal openly with what has happened, to understand that it is not their fault and to feel empathy with their inner vulnerable child. The sexual education, where we show clear limits but also accept sensations of sexual pleasure, may also have helped to diminish sexual acting out.

Final comment

Spontaneity and creativity are crucial elements in Moreno's theories of healthy functioning (Moreno 1993). These factors have often been impaired by the abuse and consequently many children have lost their ability to play in a creative way. I think this ability has been repaired for many children in the groups. To make that possible we had well structured meetings and inside these boundaries the children were safe enough to enact psychodramas and to play without overwhelming anxiety.

Moreno was inspired by the play of children when he developed psychodrama. In this way Moreno's ideas have been brought back to the children. That seems logical. The circle is closed.

References

Bannister, A. (1997) *The Healing Drama: Psychodrama and Dramatherapy with Abused Children.* London and New York: Free Association Books.

Finkelhor, D. and Browne, A. (1985) 'The traumatic impact of child sexual abuse.' *American Journal of Orthopsychiatry 55,* 530–541.

Jansson, T. (1973) 'The Invisible Child.' In *Tales from Mumin Valley.* Harmondsworth: Puffin Books.

Johnsen Christie, H. (1999) *Training lecture: working with traumatised children and their parents in a child and adolescent psychiatric unit.* Ubi, Stockholm: Unpublished.

Moreno, J.L. (1993) *Who Shall Survive?: Foundations of Sociometry, Group Psychotherapy and Sociodrama.* Student Edition, McLean, VA: ASGPP.

Patterson, S. and Needham Krupp, M. (1993) *Nono and the Secret Touch.* Junior League of Nashville (INSERDC, Uniquity, PO Box 10, Galt. CA 95632).

Schore, A.N. (1994) *Affect Regulation and the Origin of the Self: The Neurobiology of Emotional Development.* Hillsdale, NJ and Hove: Laurence Erlbaum Associates.

Terr, L. (1988) 'What happens to early memories of trauma? A study of 20 children under age five at the time of documented traumatic events.' *Journal of the American Academy of Child and Adolescent Psychiatry 27,* 96–104.

Yalom, I. (1975) *The Theory and Practice of Group Psychotherapy.* New York: Basic Books.

Part IV
The Curtain Falls

CHAPTER 14

Resisting Change
What Stops Us Acting for Young People

Annie Huntington

No longer are we content to be the lawgiver and judge over them but rather someone that travels along with them… This is the fullness of any adult child relationship, an interchange of experience in which each draws something of inspiration from the other… (Hostler 1953, p.10)

Introductory comments

This chapter will explore some of the obstacles facing adults attempting to use action methods with young people[21] as I focus on separate, yet interconnected, layers that shape and influence the ways in which adults respond to young people's needs.[22] The chapter will draw on a range of material, for example research findings and theoretical frameworks, in order to highlight the importance of focusing on differing levels of analysis when thinking about what facilitates or inhibits adults in their use of action methods with young people. Specifically it will focus on:

- the impact of wider structuring systems that fundamentally shape the terrain for practice

- local social, community and organisational issues that frame interactions between young people and adults

- intra-psychic issues and inter-personal concerns as adults seek to (re)configure their relationships with, and ways of relating to, young people.

My approach to analysing and commenting on human experience rests on the adoption of a systematic[23] approach to understanding the world, which is clearly not new. Other writers have used this model to explore, examine and explain specific aspects of experience – for example, through the expression of an ecological approach to child development (Bronfenbrenner 1979). Central to this approach is a concern with the interface between individual experience and the social context that shapes, restricts or otherwise influences an individual's passage through his/her world. Otherwise stated, those adopting a systematic approach to understanding human experience focus on the interaction of the internal (psychological, emotional, intellectual, biological) and external (social, cultural, economic, political) world (e.g. Bettelheim 1950; Miller 1987a; 1987b; 1997).

A key variable evident when assessing contrasting descriptions and analysis of human experience, that might come under the 'systemic' umbrella, is the question of emphasis and the extent to which wider structuring systems, for example political, are accounted for when exploring and explaining individual and/or group experience. Differing explanations focus attention at different levels. This in turn influences the nature of proposed solutions to address individual or collective problems. For example, some approaches to work with families where sexual abuse was an issue drew on two traditions, systems theory and psychoanalytic practice (White 1997). These families were offered family therapy after abuse had been recognised as an issue. Unfortunately, some practitioners applied systemic thinking without taking account of the impact of wider structuring systems, in particular patriarchy, and the differential power relationships evident within families. The system was the family and the family was a bounded entity. Professionals working with families using this model attracted criticism because of this omission (Waldby *et al.* 1989). Re-interpretation and re-focusing of systems thinking for family therapy followed in the light of feminist critics of professional practice (e.g. Bentovim 1992).

In this instance a political discourse was influential in formulating a challenge to those whose work, rooted in the application of the pathogenic[24] medical model, was viewed by some as oppressive to children and women. Failure to take account of wider political issues left practitioners vulnerable to legitimate criticisms when intervening in family life where adult:child sexual contact had been identified as an issue. However this only became apparent when macro concerns, in this instance the gendered nature of familial relationships and the workings of power in family systems, were brought to the fore by radical feminists (Itzen 2001).

Where we[25] stand affects what we sense, and our thoughts and feelings affect how we respond to the world around us. My exploration reflects this belief and attempts to explore the importance of taking a multi-faceted look at the differing domains that frame action work with young people. Material explored below is neither exhaustive nor definitive. Rather, it is an example of the application of systemic thinking – in this instance to explore potential blocks to using action methods with young people.

Wider structuring systems

Local responses to the needs of young people are shaped by wider agendas that reflect particular attitudes, values and beliefs about how the world could, or should, be organised. Unfortunately, young people remain relatively powerless and this means they are vulnerable to the vagaries of adult logic and behaviour that often denies them the status of full and active actors on the stage of life. As such they largely remain at the mercy of adults who continue to act, either individually or collectively, as 'law giver and judge' (Hostler 1953). Adults are generally positioned as arbiters of acceptable behaviour and guardians, or dictators, of the next generation's education – moral, social, emotional or intellectual. Many never question this positioning nor think about the legitimacy of such privileged status. Exploration of one issue within one national context, Britain, will highlight the impact, potential or actual, of wider agendas when working with young people using action methods.

Despite the UN convention on the rights of the child, children have few rights and many continue to grow and develop in less than optimal circumstances, this includes within environments where they are abused by parents or carers (Department of Health 2000a). Concerns about child abuse contributed to the establishment of the National Commission of Inquiry, chaired by Lord Williams of Mostyn QC, in 1994. The commission's brief was to consider 'current provision and make recommendations for a national strategy for the prevention of child abuse and neglect' (King 1997, p.5). A key finding was that most forms of abuse are preventable 'provided that responsibility for this is accepted by all sectors of society, from national government to individuals' (King 1997, p.4). Child abuse is then everyone's concern not just the concern of those child care professionals charged with mediating the relationship between the family and the state through their role as street level bureaucrats (Lipsky 1993). Primary prevention is central as 'the most effective means of preventing abuse is the active promotion of the wellbeing of all children, and a refusal by society as a whole to tolerate conditions and systems known to harm them' (King 1997, p.9).

Safe and healthy development is then not simply linked to just the direct caring or parenting offered to individual children. Adults need to acknowledge the impact of a wide range of issues that affect children's development – some examples being poverty, homelessness or racial harassment. One way forward for individuals, to actively promote the interest of all children, is the establishment and maintenance of 'child friendly communities'. These would provide support for parents and carers as adults develop 'a shared view of children's needs and how they may best be met, rethinking the place of children in society and persuading all those whose actions affect children to re-consider their personal and professional responsibilities' (King 1997, p.16). Unfortunately, as Walby (1998, p.83) stated, when discussing the findings of the National Commission of Inquiry, we are a long way from the creation of child friendly communities as advocated:

> The facts and evidence presented to the commission led to the inescapable conclusion that the present high social and political tolerance of the suffering of children, through inadequate or actively detrimental policies and provisions, has a direct bearing upon what we now commonly call child abuse.

One example of the sort of detrimental policies and provisions highlighted is government consultation on a range of proposals to modernise the law relating to the physical punishment of children. These follow the outcome of a case heard by the European Court of Human rights: A v UK (DOH 2000b). On this occasion, the court ruled that, on the particular facts of the case, UK law had failed to protect the boy, who had been repeatedly and severely beaten by his stepfather with a cane. Although the stepfather had been charged with assault occasioning actual bodily harm (Offences Against the Persons Act 1861: Section 47) he pleaded the defence of reasonable chastisement and was found not guilty by a jury.

The government's response to this finding was to issue a consultation document addressing itself to the issues raised by this judgement. However, rather than starting from the premise that all physical punishment is a violation of children's rights and exploring the option of outlawing physical punishment, the government made clear 'that we do not consider that the right way forward is to make unlawful all smacking and other forms of physical rebuke' (DOH 2000a, p.2). This effectively ruled out the possibility of outlawing adult chastisement of children. This stance informed articulation of options in the consultation document, which states that 'the defence of reasonable chastisement' should be preserved (Children are Unbeatable! Alliance 2000). This was despite evidence from other countries that formally challenging the socially and legally sanctioned physical punishment of children does not necessarily lead to the persecution of parents, as some fear, but rather results in the development of differing child care patterns, patterns which afford children similar protection to that enjoyed by adults (Lyon 2000). There was also material containing statements by young people who want the law to stop discriminating 'against them on the grounds of age' (Lyon 2000, p.38) and studies that have demonstrated causal relationships between parental physical punishment and children's anti, rather than pro, social behaviour (e.g. Patterson, Dishion and Bank 1984). Maybe the most important evidence of all is young people's own understanding of, and response to, the dynamics of physical punishment. The principle message from them is that it is wrong, it hurts, and parents smack you 'because they are bigger and older' (Lyon 2000, p.37).

Why is this important when thinking about what may help or hinder us as we seek to use action methods with young people? It is possible to argue that children have been, and continue to be, 'demonised' by politicians, sections of the media, and established religions as well as other significant sectors of the population, rather than 'valued, celebrated, respected and included' (Newell 2000, p.23). The history of adult responses to young people is shot through with ambiguities and tensions (Corby 1993), which is unsurprising when we consider the extent to which childhood is itself a socially constructed and reconstructed category (James and Prout 1990). Children can be, and have been, viewed as victims, villains or both – for example, when thinking about how we respond to young people who sell sex (Department of Health *et al.* 2000). The British Government's consultation exercise, as outlined above, is rooted in deep-seated adult ambiguity about young people. Do we really want to build 'child friendly communities'? If we do, can continuing to legitimate physical punishment of children be a route to this?

Working with young people in ways that encourage them to act spontaneously, engage creatively, feel empowered, use and trust all their senses can be a threatening prospect for individual adults or communities of adults. Action methods lead us to engage with young people on their terms as well as our own. They demand that we work in partnership with young people, sharing power and authority with them in ways that honour their, and our, abilities. This can be disorientating and even frightening for those who believe young people are incapable of self-regulation or self-control (as exemplified in texts like *Lord of the Flies*[26] which presents a picture of young people as innately destructive).

Hence the need to uphold the right of adults to physically punish children. If adults, either individually or collectively, believe that children need to be contained and controlled or they run amok destroying the fabric of civilised adult society, then the physical punishment of some of our most vulnerable members of society is not too high a price to pay.

Many of the contributors to this book (e.g. Gagani and Grieve Chapter 7 and Smith Chapter 4) have demonstrated their commitment to being with, rather than doing to, young people. To find ways to communicate with them that honour their innate capacity for self-regulation and healing. Such approaches offer a challenge to the dominance of expert models – either of parenting or professionalism – that result in the construction of hierarchies of experience and expression that are more congruent with purely verbal approaches to working with young people than they are reflective of the use of action methods. If we work only with words then we impoverish our interactions with young people because we engage on our terms alone and expect them to respond in kind.

Using action methods with young people puts them at the centre of interactions with adults as they mirror child-centred ways of being in the world (Bannister Chapter 2 this volume). However, they also challenge precious and well established patterns of relationships that contribute to the on-going justification of adult physical punishment of children, as discussed above. When we work in action we may, knowingly or unknowingly, challenge deep-seated beliefs about what children 'are' and what adults should 'be' or 'do' in relationship to them. Working in action often means we encourage young people to take centre stage as they present and explore their life dramas. This reflects Morenian approaches to work with people. As Clarkson (1994, p.19) states 'Moreno was arguably the first psychiatrist to put "the patient" in a centrally responsible role in his own life drama. He worked with people to empower them to do their own healing.' Furthermore, he used action methods to communicate with young people about their everyday concerns, to get alongside them and take seriously what they had to say about their world(s) (Marineau 1989). Employing action methods with young people, as discussed in this book, carries on that work and offers a challenge to wider structuring systems that legitimate the continuing treatment of young people as less than, rather than different to, adults.

Local social, community and organisational concerns

There are many areas of concern that I could address within this section to highlight the impact of more localised agendas that may limit or facilitate the use of action methods with young people. For example, whether health or education providers embrace or reject the type of work discussed by Luxmoore (Chapter 6 this volume) or Kirk (Chapter 5 this volume). Justifying doing something different, and using action methods is often construed as 'different', can be a time-consuming and at times frustrating task as staff have to demonstrate to those with power, such as head teachers or hospital managers, that what they have to offer is safe, effective and likely to provide value for money. Engaging with explicit agendas that affect what can be provided by whom, particularly in the current climate where evidence based practice and the need to legitimate interventions with reference to research dominate the agenda (e.g. DOH 2001), is time consuming.

Choice then, in terms of the examples I have selected for exploration here, is inevitable. My focus on therapeutic modalities and questions of legitimacy follows from an acknowledgement that adults that are respected and empowered in their work are more, rather than less, likely to respect and empower those they work with. As Rose (1999, p.81) states, 'the individual member of staff also needs sustenance. He or she needs the affirmation of the staff peer group, in recognition of the worth of his or her loving, professional skills.' Further, as Coulshed (1990, p.13) makes clear when discussing management issues in social work, 'insecurities and pressures often filter down and are reflected in the service given.' This is arguably true at all levels within organisations. Powerless professionals, like powerless parents, must struggle with the tensions and contradictions associated with their role if they are to contain pressures and not engage in oppressive interactions with those with less power – for example, patients and children respectively. Individuals have to work to ensure they don't physically or psychologically 'kick the cat', or even the child, following a bad day, week, year or even life.

Whether or not staff can contain tensions and contradictions generated, particularly at a time when change seems the only certainty for many employees, is an ongoing concern. As Handy (1990, p.3) argues when discussing psychiatric services, the dynamics of that system, like many others, militates against meeting the needs of service users or those that 'labour within it'. A concern echoed by Van Deurzen Smith (1996, p.73) who states, 'paradoxically, the institutions in our society often seem to encourage the very opposite of what they are supposed to be about'. As Thompson (2000, p.9) states, if profes-sionals do not find ways to hold onto their compassion and humanitarian prin-ciples they are likely to become 'functionaries', doing little more than negotiate the web of bureaucratic 'routines, procedures and standards' associated with their role. When this happens individuals are more likely to conform to 'or-ganisational expectations and interests' even if, or when, they are incompatible with the interests of individuals or groups to whom those services are offered.

Most work with young people using action methods takes place in some sort of organisation, as contributions to this volume demonstrate. As Hoey (1997) argues, organisations can either foster or stifle adult creativity as people negotiate their way through the rules and norms associated with occupational roles, particularly if we want to engage with children using non-traditional, or less well-known, methods like action approaches. Even if people appropriately use supervision or other support mechanisms to avoid 'loss of heart' or 'burnout' (Thompson 2000, p.9) the impact of the steady drip of other peoples' negativity can undermine the best of intentions. Empowering organisational cultures, that value what staff have to offer, are more likely to lead to better quality services and good outcomes for young people, for example when they are cared for away from home (DOH 1998).

Yet, the problems inherent in ensuring that positive, rather than negative or even abusive, cultures flourish within organisations, particularly but not exclu-sively total institutions (Goffman 1961), has been well documented. If institu-tions do not value action methods then staff within them will have an uphill struggle when they seek to use them in work with young people. Energy that could be used providing services is wasted legitimising the use of action methods to those with power or responsibility for decision making. Whether or not a particular approach to work is or is not seen as legitimate is not just a technical issue; again, questions of power and legitimacy shape the space within which interventions are offered.

Therapeutic approaches to work with young people

The rise to dominance of particular approaches to therapeutic work, for example those rooted in behaviourism, often deny or negate insights generated through the application of alternative frameworks, such as psychodynamic or humanistic, in order to understand human experience (Temperley 1979; Elliot 1987; Meldrum 1994). This is unsurprising when we consider the rise to prominence of market principles in the health and social care arena and the hierarchies of legitimacy constructed to justify the dominance of particular professionals, or professional groups, in terms of relationships with other professionals or those using services. As Plummer (1995) made clear we tell our stories, present narratives and make meaning, within the streams of power that flow through negotiated social orders. Further, as Taylor and White (2000) argue, competing versions of events often co-exist and we put forward our 'truth claims' in ways that are likely to lead to our version of reality being accepted. Those positioned at the bottom of socially constructed hierarchies have less chance that their story (or version of reality) will be heard as their claims are undermined by those of others with greater status and power (Taylor and White 2000). 'The power to tell a story, or indeed to not tell a story, under the conditions of one's own choosing, is part of the political process' (Plummer 1995, p.26).

Consideration of the extent to which those who employ action methods are allowed to construct their own narratives about their work, whether individually, collectively and/or in partnership with those who use services, is an important issue. As O'Brien (1994) stated changes in the organisation and delivery of health and personal social services has led to a struggle for control by staff, as closure is a way to ring-fence professional expertise and employment opportunities. Those professions, for example social work, or those modalities, for example psychodrama, that are judged to be marginal rather than mainstream are vulnerable to attacks in ways that other professions, such as medicine, or modalities, such as psychoanalytic, are not (Rojeck, Peacock and Collins 1988; Watson 1993). Power is claimed and exercised, both by individuals and groups, within the 'caring professions' in complex and multi-faceted ways (Hugman 1991). Attempts at differentiation and legitimisation of therapeutic approaches are as much about 'power, ideology, money, status, employability and snobbery' (Clarkson 1994, p.7) as they are about theory, research or practice wisdom and 'boundary disputes' continue to be part of the terrain for practice (Pilgrim 1996, p.7). As in the research arena arguments can be made about the existence of a 'gold standard', which offers a blueprint against which all else is judged, or the importance of selecting methods, without recourse to hierarchical typologies, to fit purposes (Bryman 1988; Hunter 1998). Authors (e.g. Watson 1993) have argued that some approaches to working therapeutically are situated on the high ground of the centre whilst others, like psychodrama, are positioned in the margins.

Adopting a 'gold standard' approach to the provision of services to young people is unlikely to lead to the valuing of action orientated approaches, like psychodrama, that defy easy schematisation (Kellerman 1992) and are therefore less amenable to outcome orientated research that legitimates use in hard pressed, and often underfunded, organisations. As Yalom (2000) makes clear:

> The contemporary managed care movement in health care poses a deadly threat to the field of psychotherapy... The profit hungry health care executives and their misguided professional advisors assume that successful therapy is a function of information obtained or dispensed rather than the result of the relationship between patient and therapist. (p.52)

Such an actuarial approach to therapeutic work, wherein psychotherapy is reduced to a sort of data-bank activity as information deposits and withdrawals become the currency of interactions, is inherently problematic for those whose work, like those in this volume, is rooted in humanistic principles. This information processing approach is, in Yalom's terms, de-humanising and antithetical to his understanding of the core role of relationships and service within therapeutic encounters. Something similar could be said about all work with young people in whatever setting. Further, an actuarial approach is likely to lead to the legitimisation of approaches to intervention that lend themselves to outcome orientated, rather than process orientated, evaluations as outcomes can be measured against set criteria and boxes ticked as symptoms abate, facts are learned or behaviour modified. Attention is then fixed on behaviour rather than the causes of behaviour and uncritical acceptance of this focus privileges some modalities, for example cognitive behavioural therapy, at the expense of others, such as psychodrama.

Although behaviour is important there are other less tangible aspects of experience that need to be acknowledged and addressed, such as emotional interchanges between protagonists (Sands 2000), that defy attempts to quantify them. Unfortunately, in the current climate, such understanding is easily lost and approaches to work may be excluded or marginalised because 'evidence' is not available to legitimise their effectiveness (e.g. DOH 2001). Although attempts to generate empirical evidence that demonstrates the efficacy of action methods are evident (e.g. Baim et al. 1999; Bannister Chapter 2 this volume) the historical legacy of the past will not be easily shifted, either in terms of the impossibility of 'catching up', given some modalities have a long history of attracting money to undertake research for practice, or in terms of challenging entrenched views and well established beliefs about what constitutes a legitimate approach to work with young people across service sectors.

Against this backdrop many committed and conscientious practitioners struggle to legitimate use of action methods in their work with young people.

Intra-psychic issues and inter-personal concerns

Seeing through the eyes of a child in everyday encounters (Hostler 1953), as a route to understanding and appropriate responses as they grow and develop, is not easy. The pressures of the adult world hinder adults who must juggle the contradictions of daily life – including the vagaries of the labour market and their own position within it. As adults try to manage the hustle and bustle of the world they must also develop and maintain the capacity to change pace, to see with different eyes, to make space for, and to accommodate, young people who experience and respond to the world differently. Engaging in creative and productive here and now encounters with young people is a cornerstone of development – theirs and those of adults. However as Axline (1947) makes clear a key question is whether adults can leave behind adult concerns long enough to make those connections. For example, whether they take young people's concerns seriously, even when they are not their own concerns, and join with them in sense making activity in their relationship based interactions in daily life is often neither easy nor simple. As I argued (1998), when discussing the departure of Geri Halliwell from the Spice Girls and the impact of this on pre-pubescent female fans, there are many blocks that impede positive interactions around seemingly mundane topics. Some of these are practical, there are just not enough hours in the day. Others are more fundamental, how can we talk about loss, even at a distance, in ways that threaten to overwhelm neither us nor them.

These sorts of dilemmas and contradictions are amplified when working therapeutically with young people. Working as a therapist means you open yourself to the expression of strong emotions, as those who have sought, or been directed towards, therapy are empowered to revisit often difficult and painful aspects of their experience within the context of a containing relationship (Hawkins and Shohet 1989). Therapy is 'concerned with strong emotions, insight, intellectual appreciation and change' (Meldrum 1994, p.16) and central to therapy is the relationship between therapist and the other (however labelled), as the therapist acts as guide or mentor on the therapeutic journey through life 'stages and changes' (Cattanach 1994a, p.39). The therapist is a companion on the client's journey, a person of integrity and strength who does not impose their view on the other but rather allows them to develop their own understandings of themselves and the world around them (Sands 2000). As such they need to have made their own journey, to have re-visited their own formative and subsequent experiences, making sense of what was, maybe mourning and celebrating along the way but always seeking understanding. To do otherwise is to leave themselves vulnerable to repeating the past, including in relationships they make with those who use their services.

To go back to an earlier concern, the physical punishment of children, as Lyon (2000, p.50) states: 'studies have shown that the degree to which one was physically punished as a child is an important predictor of one's support for corporal punishment as an adult.' The compulsion to repeat, even if the adult believes they do not want to replicate experiences they may have found difficult or painful, is a powerful one. The need to repeat, as a defence against an internalised sense of powerlessness that may result from abusive formative experiences, is even stronger – as evidenced by the actions of many adult sexual offenders.

Whatever role is assumed, for example teacher or therapist, individuals bring to that role the 'self'. People may have had early experiences that have sensitised them to oppressor and oppressed roles, for example if domestic violence was a feature in their birth family, in ways that fundamentally shape their inner landscape. Whether or not people have had particular experiences that have had a powerful impact, 'in childhood, we frequently feel we have little control over or influence on the behaviour of others and on the course of events (Sands 2000, p.134). To face the pain and suffering of the powerless child, which I would argue is every child at some point and to some degree, requires courage, strength and supportive networks or it may be too much to bear, particularly when using action methods as these bring their experiences to life in front of us. As Chesner (1994, p.115) states, 'in both dramatherapy and psychodrama the physicality of the experience brings the emotions or the unconscious onto the therapeutic stage.' Distancing is then less likely as action often engages people at a visceral level. In the process, adult defences may be ruptured as raw emotions, associated with unprocessed experience, confront and challenge.

Exploration of the clients' world in action within a safe therapeutic space opens up possibilities for freer exploration and expression than might otherwise be the case. When working with young people action methods offer a structured approach to work that reflects the child's natural route to expression and understanding: play (Cattanach 1994b, p.134). Engaging with young people using action methods offers adults a route to enhance their development and, when necessary, engage them in healing themselves. However, it is work that demands adults do not set themselves up as 'law giver and judge'. Occupation of such distancing roles is antithetical to the theory and practice of action work with young people. However, the role expansion that results when any adult steps outside stereotypical conceptions of adult:child relationships means they must undertake, and maintain, their own journeys to healing if they are to keep corrosive messages, as evidenced by the discussion in the first section of this chapter, at bay.

To really get alongside children of the present means adults must explore and understand the child of the past, that is, their own experiences. If adults have developed patterns of behaviour or ways of coping with their own pain and suffering that lead them to minimise or deny the existence of pain in those they work with, they need to acknowledge, address and find ways to move on from these experiences, not forget them. As Jennings (1994, p.6) states, insight alone is not 'enough to bring about lasting change'. Peer support, appropriate supervision, further training, reading and reflection are all routes to achieving and maintaining change.

Concluding comments

There are many sources of knowledge for practice that adults may draw on as they seek to work in creative and empowering ways with young people. At times it seems as if the struggle to understand and apply differing frameworks and available, information (for example, theories, research findings, first person narratives) to enhance responses to those encountered in practice, is an impossible task. Yet if knowledge is to be constructed and used in a fluid rather than fragmented way (Munro 1998) we need to deconstruct and reconstruct our understanding of the world around us as we critically interrogate bodies of information in a reflexive way (Taylor and White 2000). The plausibility and believability of competing claims (whether made by people we work with or people who write about the work we do) is a key concern for health and welfare professionals who have to make complex judgements, often in unpredictable and uncertain situations (Coulshed 1990). The contributors to this book have attempted to assertively demonstrate the appropriateness of using action methods when working with young people. They have stated their truth claims through exploration of real life examples of work and reference to theoretical frameworks that underpin their interventions. Whether or not you, the reader, believe they have done so credibly is for you to decide. It is also for you to decide whether I have outlined the importance of considering the differing intersecting systems that frame responses to current and future generations in a consistent, comprehensive and coherent way.

References

Antonovsky, A. (1979) *Health, Stress and Coping.* London: Josey Bass.

Axline, V. (1947) *Play Therapy.* London: Churchill Livingstone.

Baim, C., Allam, J., Eames, T., Dunford, S. and Hunt, S. (1999) 'The use of psychodrama to enhance victim empathy in sex offenders: an evaluation.' *The Journal of Sexual Aggression 4*, 1, 4–14.

Bentovim, A. (1992) *Trauma Organised Systems: Systemic Understanding of Family Violence. Systemic Thinking and Practice.* London: Karnac Books.

Bettelheim, B. (1950) *Love is Not Enough.* London: Free Press.

Bronfenbrenner, U. (1979) *The Ecology of Human Development.* Cambridge, MA: Harvard University Press.

Bryman, A. (1988) *Quantity and Quality in Social Research.* London: Routledge.

Cattanach, A. (1994a) 'The Developmental Model of Dramatherapy.' In S. Jennings, S. Mitchell, A. Chesner and B. Meldrum (eds) *The Handbook of Dramatherapy.* London: Routledge.

Cattanach, A. (1994b) 'Dramatic Play with Children: The Interface of Dramatherapy and Play Therapy.' In S. Jennings, S. Mitchell, A. Chesner and B. Meldrum (eds) *The Handbook of Dramatherapy.* London Routledge.

Chesner, A. (1994) 'Dramatherapy and Psychodrama: Similarities and Differences.' In S. Jennings, S. Mitchell, A. Chesner and B. Meldrum (eds) *The Handbook of Dramatherapy.* London: Routledge.

Children are Unbeatable! Alliance. (2000) *Moving on from Smacking: Children are Unbeatable. Response to the Department of Health's Consultation Document on the Physical Punishment of Children.* London: NSPCC.

Clarkson, P. (1994) 'The Nature and Range of Psychotherapy.' In P. Clarkson and M. Pokorny (eds) *The Handbook of Psychotherapy.* London: Routledge.

Corby, B. (1993) *Child Abuse. Towards A Knowledge Base.* Milton Keynes: Open University Press.

Coulshed, V. (1990) *Management in Social Work.* London: BASW/MacMillan.

Department of Health (1998) *Caring For Children Away From Home. Messages From Research.* London: Wiley.

Department of Health (2000a) *Assessing Children In Need and their Families.* London: HMSO.

Department of Health (2000b) *Protecting Children, Supporting Parents. A Consultation Document on the Physical Punishment of Children.* London: HMSO.

Department of Health, Home Office, Department for Education and Employment and the National Assembly for Wales (2000) *Safeguarding Children Involved in Prostitution. Supplementary Guidance to Working Together to Safeguard Children.* London: HMSO.

Department of Health (2001) *Treatment Choice in Psychological Therapies and Counselling. Evidence Based Clinical Practice Guidance.* London: HMSO.

Doyal, L. and Gough, I. (1991) *A Theory of Human Need.* London: MacMillan.

Elliot, B. (1987) 'Is unconscious really a dirty word?' *New Directions* (December) 10–15.

Goffman, I. (1961) *Asylums. Essays on the Social Situation of Mental Patients and other Inmates.* London: Penguin Books.

Handy, J. (1990) *Occupational Stress in a Caring Profession. The Social Context of Psychiatric Nursing.* Aldershot: Avebury.

Hawkins, P. and Shohet, R. (1989) *Supervision in the Helping Professions.* Milton Keynes: Open University Press.

Hoey, B. (1997) *Who Calls the Tune? A Psychodramatic Approach to Child Therapy.* London: Routledge.

Hostler, P. (1953) *The Child's World.* London: Penguin Books.

Hugman, R. (1991) *Power in Caring Professions.* London: MacMillan.

Hunter, D. (1998) 'The new health policy agenda: the challenge facing managers and researchers.' *Research Policy and Planning 16,* 2, 2–5.

Huntington, A. (1998) 'On Loss, Grief and the Spice Girls.' *Practice 10,* 3, 5–12.

Itzen, C. (2001) *Home Truths about Sexual Abuse influencing Policy and Practice. A Reader.* London: Routledge.

James, A. and Prout, A. (1990) 'A New Paradigm for the Sociology of Childhood? Provenance, Promise and Problems.' In A. James and A. Prout (eds) *Childhood. Contemporary Issues in the Sociological Study of Childhood.* Hampshire: The Falmer Press.

Jennings, S. (1994) 'Prologue.' In S. Jennings, S. Mitchell, A. Chesner and B. Meldrum (eds) *The Handbook of Dramatherapy.* London: Routledge.

Kellerman, P. (1992) *Focus on Psychodrama. The Therapeutic Aspects of Psychodrama.* London: Jessica Kingsley Publishers.

King, S. (1997) *Childhood Matters. The Report of the National Commission of Inquiry into the Prevention of Child Abuse.* London: HMSO.

Lipsky, M. (1993) 'Street Level Bureaucracy: An Introduction.' In M. Hills (ed) *The Policy Process. A Reader.* London: Harvester Wheatsheaf.

Lyon, C. (2000) *Loving Smack or Lawful Assault. A Contradiction in Human Rights and Law.* London: Institute for Public Policy Research.

Marineau, R. (1989) *Jacob Levy Moreno 1889–1974. Father of Psychodrama, Sociometry, and Group Psychotherapy.* London: Tavistock/Routledge.

Meldrum, B. (1994) 'Historical Background and Overview of Dramatherapy.' In S. Jennings, S. Mitchell, A. Chesner and B. Meldrum (eds) *The Handbook of Dramatherapy.* London: Routledge.

Miller, A. (1987a) *For Your Own Good. The Roots of Violence in Child Rearing.* London: Virago.

Miller, A. (1987b) *The Drama of Being A Child.* London: Virago.

Miller, A. (1997) *Breaking Down the Wall of Silence.* London: Virago.

Munro, E. (1998) *Understanding Social Work. An Empirical Approach.* London: Athlone Press.

Newell, P. (2000) *Taking Children Seriously. A Proposal for a Children's Rights Commissioner.* London: Calouste Gulbenkian Foundation.

O'Brien, M. (1994) 'The managed heart re-visited: health and social control.' *Sociological Review 42,* 3, 393–413.

O'Brien, M. and Penna, S. (1998) *Theorising Welfare. Enlightenment and Modern Society.* London: Sage.

Patterson, G.R., Dishion, T.J. and Bank, L. (1984) 'Family interaction: a process model of deviancy training.' *Aggressive Behaviour 10,* 253–267.

Pilgrim, D. (1996) 'British Psychotherapy in Context.' In W. Dryden (ed) *Handbook of Individual Therapy.* London: Sage.

Plummer, K. (1995) *Telling Sexual Stories. Power, Change and Social Worlds.* London: Routledge.

Rojek, C., Peacock, G. and Collins, S. (1988) *Social Work and Received Ideas.* London: Routledge.

Rose, M. (1999) 'Children and Adolescents: The Renaissance of Heart and Mind.' In P. Campling and R. Haigh (eds) *Therapeutic Communities. Past, Present and Future.* London: Jessica Kingsley Publishers.

Sandford, L. (1991) *Strong at the Broken Places.* London: Virago.

Sands, A. (2000) *Falling for Therapy. Psychotherapy from a Client's Point of View.* London: MacMillan.

Taylor, C. and White, S. (2000) *Practising Reflexivity in Health and Welfare. Making Knowledge.* Buckingham: Open University Press.

Temperley, J. (1979) 'The implications for social work of recent psychoanalytical developments. Conference Paper: *Change and Renewal in Psychodynamic Social Work.* St Edmund Hall Oxford, 22–26th August.

Thompson, N. (2000) *Understanding Social Work.* London: MacMillan.

Van Deurzen Smith, E. (1996) 'Existential Therapy.' In W. Dryden (ed) *Handbook of Individual Therapy.* Sage: London.

Walby, C. (1998) *Childhood Matters. The Report of the National Commission of Inquiry into the Prevention of Child Abuse.* London: NSPCC.

Waldby, C., Clancy, A., Emetchi, J. and Summerfield, C. (1989) 'Theoretical Perspectives on Father-daughter Incest.' In E. Driver and A. Droisen (eds) *Child Sexual Abuse. Feminist Perspectives.* London: MacMillan.

Watson, R. (1993) 'The illusions of psychodrama: a study in the psychology of psychodramatic representation.' *British Journal of Psychodrama and Sociodrama 8*, 2, 5–46.

White, J. (1997) 'Family Therapy.' In M. Davies (ed) *The Blackwell Companion to Social Work.* London: Blackwell.

Yalom, I. (2000) *Momma and the Meaning of Life: Tales of Psychotherapy.* London: Piatkus.

Endnotes

Chapter 1

1   The editors are indebted to Dr Anne Ancelin Schützenberger for all the information about Dr Francoise Dolto, with whom she trained.

Chapter 2

2   These were simple self-esteem scales, with locus of control items, which children completed themselves, with a therapist available to help, at the commencement and end of the group (Maines and Robinson 1988).

3   Liaison between the group staff and this boy's family, social worker and teacher continued, to ensure he still received adequate support.

Chapter 4

4   Talitha and Connor (the names of two special family members, my niece and godson) are pseudonyms.

5   The terms 'stammering' (stammer) and 'stuttering' (stutter) refer to the same condition. Stammering is used in the UK and stuttering in the USA. The author has chosen the former to refer to the condition throughout this chapter. However, 'stuttering' appears in some quotations.

6   'Dysfluency' (dysfluencies) refers to the speech behaviours that interrupt the forward flow of speech such as repetitions, prolongations, blocking behaviours, general hesitations, revisions of phrases and sentences. These behaviours are (for the most part) the same as stammering speech behaviour. However, the term 'dysfluency' is typically used with children who are diagnosed as having 'early dysfluency' (see Turnbull and Stewart 1996). Stammering is used with children who show persistent or chronic stammering patterns.

7   Contact addresses for speech and language therapy: Royal College of Speech and Language Therapist, 2, White Hart Yard, London, SE1 1NX. Tel: 020 7378 1200. Web-site: http://www.rcslt.org Information about speech and language therapy

services in other countries can be obtained from the RCSLT's web-site or the head office.

8   All references to 'therapy' in this chapter refer to speech and language therapy.

9   'Escape behaviours' refer to any behaviour or speech related strategy that helps a person to avoid, or be released from a moment of stammering.

10 Stammering is not a progressive or linear condition. Stewart and Turnbull (1996) propose a three stage model consisting of 'early dysfluency', 'borderline stammering' and 'confirmed stammering.' They give a detailed description of each stage in their book *Helping Children Cope with Stammering* (see references).

11 The term 'protagonist' refers to the person, adult or child, who is exploring some aspect of their life in action through the method of psychodrama. He/she is the main focus of a psychodramatic session.

Chapter 5

12 'Prognoses' means the predictions as to the outcome of the illness.

13 ME stands for Myalgic Encephalomyelitis, also known as Chronic Fatigue Immune Dysfunction Syndrome (CFIDS) or Chronic Fatigue Syndrome (CFS).

14 Systemic Lupus Erythmatosus (SLE) is an auto-immune condition affecting many parts of the body including joints, skin, kidneys, spleen, heart and nervous system. Commonly occurring in young women aged between 20 and 40, it is a chronic illness with periods of remission and degeneration. Renal failure is the commonest cause of death.

15 Acute lymphoblastic leukaemia is most common in children. It is simply a cancer of the blood, where there is uncontrolled proliferation of white blood cells forming in organs other than the bone marrow. It is a progressive and potentially fatal condition.

Chapter 7

16 Moreno differentiated between two types of acting out: '*irrational, incalculable acting out* in life itself, harmful to the patient or others, and *therapeutic, controlled acting out* taking place within the treatment setting' (Moreno, 1994, p. X).

17 Moreno (1994) spoke of somatic, social and psychodramatic roles. Developmentally, the first roles that are developed are the somatic roles, since they are essential for the infant's survival.

18 Parten (1932) emphasised the role of play in children's social world and by observing children during free play at nursery school, he classified developmental stages of play ranging from solitary play, where the child plays alone, through to associative play, where the play is interactive but with little or no organisation and finally to co-operative play, which involves interactive and organised play.

Chapter 9

19 It is possible to go on creating exercises of this type almost indefinitely, each calling for a memory or relationship or other aspect of family life which emphasises the strongest and most positive points associated with being in the family. In other situations and contexts the director might well want also to explore some of the less positive, more conflicted memories as well.

Chapter 13

20 Marianne Hirn and Bengt Söderström. Marianne is a veteran psychologist in child psychiatry. She has worked extensively with both traumatised and other children mostly in individual therapy. Since 1991 she has lead psychotherapy groups, together with a co-therapist, for sexually abused teenage girls. She has worked at the Vasa clinic since it started in 1994. Bengt, psychologist MS, has prior experience of working in various child psychiatric treatment centres. He came to the Vasa clinic in 1997 and has worked mostly with younger children and children who sexually abuse others. He has been head of the clinic since 1999.

Chapter 14

21 The term 'young people' will be used throughout this chapter to describe children and young people.

22 As Doyal and Gough (1991) state: values, beliefs and attitudes shape the ways in which we seek to define and respond to the needs of all 'citizen consumers' within contemporary society. Differing 'conceptual lenses' (O'Brien and Penna 1998) are available to us and needs are (re)produced through political struggles about meaning that reflect the articulation of particular worldviews. For example, classic liberalism and state socialism offer differing political frameworks for understanding the relationship between the individual and the state. Decisions made then lead to differing approaches to the provision of material services to meet identified human needs.

23 Early systems theory was associated with the work of Talcott Parsons (sociologist) and other proponents of his approach. Although justified criticisms of systems theory have been articulated, for example on the basis that it reflects inherently conservative assumptions about the integration of social systems, contemporary theorists, like Jurgen Habermas, have recycled systems thinking and used it in radical ways.

24 Antonovsky (1979) articulated the difference between pathogenic (disease focused) and salutogenic (health focused) medical models and challenged the dominance of the pathogenic model, which focuses our attention on the origins of (dis)ease rather than health. Sandford (1991) refers to this distinction when discussing the impact of child sexual abuse and the dominance of deterministic formulations and prescriptive explorations of the impact of abuse that often position those who have been abused as 'damaged goods' – unlikely or unable to live happy, healthy and fulfilled lives. As Sandford argues, maybe the question is not what makes people sick but rather how is it so many are well despite the widespread sexual assault of children.

25 Use of 'we' in this chapter refers to adults as a distinct group.

26 One might read *Lord of the Flies* as an indictment of capitalist societies that structure all human relationships in hierarchical ways and create relationships of domination and subjugation as a norm. Young people are then expressing what they have learnt not what is innate and as such can be seen to be no more or less 'uncivilised' than the (un)civilised adults responsible for their socialisation. However, this is not, as far as I understand it, how this text is routinely presented or read. Rather, it is offered as some sort of salutary tale that delineates the perils that await if young people, or should I say young men, are left to their own devices. Ultimately, this can 'only end in tears' as they, like other uncivilised groups, cannot be trusted to manage their own affairs in ways that do not lead to death and destruction. Enter the saviour – 'daddy.After all he does 'know best'.

List of Contributors

Anne Bannister, UKCP, CPSM, CQSW, is a psychodramatist, dramatherapist and playtherapist. She founded and managed the Child Sexual Abuse Consultancy for the NSPCC for many years and is now a freelance consultant and supervisor. She is the author of many articles, book chapters and books, on child protection and therapy with children. One example is: *The Healing Drama: Psychodrama and Dramatherapy with Abused Children* (1997) Free Association Books. She is a research fellow of the University of Huddersfield where she is now completing her doctoral research on the effects of creative therapies with children who have been sexually abused.

Chip Chimera, CQSW, Dip.ASS, MSc, is a systemic psychotherapist in private practice. Chip teaches family therapy and systemic practice at the Institute of Family Therapy in London and the Tavistock West Sussex Diploma in Systemic Practice in Brighton. She has many years of experience in the fields of child care and child protection. She now frequently acts as an expert witness in court proceedings under the Children Act, 1989. Chip is a senior trainee in psychodrama and group psycho-therapy and is the UK co-ordinator for the Therapeutic Spiral International.

Christina Citron, MD, is a child and adolescent psychiatrist, group therapist, psychodramatist and symboldramatist. For 20 years she has been engaged in the management of child sexual abuse and started the first Swedish project working with group psychotherapy for sexually abused children and their mothers. She promoted the foundation of the Vasa clinic in Stockholm and has been employed there since its inception in 1994.

Mario Cossa, MA, RDT/MT, TEP, is a psychodramatist and drama therapist and creator and Director of ACTINGOUT, a programme for youth in southwestern New Hampshire (USA) which combines expressive therapies and theatre education. He serves on the executive council of the American Society for Group Psychotherapy and Psychodrama and as Chair of the Advisory Committee for Training of Therapeutic Spiral International. Cossa is senior author of *ACTINGOUT: the workbook – A Guide to* the *Development and Presentation of Issue-oriented, Audience-interactive, Improvisational Theatre* (1996, Taylor & Francis).

Sue Curtis MA, SRDMT, is a senior registered dance movement therapist working with a range of children, with emotional, phyisical and learning difficulties, in mainstream and special schools. She trained at the Laban Centre London, where she has lectured and supervised for many years on the MA Dance Movement Therapy course. She currently lectures at Goldsmiths College on the new Dance Movement Therapy course. Her particular interests are therapy with children who are in foster care and children who have been abused.

Ioanna Gagani, BA, MA, is a psychodramatist and a member of the International Association of Group Psychotherapy. She has studied Acting, Theatre Studies and Psychology and Spanish in Athens, Paris and Melbourne respectively. She currently works at a school for children with autism and intellectual disabilities in Melbourne, co-ordinating the department responsible for the one-to-one therapy of the young autistic students. She will be returning to Greece in 2002, after a six-year absence, where she will focus on the early intervention for children with autism. She has published an article in the *Australia and New Zealand Psychodrama Association Journal*.

Sandra Grieve, Dip.Ad. P.C.C., Ad. Dip.Psych., Cert. Sup. is a person-centred psychotherapist and psychodramatist. She is the Director of Matrix Therapeutic Services in Lanarkshire, Scotland. In addition to working with children with autism, she works with young people in Ridgepark School, a school for children with social, emotional and behavioural difficulties. Sandra also works with adults as a trainer and supervisor.

Andy Hickson, MA, has written extensively for the theatre, and has published with Winslow Press, Speechmark and Routledge. Shows directed include *Jacques and His Master, Silent Scream, 1bl, Race!* and *33 Skins. Angel High* and *2bl* were shows produced by Tie Tours Theatre Company in 2001. For more information about Tie Tours please visit their web-site: www.tietours.co or e-mail tie@tietours.com

Erica Hollander, MA, JD, CP, is a practising lawyer, certified psychodramatist and also teaches public speaking and presents clinical legal education seminars for trial lawyers. She assists her husband, Carl, in offering psychodrama workshops and training at the Hollander Institute for Human Development and Family Growth and together they have authored a chapter on conjoint therapy, using psychodrama in *Action Methods in Conjoint Psychotherapy*, to be published by APA Books in 2002. Erica is currently working on a doctorate in human communication studies at the University of Denver, USA.

Paul Holmes, BSc, M.B., B.S., PhD, M.R.C.Psych., is a child and adolescent psychiatrist who is trained as a psychodrama psychotherapist and as a psychoanalytic therapist.

He is the project leader and clinical supervisor of the Attachment Project in the city of Brighton and Hove. He is also the consultant psychiatrist to the Family Futures Consortium in London.

Annie Huntington, PhD, MSc, BA (Hons), DipSW, UKCP, RGN, CertEd, is currently employed as a lecturer in the Directorate of Social Work and Social Care at the University of Salford. She has been employed as a nurse, social worker and psychotherapist in a range of organisations over the last 20 years. Recent publications include book chapters, for example 'Real Records, Virtual Clients', with Bob Sapey and journal articles, for example 'Childhood maltreatment and adult self injury: a woman's account'.

Sue Jennings, PhD, is a professional actor and author. She runs training groups and offers supervision in Glastonbury. She is currently researching the eco-context of therapy and theatre, and the environment in the education of young people. She has published extensively on drama, play and theatre. She may be contacted at drsuejennings@hotmail.com

Kate Kirk, PhD, MA, Ad. Dip.Psych., RGN, RM, RHV, currently works as a psychodramatist for the Isle of Man Child and Adolescent Mental Health Service. She previously worked for Salford Palliative Care Counselling Service with adults and young people post-diagnosis of life-threatening illness on through to the end stage of illness. Recent publications include a co-authored chapter with Maria Lever, 'Palliative Care Counselling: Emotional and Psychological Support from Diagnosis to Death' (2001) in K. Etherington, (ed) *Counselling in Medical Settings*, Jessica Kingsley Publishers.

Nick Luxmoore, BA, PGCE, UKCP, is currently employed as leader of East Oxford Schools Inclusion Project. He has previously worked as a teacher in school and in prison, as a youth worker, school counsellor and manager of a young people's counselling and information service. He recently published *Listening to Young People in School, Youth Work and Counselling* (2000) Jessica Kingsley Publishers.

Gail Smith, Bsc (Hons), NNEB, holds a specialist speech and language therapist post working in Hull with adults who stammer and is part of a team in Leeds offering specialist services to children and adults who stammer. She also works as a paediatric therapist with babies and children with disorders of communication and feeding skills. She regularly presents workshops at national and international conferences that explore the application of action methods with people who stammer. She has published a number of articles exploring the use of psychodrama with people who stammer.

Subject Index

Author Index